then offers insigl
writers like Kurt
Burgess are cross
tween sf and "m;
section covers sf
radio, and televis.

The book is the first to deal with the science in science fiction. The engrossing survey of the evolution of scientific ideas and their impact on literature is written with the layman very much in mind.

Finally the book considers the forms, themes, and social concerns of science fiction and provides critical readings of ten major novels, including *The Time Machine, We, Star Maker, A Canticle for Leibowitz,* and *The Left Hand of Darkness.*

Valuable aids for the reader include an index to authors, titles, and recurring themes, and extensive bibliographies.

About the authors:

Robert Scholes is Professor of English at Brown University. He is the author of many books, including *Structural Fabulation* and *The Nature of Narrative.* Eric Rabkin is Professor of English at the University of Michigan, Ann Arbor. His books include *The Fantastic in Literature* and *Narrative Suspense.*

SCIENCE FICTION

SCIENCE FICTION:

HISTORY · SCIENCE · VISION

ROBERT SCHOLES

BROWN UNIVERSITY

ERIC S. RABKIN

UNIVERSITY OF MICHIGAN

NEW YORK

OXFORD UNIVERSITY PRESS

1977

This book is dedicated to

DAVID IVAN RABKIN

and

RACHEL ANN RABKIN

> *" 'Enjoy them while you may. . . .' "*

and to

JO ANN S. PUTNAM-SCHOLES

> ἐρωτοδιδάσκαλος

FOREWORD

OR THE PAST CENTURY AND A HALF, writers of what we have learned to call "science fiction" have been trying to create a modern conscience for the human race. In this same period many writers in the field have also produced trivial, ephemeral works of "popular" fiction which are barely literate, let alone literary. The premise upon which this book is based is that a sufficient number of works of genuine merit have been produced in this field to justify its study as an aspect of modern literature as well as an important feature of contemporary culture. But the authors recognize as well that certain elements of science fiction are sufficiently peculiar to this literary form to require special treatment. Thus the book has been divided into three parts in order to approach the subject comprehensively.

The first part undertakes to provide a history of science fiction as an aspect of the history of fiction as a whole, concluding with a short chapter on science fiction in comics, film, radio, and television. The second part offers discussion of those aspects of the sciences themselves most important for an understanding of science fiction. The third part returns to the consideration of science fiction as literature, with Chapter 4 covering the typical forms and themes of this kind of fiction and Chapter 5 presenting brief interpretive studies of ten representative novels from the past century and a half.

We have tried to produce a volume that might be read through from beginning to end, but we have also kept in mind the needs of some readers for specific and limited information. Hence, the detailed table of contents, the index, the bibliographies, and the frequent cross-references within the text itself. Hence also a certain amount of repetition from one section to the next—which we have tried to keep to a minimum. (We should also acknowledge that a few paragraphs on Ursula K. Le Guin are very close to some that were included in an article in the *Hollins Critic* and appeared in Robert Scholes's *Structural Fabulation*. Everything else in the book has been prepared especially for this occasion and has not appeared elsewhere.)

Writing a book such as this, authors incur more debts than are easily acknowledged. We have tried to cite specific indebtedness to our predecessors in this field by notes in the text and to acknowledge less precise instances of assistance by inclusion of works in our bibliography. We are also generally indebted, of course, to colleagues and students who have influenced our thinking about science fiction, and specifically to three who read significant portions of the manuscript and made numerous helpful suggestions and criticisms: James Gunn, Frank D. McConnell, and Khachig Tölölyan. It is a pleasure, in addition, to acknowledge the extraordinary assistance of our editor, John Wright, whose guidance with difficult problems of order and structure has been invaluable. And finally we wish to thank the writers of science fiction themselves, for making this task so rewarding, especially the members of the Science Fiction Writers of America—one of the most well-informed and humane professional groups in the world.

R.S.

E.S.R.

CONTENTS

I. HISTORY

1. A BRIEF LITERARY HISTORY OF SCIENCE FICTION

THE BEGINNINGS

THE HISTORY of science fiction is also the history of humanity's changing attitudes toward space and time. It is the history of our growing understanding of the universe and the position of our species in that universe. Like the history of science itself, the history of this literary form is thin and episodic until about four centuries ago, when the scientific method began to replace more authoritarian and dogmatic modes of thought, and people at last could see that the earth is not the center of the universe with the sun, moon, and stars all spinning round it for the edification of mankind.

Once upon a time human beings felt the world to be alive with spiritual presence; divinities inhabited every bush and waterfall. People learned to fear and worship especially those gods they sensed behind the most awesome of natural phenomena—tempest, earthquake, and the fertility of plants and animals. Our primitive ancestors knew a world that was timeless in one sense and tightly bound up by time in another. It was a world without history, with no sense of historical change that might lead to situations different from those which people already knew. And it was also a world bound to the seasonal flow of time, planting and harvesting, sweating and shivering, thanking the gods for blessings and begging them to end punishments. The seasons required religious rituals, which were held to contribute to the great temporal cycle, without which humanity would surely perish. The rituals enacted episodes from the lives of the gods, explaining the creation of the world, and preserving in the memory of humanity the values of which the gods were believed to approve. These memories and values, when separated from their ritual enactment, we call myths. They are supernatural stories that preserve tribal values and explain a world that is assumed to continue unchanged until some point when the gods tire of it or lose their own power to preserve it.

Myths are the ancestors of all other fictions. But they are also very different from modern kinds of fiction in ways that are important for us to understand. Myths are neither speculative nor playful. They have immense inertia, persisting in time as a conservative force, teaching the old values, the old ways—resisting the new. They do not deal with individuals but with prototypic figures who enact adventures on behalf of a whole tribe or race. They are not cast in a particular set of words but are told over and over again, preserving their form through countless repetitions in the words of countless tellers. If a myth changes, it changes so slowly that no one is aware of this. Everyone believes it has always been as it now is, just as the world has always been as it now is—since the creation.

A truly mythic culture has no writing and hence no way of recording history or measuring change. In all human cultures the introduction of writing is itself a change of extraordinary impact. It is one of the great technological changes that alters the face of the world. It is almost as significant as the development of speech itself, and in the speed with which it changes the world it is more dramatic in its impact. From the point of view of literature, writing encourages individualism in authorship. Where a myth is always traditional, belonging to the group rather than to any single member of it, a written story is committed to a durable form by someone, and to the extent that he invents its details or its language the story becomes his.

It is the same with the characters of fiction as it is with authors. Writing leads toward individualizing, toward making a unique story, the product of a single mind, presenting a unique character or characters who will be associated with their particular author in the minds of readers. And the preservation of written works over a period of time enables readers to see and feel the changes that humanity has passed through from one writer's lifetime to another's.

Obviously, this is not the place to trace the whole history of literature, but we must have at least some sense of the history of fiction in order to see the role of science fiction in the larger structure of our literary heritage. Perhaps the simplest way to understand the history of fiction is to see it as a movement away from mythology. The history of fiction is the story of humanity's development from a mythic way of seeing the world to a rational or empirical way of seeing it. As human science developed, human fictions changed with it. The history of fiction can be seen as a steady movement away from myth toward realism. This movement involves a change in the world represented in fiction from one which lacks a clear distinction between natural and supernatural to a world in which the distinction is very clear and from which supernatural events are excluded. Curiously, as realism developed, so did its opposite—fiction which is aware of the difference between natural and supernatural but deliberately presents supernatural events. We call this kind of fiction "fantasy," and we distinguish it from myth and legend precisely because of its deliberate inclusion of supernatural elements in its fictional world.

As scientific ways of understanding the world developed in the seventeenth and eighteenth centuries, fiction became more and more realistic, and the realistic novel came more and more to dominate the world of fiction. Fantasy was considered a minor form, suitable for children or as light reading for adults, but not really "literature," not really serious. In the nineteenth century, realism developed new techniques for representing a whole social scene accurately and finally new ways of making individual psychology available to readers. The realistic novel presented *this* world in *this* time, competing with history and journalism as a way of recording the truth of contemporary experience. So powerful was this fictional form, that many writers and critics believed it to be the end of a long process of evolution. At last we had learned how to tell the truth in fiction! But truth is elusive and has a way of turning to dust and ashes whenever we try to stop it from growing and changing.

All during the time of the rise of realism, a number of things had been going on which tended to counteract the realistic movement and prepared the way for a great shift in human awareness. The physical scientists, as they perfected their instruments of vision and measurement, began to explore worlds which in relation to ordinary human experience seem fantastic. Cosmic space and atomic space began to reveal their secrets, and in doing so posed problems which only "fantastic" speculation seemed able to solve. The theory of evolution and the origin of species began to change our sense of human time. The pace of technological change led people to wonder about the shape of the future. The notions of natural and supernatural, which had seemed so firm when science was merely experimenting and measuring, became shaky when science began constructing and destroying. Things that had seemed fantastic became actuality, from planes and rockets to wonder drugs and super bombs. In response to this sense of technological change and fantastic possibilities in a future that became increasingly more real, new fictional forms began to emerge.

From the time of Galileo onward, prototypes of modern science fiction appeared, but most literary historians agree that the first work of fiction that has all of the characteristics of the science fiction genre was written by a woman born shortly after the political revolutions in the United States and France had changed in the most concrete way possible humanity's sense of the future. Mary Shelley's *Frankenstein* (1818), often taken for a mere literary monster, has had so many offspring that we now recognize it as the progenitor of a species rather than a genetic freak. A new species is simply the result of a mutation which proves reproductively sound. A monster is an unsuccessful mutation. The race of *Frankenstein* has proved viable and now contends with traditional realism on a nearly equal footing. (See pp. 191–96 for a discussion of this novel.)

Some historians, of course, have sought a more ancient pedigree for science fiction, in fabulous tales of imaginary voyages or in utopian fictions that imagined ideal societies as a way of criticizing the world in which their authors were forced to live. Both these fictional forms are powerfully alive in Swift's *Gulliver's Travels* (1726), which was written a century before *Frankenstein*. Swift's book is rightly considered one of the wonders of the literary world. And its ancestors in the literature of travel and utopia include works of sufficient genius to be of current interest. The *Utopia* of Thomas More (written 200 years before *Gulliver*), the satires of Lucian (second century A.D.), and *The Republic* of Plato (fourth century B.C.) are sometimes included in genealogies of science fiction—obviously to add distinction to the pedigree. But a new species needs no pedigree. Its ancestry is interesting but the mutation that constitutes its special generic quality is much more important. With all due respect for its prototypic predecessors, science fiction is a distinctly modern form of literature.

The palpable progressiveness of science and technology, and the similar concreteness of political change in revolutionary Europe and America at the end of the eighteenth century, forced people to begin perceiving the world in new ways. Above all, humanity was finally faced with a future at once real and unknown, stimulating and terrifying. The shock involved in this new concept of the future can hardly be realized by those of us who accept the notion of future shock as a commonplace. But it was a great shock indeed, and stimulated some imaginations powerfully.

In order to appreciate the nature of the first future shock we must imagine how people of the pre-modern era visualized the future. In ancient times most people saw the future as being simply a continuation of the present—until the end of the world. For many, the myth of a golden age, from which men had fallen and to which they might be restored at the end of time, provided some comfort. But the notion that the world would change regularly is simply not a part of human thought until modern times. Plato, who saw as far as anyone, saw only cycles—as tyranny, oligarchy, democracy, anarchy, and, once again, tyranny succeeded one another in time. Others saw history as having involved a steady decay from gods to heroes to men, which could only be renewed by the gods returning to earth, possibly destroying it, and beginning the cycle again. The idea of steady and irreversible growth in human capabilities was unthinkable until a few hundred years ago, and the idea of humanity as the product of an evolution from less highly organized forms of life would have seemed fantastic beyond blasphemy until the last century.

The point of this brief dip into human concepts of time and history is that science fiction could begin to exist as a literary form only when a different future became conceivable by human beings—specifically a future in which new knowledge, new discoveries, new adventures, new mutations, would make life radically different from the familiar patterns of the past and present. Once it becomes possible to think in this way, the division between realism and fantasy begins to fade, and we can see that realism depends upon a view of the world that largely ignores the future. Once we acknowledge that the very concepts of natural and supernatural are subject to historical change, then a change in time becomes a license for a change in the boundary between natural and supernatural. Once we understand this we can see how Mary Shelley changed her reality by simply projecting a scientific advance that *might* be made *some* day upon her own historical time. She introduced a piece of a possible future into her own world and altered forever the possibilities of literature.

THE FIRST CENTURY A.F. (AFTER FRANKENSTEIN)

When Mary Shelley wrote *Frankenstein,* science fiction had neither a name nor any recognition as a separate form of literature. This situation lasted for a century: a century of extraordinary scientific discovery by Pasteur, Darwin, and Einstein among others; a century of tremendous technological and social change, including the development of steam engines, mills, factories, railroads, automobiles, and culminating with man's first hesitant ventures toward space—first in balloons and finally in winged vehicles that were heavier than air. During this century many of the most respected writers in America, England, and Europe tried their hands at fiction that played with the fantastic possibilities suddenly made available by new scientific ideas and technological discovery. The human imagination is *always* heavily influenced by the world-view that is dominant in its time. And in the nineteenth century traditional world-views were shaken as never before, inviting speculation to fill the great gaps opening in traditional wisdom.

To follow the details of these adventures in speculation would be both time-consuming and confusing. But we can single out four authors who wrote in the century after *Frankenstein* whose work illustrates the major directions taken by the speculative imagination in the fiction of that century. And these directions will prove to be helpful guideposts in developing a sense of the history of the literary form that has come to be called science fiction. These four writers are Edgar Allan Poe (American, 1809–49), Jules Verne (French, 1828–1905), Edward Bellamy (American, 1850–98), and Edgar Rice Burroughs (American, 1875–1950).

Edgar Allan Poe, though perhaps best known to us as a writer of stories designed to produce a chill of terror or horror, also worked with two other forms of fiction that were largely his own inventions. He wrote the first fully achieved detective stories, initiating a special form of fiction which is still going strong. And he perfected a certain kind of speculative tale based on scientific or philosophical ideas, which although less durable has some very distinguished modern practitioners, such as the Argentine writer Jorge Luis Borges. We may call this sort of tale metaphysical fiction, since it involves speculation about the nature of the universe which goes beyond the bounds of any known science. Poe, in fact, worked out of a philosophy which was materialistic but insisted on the existence of a "rarified matter," which was "unparticled" and hence beyond the detection of our clumsy scientific instruments. Presumably, the two spirits of his tale "The Conversation of Eiros and Charmion" are beings who after "death" have been translated to a more "rarefied" form of existence. In the tale, they meet and discuss the recent end of the world, caused by a collision with a comet that removed the nitrogen from earth's atmosphere, setting the globe afire in a field of pure oxygen. This combination of science with notions that transcend science is typical of Poe, and represents a persistent feature of contemporary science fiction. The end-of-the-world motif, needless to say, has also been a persistent preoccupation in science fiction, since Mary Shelley's *The Last Man* (1826). But Poe's unique combination of idealism and materialism has never been recaptured—which is perhaps just as well, since it means that no other writer has had to pay quite the same price in the psychological tension produced by that unique combination of values. Poe's philosophy has been ably summarized by David Ketterer in the following words:

> It is Poe's basic assumption that man lives in an inevitable state of deception as a result of the subjective, ideopathic nature of his awareness, which is limited externally by his circumscribed place in space and time, and internally by his personal experience, eccentricities, and in particular his erratic, dissecting, and gullible reason. (*New Worlds for Old*, p. 53)

Such a distrust of that very "ratiocination" which he dearly loved was an important part of Poe's mental equipment. A similar admiration for scientific thinking coupled with a vivid sense of its limitations is part of the equipment of many a modern writer of science fiction.

It is hard to think of anyone more different from Poe than Jules Verne, whose works have been aptly called (by Darko Suvin) "an epic of communication for the age of industrial liberalism." As Poe has roots in Swift and the prophetic books of Blake, Verne descends from Defoe and the positivism of Auguste Comte. Defoe's *Robinson Crusoe* (1719) is an extraordinary voyage in which a matter-of-fact, ordinary man subdues a new world with the help of a conveniently inexhaustible supply of hardware. It is *not* fantastic, but it is extraordinary. Verne took the Crusoe tradition and stretched its dimensions—around the world, inside the earth, under the sea, through the air, around the moon. As Suvin has shrewdly observed, "Verne's voyages fill in the white spots of already sketched space, but they do not reach new imaginative space" (from an article in *Clio,* IV/1, pp. 51–71). Verne is the poet of hardware. He loves to dilate on the technology of his adventures, and this technology is for the most part closely limited by the science of his own time. His fiction is resolutely unspeculative. After all, a speculative Robinson Crusoe would no doubt have perished from an acute sense of his own loneliness and isolation. Like Crusoe, Verne's characters are busy, busy, busy with material things, in a world that is very solid. Verne's universe is on the verge of complete subjugation by a science still in the stages of quantification and classification. And he thrills with participation in this material progress. He participated, of course, not only through his imaginary voyages. He was also a commercial success. He was thus the first writer of science fiction to make a fortune through his writing. For this alone he might have been remembered. But his works, too, have survived, for a time mainly as children's books, but now rediscovered and examined seriously by such influential critics in his own country as Michel Butor and Roland Barthes. And surely Verne is very much alive in all those literary descendants of his who delight in the technical side of science fiction and tend to ignore the problematics of human motivation and the cost of technological progress. (See pp. 196–200 for a discussion of *20,000 Leagues Under the Sea*.)

If Verne represents the physical dimension of nineteenth-century science fiction, with his emphasis on the conquest of local space, and Poe represents a metaphysical aspect of this new literary phenomenon, Edward Bellamy represents a third dimension of social concern and commitment—and a fourth dimension, *the* fourth dimension: time. More than anything else, the new senses of time developed in the nineteenth century and the beginning of the twentieth have enabled—or required—a science fiction to deal with them. Bellamy wrote a single book of uncalculable influence, which sprang from the sort of political concern that generated the socialistic and communistic movements of the nineteenth century. This concern alone could not have produced a work of such immediate impact. The ideas of Karl Marx have done more to change the world than the similar ideas presented by Bellamy in *Looking Backward* (1888). But *Looking Backward,* set in the year 2000, found a style, a form for social vision, which gave it an emotional coloring that no work of pure political economy could hope to match.

The book's impact was extraordinary. In popularity as measured by sales, only *Uncle Tom's Cabin* and *Ben Hur* exceeded it. It was translated into over twenty languages. In the United States alone, during the dozen years between its appearance and the turn of the century, some forty-six other utopian works of fiction were published in imitation of it. Between 1890 and 1891 in this country 165 Bellamy Clubs were founded in response to *Looking Backward*. And later social critics like John Dewey, William Allen White, Eugene V. Debs, Norman Thomas, and Thorstein Veblen all acknowledged the influence of Bellamy's book. This influence is the result of an aesthetic break-through, a burst into new literary territory which had a profound effect on the future of literature. The tradition of utopian fictions, ideal worlds invented to illustrate political theories, is as old as Plato. But the utopian tradition until the eighteenth century had always located its ideal worlds in "another place," on the moon, inside the earth, around the globe. Bellamy located his in Boston, Massachusetts, in a time a little over a century after the date of his book's publication. (Some French writers had anticipated him in the revolutionary period, and doubtless there were other hints from various quarters, but he was the first significant writer in English to bring Utopia home, to present it as lying ahead in our path—and in Boston!)

By entrusting his tale to a time-traveling hero—born in 1857 and mesmerized by a quack doctor on 30 May 1887 only to find himself alive on 10 September 2000—Bellamy revolutionized utopian fiction. After its shocking beginning the book became more of a guided tour than a story—as is the way with utopian fictions, for the most part—but in the course of the tour, Bellamy's own world was tried and found wanting when measured by the standards of the year 2000. The formula proved irresistible, and time travelers began flying about the literary universe with astonishing frequency. Mark Twain sent his Connecticut Yankee back to Camelot. And even Henry James, on his death bed, was in the process of getting a more modest voyager back to the eighteenth century in *The Sense of the Past* (1917). William Morris sent a man for *News from Nowhere* (1890) into a future that looked like the best features of the Middle Ages combined with labor-saving machinery. Bellamy had brought the vision of a better world into close proximity with humanity's growing sense of time as an inexorable voyage into the unknown. In his hands the unknown was largely benevolent—a consummation devoutly to be wished. Not everyone saw it that way, of course. Even in Bellamy's time, some readers found his utopia itself unattractive as a possible future. But by bringing together a setting in the near future and a utopian social consciousness, Bellamy had created a fictional form of enormous potency. He had not, however, solved all the problems of his form *as* fiction. The social vision was incredibly stimulating—in 1888. When the vision lost some of its freshness, the work had little in the way of fictional quality to preserve it, and it sank into near oblivion: immensely influential, but dated, dead. Now it is a document in social and literary history, while the boy-scout adventures of Jules Verne are studied by the most sophisticated literary scholars. If there is a moral here, it is not easy to draw. Verne himself is more alive than his tradition. Bellamy's tradition is still producing works of power and interest. But the visions are darker now.

What Bellamy lacked or spurned was possessed in abundance by a host of writers who did not have his concern for social evolution. As space and time were opened for literary exploration, popular writers of adventure stories began poaching on that territory, and of these the most popular was Edgar Rice Burroughs. Later so familiar that his fans referred to him by his initials alone, ERB began his career with a story in a pulp magazine, *All-Story,* in 1912. (Of the pulps, more later.) This tale, called "Under the Moons of Mars" and later published as a novel under the title *A Princess of Mars* (1917), was the first of a whole series of Martian novels. *All-Story* also published ERB's second story, "Tarzan of the Apes," which led to another series. A third series set in the center of the world began with *At the Earth's Core* (1914). In 1923 he started a moon series with *The Moon Maid,* and in 1932 a series set on Venus began with *Pirates of Venus.* He wrote other fiction, not part of a long series, including *The Land that Time Forgot* (1924), which many believe to be his best work. It is estimated that total sales of all editions of his works have now passed the hundred million mark. He described himself as having been born in Peking and raised in the Forbidden City, but actually he came from Chicago. He died in bed at the age of seventy-four while reading a comic book, leaving behind a flourishing business empire in Tarzana, California and about a dozen novels which were published after his death, bringing his total output up to around seventy books. Not bad for an ex-cavalryman, gold prospector, railroad cop, and candy man.

He must have been doing something right, though no literary critic can speak of his work without embarrassment. Candy man was his true vocation, of course, and he remained one to the end. He was a formula writer and he knew what formulas worked: essentially a prettified violence and a tantalizing threat of sex—the same combination that popularized Greek romances all over the Mediterranean world two thousand years ago. One critic has counted seventy-six threatened rapes in ERB's output of four years (1912–15), without a single consummation. The women in these tales are tantalizing and scantily clad. They are threatened by hideous monsters out of fairy tales and the Arabian Nights, and protected by muscular heroes who also long to possess them but respect their virtue utterly. That these scenes take place on Mars or Venus signifies little. Any strange place would do. But "Mars" provides a kind of license for the monstrous variations of humanoid and animal creation that ERB's sense of wonder required. There is a strong temptation for the critic to write him off as a hack who has taken shrewd advantage of a weakness in human nature. But this would be most unwise, for what he represents is a vital part of all fiction and especially of science fiction. And his work, despite clumsy prose and obvious appeals to simple emotions, has certain redeeming features that may have as much to do with his survival as the formulas he employs.

His greatest strength is a genuine inventiveness that many "serious" writers might envy. This is not the ingenuity which creates memorable individuals, nor is it a keen eye for social types. Burroughs creates whole species which are the embodiment of ideas—frequently revealing a horror which is *in* the ideas but not so noticeable. Consider two examples: the Lotharians in *Thuvia, Maid of Mars* (1920) and the Kaldanes of *The Chessmen of Mars* (1922). Both are based on a similar notion, an exaggeration of the mental at the expense of the physical, but their conception is strikingly different and suggests at least a measure of the author's imaginative power. The Lotharians are a race of extensive mentalization. Most of them have died but they maintain the appearance of life in their city by imagining its citizens; they even defend it successfully with imaginary warriors, whose fictional arrows kill real men because these men believe in the reality of the fictions. In doing this the Lotharians are careful not to allow their imaginary soldiers any supernatural activities, for that might shatter the illusion. They must even seem to die if wounded in combat. Within the city there are two parties of survivors: realists and etherealists. The etherealists do not eat anything, while the realists must create and ingest imaginary meals in order to survive. The bluff Carthoris, a typical Burroughs hero, trying to understand this strange world, discovers that a monstrous animal called Komal is believed to provide the energy that powers the brains of the surviving Lotharians. "Komal is the essence," a realist tells Carthoris:

> "Even the etherealists admit that mind itself must have substance in order to transmit to imaginings the appearance of substance. For if there really was no such thing as substance it could not be suggested—what has never been cannot be imagined. Do you follow me?"
>
> "I am groping," said Carthoris dryly.
>
> "So the essence must be substance," continued Jav. "Komal is the essence of the All, as it were. He is maintained by substance. He eats. He eats the real. To be explicit he eats the realists." (*Thuvia*, Ch. 7)

It is as if Superman had blundered into a story by Borges. Only, the satire is directed *against* metaphysical supersubtlety. In the presence of the solid flesh and common sense of Carthoris, this talk of essence and substance parodies itself. Real monsters must be faced by real men. Burroughs is smarter than he usually lets us think. This passage has a touch of Swift in it as well as a touch of *The Wizard of Oz* (1900). Like L. Frank Baum, Burroughs is a master at populating imaginary landscapes. His kaldanes and rykors in *The Chessmen of Mars* take the same theme and project it more seriously. The kaldanes and rykors are symbiotic species who have developed together. The rykors are humanoid bodies without heads, and the kaldanes are large spidery creatures capable of implanting themselves on the neck of a rykor and functioning as its head, controlling its movements. The kaldanes consider this an ideal evolutionary adaptation, powerful brains with large strong bodies at their service, but they prove no match for humans whose thoughts come from their bodies as well as their brains, and whose bodies respond more efficiently to the orders of a brain that is their own. A simple moral, perhaps, but a good one, and powerfully presented. There is a balance in Burroughs between mind and body which many headier novelists lack. He is not a philosopher but a writer of amazing stories; still, some amazing stories are more fully conceived than others. His have a restraint and inner consistency that many wilder fictions lack. ERB's durability—and he is very much in print—is a measure of his mastery of the most humble but most essential task of fiction. He can tell a tale.

Thus in the first century A.F. the as yet unbaptized genre of science fiction explored its potential range in various directions. Poe's metaphysical speculation, Verne's romance of hardware, Bellamy's social criticism, and ERB's tales of exotic adventure did not flourish alone but in the midst of emulators and precursors of every sort. And if you should ask whether any person of genius during this period began to put it all together, speculation and social criticism, hardware and exotic adventure, the answer is, "Yes, someone did." Actually more than one person did, but one led all the others by such a wide margin, that students of the field are beginning to divide it historically into the period before and after this man wrote. He did some of his best work while Queen Victoria was still alive, and survived to chat personally with Lenin and F.D.R. He predicted that air warfare would come and destroy the frontiers that separated soldiers and civilians, and he lived through the bombing of London. He predicted that atomic energy would be used for bombs, and he died shortly after the first such bomb was dropped on a city full of human beings. In his later years he was much attacked because he seemed too optimistic about the future of humanity and designed a utopian vision which one critic called a "paradise of little fat men." He *was* a little fat man, though he had been an undernourished boy, and he was a remarkable writer, whose work is still insufficiently appreciated in literary circles because his greatest achievement as an imaginative writer came in the area of science fiction, which is only now beginning to receive acceptance as a serious form of fiction. His name, of course, was H. G. Wells, and he deserves a separate discussion.

H. G. WELLS (1866-1946)

Enter the hero. A scrappy little man who was destined for oblivion as an apprentice to a draper but struggled to educate himself and made the world take notice of him as a writer of fiction and a social critic. He was much acclaimed in his lifetime, but only in recent years, after nearly a century of emulation by other writers, has one aspect of his achievement been truly appreciated. Mary Shelley planted the flag on the new territories, but Wells explored them, settled them, and developed them. Writers as far apart from Wells—and from one another—in geography and temperament as Yevgeny Zamyatin in Russia and Jorge Luis Borges in Argentina called Wells master and praised his work. And his influence on the science fiction tradition in the English-speaking world is so great as to be incalculable.

Wells himself would regret our emphasizing his personal qualities and achievements. He firmly believed that conditions shaped individuals and that the times made men what they were. But if the times had made his achievement possible, as they make most scientific or artistic breakthroughs possible, he was more aware of his times than most, and he earned his achievements by this awareness. In many ways, he was ahead of his time, and he made it his business to make other citizens conscious of the future. In 1934, at the age of sixty-eight, in his *Experiment in Autobiography,* he was proposing that universities establish a new discipline, to be called "Human Ecology," which would project into the future "strands of biological, intellectual, economic consequences." Wells himself had begun such work in a book called *Anticipations of the Reaction of Mechanical and Scientific Progress Upon Human Life and Thought,* which appeared in 1900. Recalling this occasion, he later wrote, "A comprehensive attempt to state and weigh and work out a general resultant for the chief forces of social change throughout the world, sober forecasting, that is to say, without propaganda, satire, or extravaganza, was so much a novelty that my book, crude though it was and smudgily vague, excited quite a number of people" (*Experiment in Autobiography,* p. 551). In 1902 Wells presented his ideas in a Royal Institution Lecture:

> I called this lecture the *Discovery of the Future* and I drew a hard distinction between what I called the legal (past-regarding) and the crea-

tive (future-regarding) minds. I insisted that we overrated the darkness of the future, that by adequate analysis of contemporary processes its conditions could be brought within the range of our knowledge and its form controlled, and that mankind was at the dawn of a great change-over from life regarded as a system of consequences to life regarded as a system of constructive effort. I did not say the future could be foretold but I said that its conditions could be foretold. We should be less and less bound by the engagements of the past and more and more ruled by a realization of the creative effect of our acts. We should release ourselves more and more from the stranglehold of past things. (*Experiment*, pp. 553–54)

The man who was advocating human ecology and future studies so vigorously seventy-five years ago was a unique figure in English life and letters. The greatest achievements in British fiction during the nineteenth century were the work of those who because of their sex or class had been denied the privileges of a university education. Jane Austen, Dickens, the Brontë sisters, and George Eliot all wrote from outside the system of prestige and power determined by the great public schools and universities. They were far from ignorant, but their learning was different from the classical education provided by the system of which Oxford and Cambridge universities were the crown jewels. Herbert George Wells was similarly excluded from the halls of privileged learning. Like Dickens he was apprenticed at an early age. Which meant that his parents paid to have him taken on as a kind of slave for a period of years, during which, in return for working about thirteen hours a day, the boy was supposed to learn the rudiments of a trade. He lived in the house of his master, with other apprentices, and was legally bound or "indentured" to him. Wells was found unsuitable for trade after two years and released from his indenture by the owner of the Southsea Drapery Emporium.

What made Wells unique among those British novelists of the nineteenth century who were excluded from the universities was the kind of education he finally did receive. After his failure as a budding draper, his talent for schoolwork won him a job as a kind of student teacher at a small private school. And here an unusual aspect of the English educational system came to his rescue. It was possible in Wells's day for a senior teacher to earn money when his students did well on science examinations. Wells's headmaster at the Midhurst School, discovering that Wells was a sort of learning machine, who could get up a subject by himself from a textbook and do first class work on national examinations, established a number of so-called evening courses, which had only one student—Wells. The headmaster would give Wells a suitable textbook, and when Wells scored high on the exam, as he usually did, his "teacher" would pocket the reward for his "teaching."

This worked nicely until Wells's achievements were noticed and he was offered a scholarship to the Normal School of Science in London, which he was pleased to accept. At the Normal School, Wells encountered the most important educational influence in his life. He studied biology under the great T. H. Huxley, then carrying on the work of his friend Charles Darwin, who had died in 1882, a year or so before Wells began attending Huxley's lectures. Wells described his experience with Huxley in this way:

> The study of zoology in this phase was an acute, delicate, rigorous and sweepingly magnificent series of exercises. It was a grammar of form and a criticism of fact. That year I spent in Huxley's class, was beyond all question, the most educational year of my life. It left me under that urgency for coherence and consistency, that repugnance for haphazard assumptions and arbitrary statements, which is the essential distinction of the educated from the uneducated mind. (*Experiment,* pp. 160–61)

His teachers in the physical sciences proved less stimulating, and Wells himself discovered in time that he was not himself a scientist of the first rank. He married young—twice—and, desperate for money, tried his hand at what we now call scientific journalism. He began to have some success at this, and he thought of selling some works of fiction to the same papers and magazines that were accepting his articles. Earlier, he had written a piece called "The Chronic Argonauts," which was serialized in the *Science Schools Journal* for three installments, but had stopped writing it because he realized it was no good. Later he observed,

> That I realized I could not go on with it marks a stage in my education in the art of fiction. It was the original draft of what later became the *Time Machine,* which won me recognition as an imaginative writer. But the prose was over-elaborate . . . and the story is clumsily invented, and loaded with sham significance. . . . If a young man of twenty-one were to bring me a story like the *Chronic Argonauts* for my advice today I do not think I should encourage him to go on writing. (*Experiment,* pp. 253–54)

Wells is unique among the major novelists of his time because of his training in science. He was the first novelist ever to understand and accept fully the consequences of Darwin's theory of evolution, and his own personal struggle for existence had prepared him to apply Darwinian thinking to social organization in a vivid and personal way. This experience, which for his first thirty years was a long struggle with an entrenched class system, an established church, and an economy that kept the lower middle class and the working class perpetually on the edge of poverty, combined with his education to make him a formidable social critic. And social criticism became increasingly what he took his task to be from the time he found his own literary voice until his dying day.

In his middle years, Wells had a celebrated quarrel with that great master of literary style, Henry James. James admired Wells's raw talent but wished Wells would discipline himself more, construct more carefully, write more elegantly. It is widely assumed in literary circles that James won the argument, but it is probably more appropriate to say that neither won, since their views are aspects of a permanent division in the ranks of men of letters. For Wells responded to James's criticism with a strong counterattack, in which he accused James of leaving out too much of life in order to achieve a kind of fussy, old-maidish neatness:

> He omits everything that demands digressive treatment or collateral statement. For example, he omits opinions. In all his novels you will find no people with defined political opinions, no people with religious opinions, none with clear partisanships or with lusts or whims, none definitely up to any specific impersonal thing. There are no poor people dominated by the imperatives of Saturday night and Monday morning, no dreaming types—and don't we all more or less live dreaming? And none are ever decently forgetful. All that much of humanity he clears out before he begins his story. It's like cleaning rabbits for the table. (*Boon*, pp. 98–99)

The counterattack goes on, and becomes quite bitter. But the main point argued by Wells is that his own work, though imperfect and unpolished, attends to aspects of life left untouched by James.

A number of things become apparent to anyone who studies this argument. For one thing, it marks very clearly the separation between a "high," especially literary, kind of fiction and a "low" fiction, closer to journalism. Henry James saw himself as devoted to Art, while Wells thought he was in the service of Life. At this time, what had been a rich but unified tradition of realism in fiction began to split into separate forms: a psychological and poetic kind of novel on the one hand and a sociological and journalistic novel on the other. This is an important event in the history of fiction. But for our purposes what is even more important is what was omitted from the argument between these two writers. For Wells had defended himself as a realist, not as a romancer, as a reporter on life, not as a writer of imagination. There is nothing in his argument with James—or anywhere else in his writing—to suggest that he valued highly the work that has kept him alive in literature today, the novels and stories that he called his "scientific romances," most of which were written and published before 1906, while he was still in his thirties. Yet today, when his social criticism has long been out of print, and only one or two of his more realistic novels are obtainable, the scientific romances are almost all available in various paperback editions. Wells is not only a figure of importance in the history of science fiction. His work, like all truly classic work in literature, is still alive. His major works of science fiction fall into two groups, with just a slight overlap in time, as his interest moved from a fiction of wonder to a fiction of social concern and commitment.

Group 1.	*The Time Machine*	1895
	The Island of Dr. Moreau	1896
	The Invisible Man	1897
	The War of the Worlds	1898
	The First Men in the Moon	1901
Group 2.	*When the Sleeper Wakes*	1899
	The Food of the Gods	1904
	In the Days of the Comet	1906
	The War in the Air	1908

In *The Time Machine* (see pp. 200–204) Wells took the notion of time travel, which had become very popular since *Looking Backward,* and put it on a "mechanical" basis. The importance of this is not in the vague, pseudoscientific rationale he provided for the time machine in his novel, but in the fact that it *was* a machine, which could move through time under the control of its operator. The replacement of the dream, enchantment, mesmerization, hibernation or other method of reaching the future by a new mechanical agent, a time *machine,* changed the whole footing of time travel, opening up the past as well as the future, for imaginative investigation. Though Wells's traveler returns from the future only, there is speculation in the closing pages of the novel that he may also have reached the past. Later writers have been quick to pick up that hint and develop it. Wells also changed the scale of time travel. Thinking in Darwinian temporal dimensions, he projected his traveler sufficiently far into the future to discover not only social change but evolutionary biological change as well. It was Wells, more than anyone else, who introduced Darwinian thought to fiction.

The Island of Dr. Moreau is a more pointedly Darwinian and a more gruesome and grotesque tale. On a Pacific island a mad scientist vivisects animals, reconstructing them in his own image and giving them to the best of his ability powers of speech and thought. These monsters fear and worship their creator, constantly repeating prayers and enacting rituals to remind themselves that they are "men" and must not revert to animal ways. In this, his darkest vision, Wells seems to ask why man has evolved to such a tormenting state of being, with aspirations toward ideals that are continually thwarted by his animal appetites. The book horrified many reviewers upon its first appearance but has inspired later writers and remains one of Wells's strongest and most unified works of fiction.

Like Dr. Moreau, Mr. Griffin of *The Invisible Man* represents science gone astray and dehumanized by its own power. Though Wells deliberately makes the science of his books fabulous, his scientists are very real indeed. He has a vivid sense of scientific attitudes and conveys with vigor the behavior of men for whom research and discovery outweigh all human values. Griffin's invisibility makes him something at once more and less than human. His needs drive him to acts of theft and violence, of course, but his disposition as a scientist had led him to undervalue the ordinary lives around him even before he succeeded in making himself invisible. These first novels of Wells have a strong quality of fable or parable. They are brief, vivid, and present wonders to us in the most matter-of-fact manner possible.

In *The War of the Worlds* Wells is at his most matter-of-fact, when he brings Martian invaders into an astonishingly ordinary English countryside and presents these creatures and their weapons through the eyes of a plain, downright Englishman. *The First Men in the Moon* is in this style also, but since it is mostly a kind of travelogue it loses some of the dramatic quality that the earlier works possessed. It is as if Wells's growing social conscience had begun to draw his interest away from fiction which could not incorporate the kind of criticism of society he wanted to make. His narrator in this novel verges on being a mindless, purely exploitative capitalist, but Wells seems to hesitate between sympathy for him and scorn of him, as the story hesitates between a pure adventure and a commentary on the imperatives of discovery and exploitation.

In *When the Sleeper Wakes,* written and published before *The First*

Men in the Moon, Wells had already begun to move in a new direction. In this novel his hero, Graham, is an ordinary man who falls into a trance and awakes two hundred years later, in a society in which bosses and workers have divided into rigid classes and all of England lives in five enormous cities. Starvation and disease have been virtually eliminated, but "the whole world was exploited, a battlefield of business" (Ch. 14) until at last everything is owned by trusts:

> So the magnificent dream of the nineteenth century, the noble project of universal individual liberty and universal happiness, touched by a disease of honour, crippled by a superstition of absolute property, crippled by the religious feuds that had robbed the common citizens of education, robbed men of standards of conduct, and brought the sanctions of morality to utter contempt, had worked itself out in the face of invention and ignoble enterprise, first to a warring plutocracy, and finally to the rule of a supreme plutocrat. (Ch. 14)

This terrible future came to pass, as Wells makes clear, quite naturally, through the working of social forces. And something like it is really going to happen, he warned, if men do not take some thought for the future and try to plan for it.

After Graham wakes, he realizes that men like him, in his own time, had been allowing this future to gather and lie in wait for later generations:

> It seemed to him the most amazing thing of all that in his thirty years of life he had never tried to shape a picture of these coming times. "We were making the future," he said, "and hardly any of us troubled to think what future we were making. And here it is!" (Ch. 7)

From the publication of *Anticipations* in 1900, this became the major concern of H. G. Wells: how to avoid the bad future he saw as inevitable if men would not *plan* for a better one, and how to act in order to bring a better future into being. In *The Food of the Gods* he presented his planners as a new race of young giants brought into being by a nutritional breakthrough. Their size and their greater intelligence bring them into conflict with ordinary men. As the book ends they are preparing to battle the "little people" for reasons one of them expresses with considerable eloquence:

> Through us and through the little folk the Spirit looks and learns. From us by word and birth and act it must pass—to still greater lives. This earth is no resting place; this earth is no playing place, else indeed we

might put our throats to the little people's knife, having no greater right
to live than they. And they in turn might yield to the ants and vermin.
We fight not for ourselves but for growth, growth that goes on for ever.
To-morrow, whether we live or die, growth will conquer through us.
That is the law of the spirit for evermore. To grow according to the will
of God! To grow out of these cracks and crannies, out of these shadows
and darknesses, into greatness and the light! (Bk III, Ch. 5)

The issue was becoming clear. Either mankind would grow spiritually,
until it could control its own power over the material universe and shape
the world benevolently—or it would strangle and choke in the foulness of
its own unplanned growth. *The Food of the Gods* raises many questions
and provides few answers, as does *In the Days of the Comet*. This relatively undervalued work contains some of Wells's best writing. It is
autobiographical in style and in content, portraying the anguish of a
bright young man's coming of age in a social system which is repressive
to the point of madness—a madness which expresses itself in the ultimate
human madness of war. Yet the society presented is a very convincing
version of the world Wells himself grew up in, portrayed as horrible
without any of the exaggerations of satire—horrible because it wastes and
frustrates so many good instincts and hopeful qualities in its own youth.
In Wells's novel this all too real society is saved from destructive war by
gas from a comet which magically removes the poison of competitive
strife from the human psyche, enabling people to live in mutual and
benevolent harmony, even to the point of eliminating jealousy in love.
The magical unsatisfactoriness of this solution has no doubt caused the
book as a whole to be slighted—or perhaps it is the unuttered conclusion
that without such intervention it is unlikely that humanity can grow more
benevolent or that society will organize to promote what is best in men
instead of what is worst. In the last of this sequence of major science
fiction novels, *The War in the Air,* Wells turned again to what is worst,
and described with truly startling prophetic powers what air warfare
would be like when it came.

Later, Wells tried harder and harder to produce believable, attainable
versions of the future, and at last came to feel assured that a sanely
planned world would come into being after mankind had learned a few
more lessons in its own destructive power. He has been much criticized
for this optimism, and his later writings are currently held to be of little
value. This is no place to reopen the question of the later Wells, but it is
definitely right for us to affirm here the strength, originality, and durability of his early fiction, both the scientific fables and the future-oriented

social criticism that followed the fables. In a period of a little over ten years, while producing many other writings of various kinds, Wells wrote nine science fiction novels which had an immense influence on later writers and have remained highly readable for three quarters of a century. In acknowledging this it remains only to look briefly at some other aspects of this achievement and to notice some of the recognition it has received.

The great strength of Wells as a writer of science fiction, and his great contribution to the tradition, lay in his ability to combine the fantastic with the plausible, the strange with the familiar, the new with the old. We can see this at every level of his work, from the word and the sentence to the largest structural concepts. If he wishes to show us a fantastic scene, he will present it from the viewpoint of the most matter-of-fact person conceivable. If he wishes to describe an unearthly thing, he will find the most concrete and specific language for it. His Martians will invade an England that is utterly commonplace and believable. And they will strike us with a vivid horror when seen through the eyes of a calm, plain-spoken narrator:

> A big greyish rounded bulk, the size, perhaps of a bear, was rising slowly and painfully out of the cylinder. As it bulged up and caught the light, it glistened like wet leather.
>
> Two large dark-coloured eyes were regarding me steadfastly. The mass that framed them, the head of the thing, it was rounded, and had, one might say, a face. There was a mouth under the eyes, the lipless brim of which quivered and panted, and dropped saliva. The whole creature heaved and pulsated convulsively. A lank tentacular appendage gripped the edge of the cylinder, another swayed in the air. (*The War of the Worlds,* Ch. 4)

The power of this seems to come straight from the creature itself, but it is subtly reinforced by the narrator's obvious difficulty in describing it through analogies to familiar objects: it "had, *one might say,* a face." The sense of an observer trying to retain objectivity and accuracy of description when confronted by monstrosity can be far more terrifying than shouts and screams of terror. Wells exploits this beautifully.

He is superb at physical details, as a biologist ought to be, and he knows how to use them in a telling way. His invisible man, when finally surrounded and beaten to death by a frightened crowd, loses his invisibility in a terribly convincing and moving fashion. The whole scene is worth examining, for it illustrates a variety of Wellsian techniques for domesticating the fantastic:

"Hullo!" cried the constable. "Here's his feet a-showing!"

And so, slowly, beginning at his hands and feet and creeping along his limbs to the vital centres of his body, that strange change continued. It was like the slow spreading of a poison. First came the little white nerves, a hazy grey sketch of a limb, then the glassy bones and intricate arteries, then the flesh and skin, first a faint fogginess, and then growing rapidly dense and opaque. Presently they could see his crushed chest and his shoulders, and the dim outline of his drawn and battered features.

When at last the crowd made way for Kemp to stand erect, there lay, naked and pitiful on the ground, the bruised and broken body of a young man about thirty. His hair and beard were white,—not grey with age, but white with the whiteness of albinism, and his eyes were like garnets. His hands were clenched, his eyes wide open, and his expression was one of anger and dismay.

"Cover his face!" said a man. "For Gawd's sake, cover that face!" and three little children, pushing forward through the crowd, were suddenly twisted round and sent packing off again.

Someone brought a sheet from the Jolly Cricketers, and having covered him, they carried him into that house. (Ch. 28)

That the invisible man should have been an albino, separated at birth from all others of his species, lends both psychological plausibility to the character, helping to account for his indifference to other people, and physiological piquancy to the body, which is humanly pitiful in its naked, broken state, but irrevocably other, strange and slightly monstrous. And all this in the midst of domestic details—the constable, the pub with its incongruously placid name, the curious children—which suggest an England virtually unchanged for centuries. Wells is a master of contrasts of this sort. Images like this remain with us for a long time.

But the power of this writing is not simply a matter of technical skill. Nor are these stories still attracting readers just because of their suspenseful plotting. As that master of intricate philosophical fiction, Jorge Luis Borges, wrote in "The First Wells," the value of Wells's work is not simply in his ability to tell a tale:

In my opinion, the excellence of Well's first novels—*The Island of Dr. Moreau,* for example, or *The Invisible Man*—has a deeper origin. Not only do they tell an ingenious story; but they tell a story symbolic of processes that are somehow inherent in all human destinies. The harassed invisible man who has to sleep as though his eyes were wide open because his eyelids do not exclude light is our solitude and our terror; the conventicle of seated monsters who mouth a servile creed in their night is the Vatican and is Lhasa. Work that endures is always capable of an infinite and plastic ambiguity; it is all things to all men, like the Apostle; it is a mirror that reflects the reader's own features and it is also a map of the world. (*Other Inquisitions*)

The ability of Wells to produce fantasy that dramatized truths about human nature and the human situation was what endeared him to Borges. Because his early fictions approached the status of myth, Borges predicted that they would enter into "the general memory of the species and even transcend the fame of their creator or the extinction of the language in which they were written" (p. 88).

To this tribute, in concluding our chapter on Wells, we can add the prophetic words of the brilliant Russian writer Yevgeny Zamyatin, written in 1922, while Wells was very much alive, and only a year or so after Zamyatin had finished writing *We:*

> In Wells's sociofantastic novels the plot is always dynamic, built on collisions, on conflict; the story is complex and entertaining. Wells invariably clothes his social fantasy and science fiction in the forms of a Robinsoniad, of the typical adventure novel so beloved in Anglo-Saxon literature. . . . However, in adopting the form of the adventure novel, Wells deepened it, raised its intellectual value, and brought into it the elements of social philosophy and science. In his own field—though, of course, on a proportionately lesser scale—Wells may be likened to Dostoyevsky, who took the form of the cheap detective novel and infused it with brilliant psychological analysis.
>
> An artist of considerable stature, a brilliant and subtle dialectician who has created models of an extraordinarily contemporary form—models of the urban myth, of socioscientific fantasy—Wells will unquestionably have literary successors and descendants. Wells is only a pioneer. The period of socioscientific fantasy in literature is only beginning. The entire fantastic history of Europe and European science in recent years makes it possible to forecast this with certainty. (*A Soviet Heretic,* pp. 288–89)

We began this chapter, speaking of Mary Shelley as a pioneer and Wells as a settler in the territory of science fiction, who developed and exploited what she had discovered. It is fitting, then, that we conclude with the perspective of Zamyatin, who saw Wells himself as a pioneer, one who had opened up new literary territory that young men like himself would explore and develop further. In the next section we shall be investigating some of the developments that Zamyatin predicted so confidently and so accurately in 1922.

THE TWENTIES AND THIRTIES

The great achievement of Wells as a science fiction writer lay in his ability to hold together so many of the facets of this kind of fiction. He was a good storyteller, always able to engage our interest in his characters' lives and generate in us a concern for their fates. And he had a gift for domesticating the fantastic and extrapolating plausibly from extraordinary situations. His sense of human society as an eco-system helped him to project visions of the future and to make those visions convincing. But after Wells it was some time before other writers appeared who could consistently manage the same kind of synthesis of thought and action in fiction. Thus, in the twenties and thirties we find science fiction fragmented into two distinct groups, both of which owe something to the influence of Wells. In Europe we can find a number of extraordinary writers of science fiction, whose works are emotionally powerful, intellectually demanding, and socially aware. In America we have, in marked contrast, the development of mass magazines, with stables of underpaid and overworked writers, turning out fiction that emphasized wonder and horror, delighted with new gadgets and new physical concepts, and almost totally innocent of social commitment and concern. Thus, when we look at the east side of the Atlantic Ocean during the twenties and thirties we find a few isolated giants, and on the American side a horde of pygmies. In England and Europe we must consider individual authors. But when we turn to America during this period we find ourselves considering not the writers themselves but the magazines they wrote in and the editors who shaped them.

A Political Europe

While America was still relatively isolated from the rest of the world and innocent of political developments abroad, continental Europe was undergoing massive changes in social and political structure. The Communist revolution in Russia was followed by the rise of fascism in Italy, Germany, and Spain. These developments combined with certain features of fictional form to create a powerful new kind of science fiction, the anti-utopian or dystopian novel. In considering this it is important to realize that the change from utopian to dystopian fiction involves precisely the invasion of traditional utopian writing by the concepts and techniques of science fiction. Utopias from Plato onward were largely innocent of what Wells called "human ecology." They were models of human desires rather than projections of social realities. But most utopias have something repellent about them, since they involve the imposition of order on society at the expense of liberty. This order may be consciously imposed or unconscious, a matter of force or of manipulation, but every attempt to visualize a utopia which benefits all human beings involves alternatives to actual existence which will strike some readers (those most privileged in actuality) as unfortunate. And the more it is insisted that any particular utopian vision is actually lying ahead for humanity at some particular point on the road of history—the more repellent its oppressive or manipulative features are likely to seem. Thus science fiction, which changes dream into projection, forces us to face the implications of utopia in a more concrete and therefore more powerful way.

This matter is worth some thought. We all live in a cultural situation which, since we have grown up in it and been shaped by it, seems to us "natural." Any radical change in this situation, even if clearly an improvement in some respects, is likely to strike us as painful. The more honestly the price for change is reckoned, the more painful it will seem. Most utopian fictions are vulnerable to criticism upon two grounds: either they hide the price by not envisioning their world with sufficient thoroughness, or they make the price so obvious that many readers are reluctant to pay it. Even Bellamy's *Looking Backward,* which was certainly intended as a vision of a better future, inspired both kinds of criticism. It, and its imitations, also inspired a host of reactions in which the future was presented as likely to be awful. These dystopian visions followed the natural contours of the literary territory—change is frightening, and the likelier it is the more frightening it becomes—and they also extrapolated from the most threatening aspect of contemporary history, the growing totalitarianism in political systems. Where the later Wells had run from Muddle into the arms of Planning, these writers saw Liberty and Identity being destroyed by Tyranny and The State.

The tradition of dystopian writing is derived, then, in reaction to Bellamy, both in emulation of Wells and in criticism of him. Jack London, a writer still underrated in his own country, saw the possibilities of this form early and exploited them in a powerful novel called *The Iron Heel* (1906). This novel, like Wells's *When the Sleeper Wakes* and his earlier "Story of the Days to Come" (1897), is horrible enough but lacks some of the concreteness which the later masters of the dystopian form achieved, largely because the world was kind enough to provide them with examples of the horrible future close at hand. Two continental writers stand out in the period we are considering. Each produced a classic of the dystopian kind. They are Yevgeny Zamyatin (Russian, 1884–1937) and Karel Čapek (Czechoslovakian, 1890–1938).

Zamyatin was an engineer by profession. In his lifetime he had the honor of being arrested and placed in solitary confinement by the Tsarist police, because he had joined the Bolshevik faction of the Social Democratic Party, and later being arrested, imprisoned in the same jail as before, and forbidden to publish by the police of the successful Bolsheviks. Finally, he was fortunate enough to be allowed to go into exile. He died in France. Before his departure he had been a leader of the Serapian Brotherhood, an organization of young Russian writers which included the formalist critic Victor Shklovsky. Zamyatin's work has proved influential throughout the world.

He is known primarily for one book, *We* (discussed on pp. 204-207), which was denied publication in Russia in 1923. It is the most carefully constructed of all dystopian novels, and perhaps for that reason it has proven the most durable. When an English version appeared in 1924 *We* entered English literature, where its influence is visible in works from Huxley's *Brave New World* (1932) and Orwell's *1984* (1949) to Vonnegut's *Player Piano* (1952) and Burgess's *A Clockwork Orange* (1962). In Zamyatin's regimented future the most personal aspects of life and thought are controlled by the State, and individuals are "Numbers," whose lives are shaped by all the forms of social and biological pressure that Zamyatin's fertile mind could conceive. Because this novel had such a powerful political impact, critics have overlooked the extent to which its vision is the vision of a scientist and the novel itself a work of science fiction. In 1923, in an essay called "Literature, Revolution, Entropy," Zamyatin explained how art, politics, and science must be part of a single vision: "What we need in literature today are vast philosophic horizons—horizons seen from mastheads, from airplanes; we need the most ultimate, the most fearsome, the most fearless 'Why?' and 'What next?' " (*A Soviet Heretic,* pp. 109–10). Most of science fiction does not try to rise to the philosophical standards set by Zamyatin in his critical essays or in his fiction. But some of it does, and his eloquent justification of the form remains an inspiration today.

Like Zamyatin, Karel Čapek did most of his writing during the unsettled period between the first and second World Wars. He was much more prolific than Zamyatin, producing almost fifty works of fiction, drama, and journalism during his short life. Only a few of these have ever been available in English: some of the plays, especially *The Insect Play* (1921) and *R.U.R.* or *Rossum's Universal Robots* (1921); and three science fiction novels, *The Absolute at Large* (1922, also called *The Factory for the Absolute*), *Krakatit* (1924), and *War with the Newts* (1936). For some time Čapek was best known in America for his plays, especially *R.U.R.*, which was a standard high school text in the thirties and established the word "robot" as a name for mechanical creatures. Actually, Čapek's brother Josef coined the word, basing it on the old word for drudgery in Czech: *robota*. (Čapek's robots are so human in appearance that most contemporary writers of science fiction would refer to them as "androids," a special name for robots that are human simulacra.) In *R.U.R.* the robots look much like humans and finally learn to behave like humans, lusting for power and ultimately achieving it at humanity's expense.

Čapek's fiction is now coming back into print in America and it is apparent that his talents were most suited to the medium of the book and the form of the novel. His greatest work is undoubtedly *War with the Newts,* a political satire which is technically innovative as fiction and ranges from the wildly humorous to the chillingly ominous in its effects. At times, Čapek is the funniest man ever to write science fiction (with the possible exception of Kurt Vonnegut, Jr.). At other times he is the most profoundly pessimistic (again with the possible exception of K. V., Jr.). In *War with the Newts* he frequently manages to be both at the same time.

In considering this novel we need to emphasize two aspects of Čapek's achievement: the complex power of his vision and the technical ingenuity of his method. His basic idea is simple, and not very different from that of *R.U.R.,* but his execution is extraordinary. The book is divided into three parts. In the first part a stupid sea captain in search of pearls stumbles upon a race of newts or salamanders living in the lagoon of a remote oriental island. These creatures are only a little smaller than men. They live in water but can emerge from it for short periods of time. It seems that they may be capable of learning human speech and working with tools. In their native lagoon their numbers are kept down by sharks, against whom they have no weapons. The captain persuades a Czech business tycoon, G. H. Bondy, to invest in development of the Newts, initially for pearl fishing and later for other projects. It turns out that, given weapons against sharks, the Newts multiply with incredible rapidity and spread from island to island, thus becoming an apparently inexhaustible source of slave labor for human entrepreneurs who hunt and sell them.

The second part of the book, "Along the Steps of Civilization," tells the story of a worldwide exploitation of the Newts, as they are imported to every seacoast and river, used for every imaginable purpose, put in zoos, made the subject of scientific experiments including vivisection, and finally become the objects of various humanitarian groups, who want to clothe them, enfranchise them, and convert them to various religions. This section ends with Newts reading papers at scientific gatherings and beginning to convert people to their own religion. They have become indispensable to the economic systems of all the advanced nations in the world, and they have acquired a substantial amount of power, including explosives and other weapons. In the third section they begin to make war on mankind, seeking room to expand their population. They need coastlines for breeding and they plan to rearrange the continental land masses of the world in order to yield the maximum amount of coast. Nations as we know them will have to go—as will most of the human race. And there seems to be no way to stop them.

At this point, in the book's last chapter, the author's "inner voice" intervenes. All along, the book has been presented through "documentation" from newspapers and other sources, taken from all over the world, revealing the journalistic habits and cultural quirks of a variety of nations. And the author has presented himself as a mere chronicler of these events. Now he reveals himself somewhat differently. The "inner voice" treats the work as a fiction and asks the author to provide a happy ending. The author says he is just a historian. They argue:

"Wouldn't it be possible to stop those Newts somehow?"

"It wouldn't. There are too many of them. You must make room for them."

"Wouldn't it be possible for them to die out somehow? Perhaps some disease or degeneration might develop among them."

"Too cheap, my dear fellow. Must Nature always be asked to straighten out the mess that man has made? And so, even you don't believe now that they could help themselves? So you see, you see; at the end you would again like to rely on someone or something to save you! I'll tell you something: *now* when a fifth of Europe is already covered with water, do you know who is still supplying the Newts with explosives, torpedoes, and drills? Do you know who it is that is feverishly working day and night in the laboratories to invent still more efficient machines and materials for annihilating the world? Do you know who lends them money, do you know who finances this End of the World, all this New Flood?"

"Yes, I do. All the factories. All the banks. All the different states."

"So you see. If only the Newts were fighting men, then perhaps something might be done; but men against men—that, my friend, can't be stopped."

"Wait; men against men! I've got an idea. Perhaps in the end the Newts may fight the Newts." (Pt. 3, Ch. 11)

And so the inner voice convinces the author that the Newts have learned so much from men that they will ultimately indulge in the same intraspecies combat, driven by the same pressures of greed and ambition. The final war with the Newts will be Newt against Newt, allowing some remnant of the human race to survive.

In narrating this history, Čapek is able to reenact for us all the atrocities that humans have committed against other species and against less developed human cultures. His most brilliant work appears in the ironically titled second section—"Along the Steps of Civilization." Here he pretends to be basing his narrative upon the journalistic records of the era haphazardly collected by the retired porter of G. H. Bondy—a Mr. Povondra—who started the whole thing by allowing the stupid sea captain in to see the greedy financier in the first place. Povondra's files, surreptitiously torn from newspapers in coffee-houses and frequently purged by Mrs. Povondra because the filing boxes have become overcrowded, enable Čapek to create an astonishing range of journalistic pieces, in which the mannerisms and prejudices of various nations are superbly captured and pilloried. The introduction of this kind of documentation into fiction, which John Dos Passos was seriously undertaking in America at that very time, had already been reduced to absurdity by Čapek's mad but acutely appropriate parodies.

Attempts have been made to see *War with the Newts* as an attack on the rise of Nazism—but his enemy is a greater and more terrifying one. For Čapek, as for Swift, Voltaire, and Vonnegut, the trouble is not in systems but in men. Human nature is the enemy. The Newts are pitiable victims until they learn from their oppressors how to be like them. Men are incapable of acting in a genuine collective spirit, as Čapek sees them, which is why there is no ism that can save them. It would be nice to think that he is wrong.

A somewhat different view of the human situation was then being developed in a country separated from the Continent by a narrow but crucial body of water, the English Channel.

Born in 1886, two years after Zamyatin and four years before Čapek, William Olaf Stapledon was the most distinguished writer of science fiction in English during the period between the first and second World Wars, and one of the most influential ever to write in any language. Like every thinking European in his time, he was deeply concerned about the future of the human race. Like Čapek, he feared that man's power had come to exceed his ethical control. But, perhaps because he was English and the insularity of his country made the bad news less depressing, or perhaps because he was a philosopher rather than a journalist, he saw some slight grounds for hope.

Stapledon's hope is cautious, and it takes different forms in different works, but its theme is something like this. The universe itself is not simply a collection of matter but matter shaped by some power that is immaterial. This power, or Spirit, as he usually calls it, is behind all great achievements. (This view, which owes a good deal to Hegel and Nietzsche, is similar to that expressed by the young giants in Wells's *Food of the Gods.*) The purpose of humanity in the universe is to understand Spirit as fully as possible and to live in harmony with it. The universe is in a state of evolution. The role of the human species in evolution is presently in question. Mankind now has so much power that it must either destroy itself or improve itself. There are no alternatives. Stapledon suggests various versions of improvement. The mildest is simply by a spreading of education so that what moves the best minds will move a majority of minds. More drastic is an improvement through mutation. *Homo sapiens* may be replaced by *Homo superior*. This tendency may yield some sort of group mind which harnesses the power of many individual minds and generates a much more perfect vision of the universe. But in any case, if one takes a sufficiently long view of the cosmos, the human race can be seen as playing only a minute role in the grand scheme of things, which went on long before there was any life on earth and will continue long after life as we know it ceases to exist.

After publishing a volume of religious poetry and a book on the relationship between ethics and psychology, Stapledon produced his first science fiction novel: *Last and First Men: A Story of the Near and Far Future* (1930). The impact of this book on later writers is summed up in the remarks of Arthur C. Clarke in his Introduction to *The Lion of Comarre, and Against the Fall of Night* (1968):

. . . William Olaf Stapledon's tremendous saga of future history, *Last and First Men.* I came across this volume in the public library of my birthplace, Minehead, soon after its first appearance in 1930. With its multimillion-year vistas, and its roll call of great but doomed civilizations, the book produced an overwhelming impact upon me. I can still remember patiently copying Stapledon's "Time Scales"—up to the last one, where "Planets Formed" and "End of Man" lie only a fraction of an inch on either side of a moment marked "Today."

Stapledon's other major works of science fiction followed at regular intervals for the next fourteen years, interspersed with works of moral and social philosophy: In *Last Men in London* (1932) he uses one of the "last men" of the previous volume to examine contemporary life, including the experiences of a person much like the author himself. In *Odd John* (1934) he tells the story of a superior mutant who tries to found a colony on a Pacific island with a few others of his kind. This work may be seen as a development of Wells's *Food of the Gods,* but it is more subtle psychologically and avoids the problems of mere gigantism. *Odd John* has many distinguished descendants in the world of science fiction. Notable among them are Clarke's *Childhood's End* (1953) and Theodore Sturgeon's *More Than Human* (1953). *Star Maker* (discussed on pp. 212–216) appeared in 1937, *Darkness and the Light,* a story of mankind's two alternate futures, in 1942, and *Sirius,* the story of a dog with an artificially heightened intelligence, was published in 1944.

This completes the list of Stapledon's major works of science fiction. It is an extraordinary achievement in its philosophic depth and consistency, the unwavering rigor of its speculative extrapolation, and in the stoical equanimity of its vision. Where Čapek laughs and cries at human greed and folly, Stapledon calmly invites us to take a more cosmic perspective on things as a way of avoiding the despair so justified by the social and political debacle of the 1930s. Together, they produced a body of work which is a historical document of the time between the two wars and a more permanent testament to man's ability to scrutinize his own situation through the literary techniques of science fiction.

Before turning from the social and philosophical fiction of Europe to the pulp magazines of America, we should consider one more writer whose influence on later science fiction was profound. Aldous Huxley (1894–1963), the grandson of H. G. Wells's biology teacher, produced in 1932 a work of dystopian future projection so lively and so appalling that it has never been out of print. Taking his title from the exclamation of Shakespeare's young heroine Miranda ("How beauteous mankind is!

O brave new world that has such people in't" *The Tempest,* V. i) when she first sees a group of other human beings, Huxley called his novel *Brave New World.* Set six centuries A. F. (after Henry Ford), Huxley gives us a state which is not so much a political horror as a technological one. Where Zamyatin had painted a vivid portrait of oppressive totalitarianism, Huxley gave us a society run by benevolent behaviorists, which proved almost as terrifying. Both men feared the loss of freedom and individuality, but the Russian was most concerned about bureaucratic excesses and the Englishman felt that technology itself would lead to the extinction of individual behavior.

Huxley's novel begins in the "Central London Hatchery and Conditioning Centre," because this is the key to his brave new world. Here fetuses are conceived and incubated in test tubes which produce groups of up to ninety-six identical babies at a time. These groups of babies are then "predestined and conditioned." Some are deprived of oxygen, for instance, so as to produce docile workers at the more menial tasks. Others are "predestined" to thrive on heat or cold. Some are given maximum intelligence, some minimum. Once born, or rather "decanted," they are further conditioned to fit perfectly into their niches. And in later life a combination of drugs, entertainment, and sterile sexuality keeps all these creatures content—with a few exceptions which enable Huxley to give us a story instead of a travelogue.

Dystopian fiction always reduces the world to a "State," and presents us with the struggles of an individual or a small group against that State. When George Orwell wrote his famous dystopian novel *1984* in the late forties, he chose to follow Zamyatin instead of Huxley. He was much more concerned with politics than with technology. Thus, as Huxley was to observe in 1958, Orwell produced "a magnified projection into the future of a present that contained Stalinism and an immediate past that had witnessed the flowering of Nazism." This was a valid reflection of Orwell's own time which then "seemed dreadfully convincing." However, Huxley argued, later developments in science, technology, and politics suggested that the horrible future would be more like *Brave New World* than *1984*—only it will arrive much sooner than six centuries from now. (See *Brave New World Revisited,* 1958, Ch. 1.)

Huxley may or may not be right in these views, but either way they suggest that there are at least two distinct strands of dystopian fiction. One, which considers more fully what Wells called "human ecology" and is central to science fiction; and another, more purely political, which is less concerned with scientific development and the impact of technology on man, and more interested in making concrete certain tendencies in political thought. Huxley took Zamyatin's dystopian fable and made it more responsive to the impact of technological change. Orwell made the fable even more narrowly concerned with politics and power. The tendency among later British and American writers of dystopian fiction is to assume that technological and biological processes have got beyond governmental control and will effectively shape human life regardless of the nominal system of government. There seems to be very little maneuvering room left between the distinct horrors of ineffective and overeffective government. The infrequent writers who attempt truly Utopian fiction nowadays avoid seeing this as future projection but send their characters off to communes or islands where things can be achieved outside of history—until history catches up with them, as it does to the beautiful people of Huxley's *Island,* which appeared in 1962, a little over a year before Huxley died peacefully on the day John Kennedy was assassinated.

A Pulpy America

The science fiction written in Europe in the twenties and thirties was both more dignified and more durable than that produced in the United States. It was written by men of broad general culture, who were in no way cut off from the central artistic and intellectual life of their times. And though the four writers we have just discussed all knew that they were taking new fictional departures, they had no set name for what they were doing and did not think of it as any more or less literary than the work of other men and women of letters. If anything, they assumed that they were in the vanguard of a kind of fiction especially suited to the twentieth century.

In America the situation could hardly have been more different. In a country still underpopulated, untouched physically by World War I, and uncertain of its own literary tradition, serious writers were still trying to master the techniques of realism or to adapt them to American materials. The spread of public education on an unprecedented scale had given a great body of readers rudimentary reading skills but no interest in the more esoteric reaches of literature. These readers bought dime novels, Westerns, adventure stories of various kinds—whatever they could find that satisfied a basic hunger for fiction. Magazines produced on cheap paper—pulp—met some of this demand. At the same time, young semieducated Americans yearned for more information about science and technology. The achievements of Edison, the Wright brothers, and

Henry Ford were still new, and young people could seriously think of "inventor" as a vocation. Nonfictional science pulp magazines met some of this demand for information. In 1911 the editor of a radio magazine called *Modern Electrics* serialized a piece of fiction in his magazine: *Ralph 124C 41+: A Romance of the Year 2660.*

The author was the editor himself, an émigré from Luxembourg named Hugo Gernsback. The story is both simple and clumsy but it was a great success and other serialized stories were included among the scientific articles until the magazine folded in 1913. During this same period, we should remember, Edgar Rice Burroughs sold his first Martian fiction to an adventure-pulp, *All-Story*. Gernsback, who sold radios as well as magazines, wanted stories with lots of futuristic hardware. The adventure story pulps wanted action and didn't care whether it happened on Mars or Earth, now or then. Toward the end of the second decade of this century, pulps catering to yet another clearly defined market of readers had begun to establish a footing—featuring tales of unscientific supernaturalism and horror. *The Thrill Book* began in 1919, and in four more years *Weird Tales* appeared, soaring to success on the eerie fiction of H. P. Lovecraft (1890–1937) and his imitators.

These three strands of pulp fiction—adventure, hardware, and weird—dominated American science fiction in the twenties and thirties. The only element of the previous century of science fiction not vigorous in the U.S. at this time was the element developed by Bellamy, the social concern and commitment that were so important in the European fiction of this period. If Jack London had not died in 1917 at the age of forty, this strand might also have continued to be vigorous in popular American fiction, but the kind of writing Zamyatin was engaged in at this time was clearly beyond any American writer, including London, whose socialism had never been tested by living under Bolshevik rule.

Hugo Gernsback continued to experiment with fiction in his pulpy technical magazines. In 1923 he took the major step of devoting a whole issue of *Science and Invention* to stories. He called it a "Scientifiction Issue," and thus virtually baptized this new literary form. The issue was sufficiently successful to lead the enterprising Hugo to think of a magazine devoted exclusively to the new fiction, perhaps to be called *Scientifiction*. When readers of *Science and Invention* did not take to the proposed title of the new journal, it finally appeared in April 1926 under the more dashing name of *Amazing Stories,* which it kept, even after its founder lost control of it in the "crash" of 1929. At first, the new magazine relied heavily on the giants of the past, reprinting a number of short pieces by Poe, nine of Jules Verne's novels, and over thirty items by H. G. Wells, thus exemplifying concretely Gernsback's definition of "scientifiction" first spelled out in 1926: "the Jules Verne, H. G. Wells, and Edgar Allan Poe type of story—a charming romance intermingled with scientific fact and prophetic vision." Gradually Hugo found new writers to carry on this tradition, and soon after his financial debacle he founded two new pulp magazines for those writers to publish in: *Air Wonder Stories* and *Science Wonder Stories,* which soon (1930) merged into just plain *Wonder Stories. Amazing* continued, under other management, and a third journal, *Astounding Stories of Super-Science* joined the competition in 1930. The 'thirties became a decade in which *Amazing, Astounding,* and *Wonder* fought a pulpy battle for control of a small but vital segment of the American imagination.

For a time *Astounding* was controlled by Clayton Publications and offered stories with more adventure and less science than *Amazing* and *Wonder.* In 1933 it was taken over by the immense publishing house of Street and Smith, which gave it a financial advantage over its two rivals. It paid better—and much more promptly. At the same time, we must not forget, other pulps not exclusively devoted to science fiction continued to present material related to the growing body of work in the science fiction magazines. In particular, *Weird Tales,* under the domination of H. P. Lovecraft, Robert B. Howard, and Clark Ashton Smith flourished until the deaths of Howard and Lovecraft in the late thirties. And magazines like *Argosy* were publishing serializations of planetary adventures by the great ERB.

There were no water-tight divisions between these groups. Hugo Gernsback reprinted Burroughs's *The Land that Time Forgot* in *Amazing* (1927/28) and published *The Master Mind of Mars* in his *Amazing Stories Annual,* which made its only appearance in 1927, featuring the Burroughs story on its lurid cover. Other writers moved back and forth, sometimes under pseudonyms, trying to make a living at the sweatshop rates paid by the pulp magazines. But in retrospect, for those concerned with the development of science fiction, Hugo Gernsback dominated the period from 1926 to 1936. After some fumbling with "scientifiction" he established the name science fiction for the kind of writing he admired, and his journals and their imitators published the kind of science fiction favored by Hugo.

For some reason—perhaps because he got his start with technical magazines—Gernsback's name as an editor is usually associated with stories that feature hardware, as if he cared more for Verne than for Poe or

Wells. But in the confused world of the thirties, with magazines being born, dying, merging, cloning, or mutating every minute, it is hard to clarify even an editor's preference without doing violence to the facts. Hugo loved romance, technology, and vision, as his definition of "scientifiction" suggested. And when he found a writer who could combine all three, he published him with pleasure. One such writer was E. E. Smith, Ph.D., known affectionately to his fans as "Doc."

Doc Smith (1890–1965) is usually credited with starting science fiction on what Brian Aldiss has called its "billion year spree," with his first novel, *The Skylark of Space,* published as a three-part serial by Gernsback's *Amazing* in 1928. Most of Smith's predecessors had been content to stay within the solar system, restricted if not confined by the speed of light. But what Wells had done for time, Smith did for space. Aldiss has described Smith's work and its limitations better than any other historian of science fiction:

> Beneath Smith's advance, the light-years went down like nine-pins and the sober facts of science were appropriated for a binge of impossible adventure. Smith set the Injuns among the stars. . . .
>
> Doc Smith, in short, wrote the biggest games of Cops and Robbers in existence. His saga is loaded to its armpits in unstoppable forces and immoveable objects, in hyper-spatial tubes and super-weapons and planets full of stupefying life armed with terrible mental capabilities. . . .
>
> Smith took great pains with his epic, rewriting its earlier parts to hang together in one entire enormous concept. And the concept is impressive. Unfortunately, everything moves at such breath-taking speed—or else stops entirely while everyone talks and the plot catches up—that what is good in theory is by-passed in practice. The author conveys no visual experience and does not make his immense distances real. . . . (*Billion Year Spree,* Ch. 9)

After *Skylark* Smith began his *Lensman* series of novels, which grew to seven volumes in the Pyramid edition, variously serialized in the magazines over a period from 1934 to 1947. *Lensman* is an intergalactic epic which begins "Two thousand million or so years ago"—the space age version of "Once upon a time." We have learned to call this kind of science fiction "space opera" and to hold it in a tolerant contempt. But Smith's achievement is the culmination of the early phase of pulp magazine science fiction. It is what all those marvelous magazine titles proclaimed their wares to be: weird, amazing, astounding. Kids who cut their teeth on Smith and his contemporaries grew up to form the next two generations of American science fiction writers. And if some of their achievements are likely to be more permanent than his, they, and we, will still owe Smith a debt of gratitude.

In addition to providing the setting for Doc Smith and his contemporaries, Hugo Gernsback performed one other service for science fiction that has been widely recognized. Though some have disputed critic Sam Moskowitz's claim that Hugo was the "father of science fiction," everyone must admit that he was at least its benevolent uncle. His *Amazing* volumes had a letters column called "Discussions," through which readers communicated to one another about the works and ideas presented in earlier issues. This was the beginning of what developed into the most elaborate and efficient literary feedback system since the time of the oral epic poets. Columns like "Discussions" developed in other magazines, and in them readers, writers, and editors discussed matters of common interest. In time these correspondents found other ways and places to exchange ideas. Clubs were formed and mimeographed magazines written by amateurs appeared with them. In the late twenties two young men named Siegel and Shuster met through *Amazing's* "Discussions" column and founded their own little magazine, *Cosmic Stories.* Later they reached a wider public as the originators of *Superman.* Gernsback himself helped the fledgling Science Correspondence Club, which became the International Science Club and published a mimeographed news letter called *The Comet.* In the early thirties groups of science fiction fans all over the country were forming clubs and issuing periodicals of commentary, reviews, gossip, poetry, and imitations of professional fiction. In 1934 Hugo Gernsback tried to channel all this activity into a single more productive (and lucrative) super-club. He founded a group called the Science Fiction League, which was supposed to have Hugo's *Wonder Stories* as its club magazine. This never reached the size or profitability its founder had hoped for, but it gave some impetus toward larger groups and gatherings. All this feverish activity, so much of it inspired by the fans themselves, came to be called "fandom," and the magazines started by fans were called "fanzines." The fanzines proliferated, feuded, died, and persisted. Some of them, like the *Riverside Quarterly,* are still going strong, and in their letters columns one can find writer and reader, side by side, arguing like hell and enjoying it thoroughly.

Like the farm systems of the big league baseball clubs, which developed during the same era, the fanzines became the schools and play grounds for developing writers and editors. All this might have happened without Hugo Gernsback, but it could never have happened in quite the same way. He put his mark on the field as an editor and a facilitator of fandom, dominating it for over a decade with his incredible energy. So it is no wonder that when international fandom began to hold annual conventions for fans and writers, and to give awards for the best work done in the field each year, that these awards should recall the name of Gernsback. At the eleventh World SF Convention in Philadelphia, 1953, the first Hugo Awards were presented. And in 1960, Hugo himself received a Specially Awarded Hugo for his contributions to the field. He deserved it.

One other development must be noted before we can leave the pulps and fanzines of the thirties. Of the many writers who struggled along in the gigantic shadow of Doc Smith, one was to have a greater impact on the field than the galactic doctor himself. John W. Campbell (1910–71) started writing science fiction seriously as a young man. His first published story, "When the Atoms Failed," appeared in *Amazing* in January 1930, before his twentieth birthday. He quickly rose to challenge Doc Smith as a writer of super-science epics, and might have gone down in history as Smith's greatest rival as a concocter of space operas. But he did two things that changed the nature of his own contribution to science fiction, and made a permanent impact on the field. First, he began to write a different kind of science fiction—so different that it first surfaced in *Astounding* under the pseudonym of Don A. Stuart. Campbell's new science fiction nudged the form into a somewhat less juvenile pattern. Distances were smaller, characters less one-dimensional, technology closer to what current science allowed as possible. The tone was more thoughtful, sometimes elegiac. Isaac Asimov remembers reading "Stuart's" stories while still in his teens—and not liking them at all:

> The fault was mine. I have reread some of them since, and I am ashamed of myself for having remained at the lower level. I had found them too quiet, too downbeat, too moving. I wanted action and adventure and was simply incapable of following Campbell up to the Stuart level. I eventually did, but it took a few years. I was not as good a man as Campbell was. (*Before the Golden Age,* p. 794)

Other writers, notably Stanley G. Weinbaum (1900–1936) were also challenging the space opera as a fictional form. Weinbaum's first story, "A Martian Odyssey," appeared in the July, 1934 issue of *Wonder Stories* to great acclaim, and before he died of cancer less than two years later he had published enough fiction to suggest that there were alternatives to Doc Smith that even the young Asimov could appreciate. When "The Parasite Planet" appeared in *Astounding* (February, 1935) Asimov reports, it "hit me with the force of a pile driver and turned me instantly into a Weinbaum idolater" (*Before the Golden Age,* p. 579). (These and other Weinbaum tales were collected and published in a volume called *The Best of Stanley G. Weinbaum* by Ballantine Books in 1974.) Weinbaum's new mixture of science and fiction impressed Campbell too. He sought to emulate it with "The Brain Stealers of Mars," which appeared in *Thrilling Wonder Stories* (a mutated version of *Wonder Stories*) in December, 1936, which was the first of a series of tales in which two men face the hazards of life on various planets. These stories, appearing under Campbell's true name, set the tone for his future career. But that career was not the career of a writer. John W. Campbell became the acknowledged heir of Hugo Gernsback and the most influential editor in the field of science fiction when he took over the helm of *Astounding* in 1937.

Much has been written about Campbell as an editor, especially by those writers who were associated with the first decades of the Campbell *Astounding*. In 1939 he published such new figures as A. E. van Vogt, Robert A. Heinlein, Isaac Asimov, and Theodore Sturgeon—names which soon eclipsed most of those that had appeared in the previous decade and a half of magazine fiction. How did he do it? It was partly luck, of course. The second generation of writers in this tradition was coming along anyway. They had read Smith and Weinbaum and the others, loving their work but seeing ways to improve on what had moved them as teenagers. These writers would have appeared anyway. But they came to Campbell and *Astounding,* and they stayed there for a long time. Why? Brian Aldiss offers a simple explanation: "Unlike many editors before and after, Campbell knew when a story made sense and when it didn't." Judith Merril spells it out more completely:

> It may seem self-contradictory to say that Campbell is the "sociological science fiction" editor, and add that his great limitation is his essentially *engineering* frame of mind: but this is precisely the "useful limitation" I referred to earlier. In the deepest sense, Campbell was the linear and logical successor to Gernsback. He was as technology-minded and application-oriented as the rest of the field in the thirties, with this difference: that he had a broader concept of the scope of "science" (technology and *engineering*); he wanted to explore the effects of the new technological world on *people*. Cultural anthropology, social psychology, cybernetics, communications, sociology, education, psychometrics—all these, and a dozen intermediate points, were thrown open for examination.

There were two immediately noticeable effects: better stories and more and better speculative development. A third effect came inevitably on their heels: one I do not believe Campbell was looking for, and may not have noticed when it arrived—better writing. ("What Do You Mean: Science? Fiction?", in T. D. Clareson's *SF: The Other Side of Realism*, p. 67)

Under Campbell's guidance, American science fiction became more thoughtful, more speculative, and much more effective as literature—without losing its sense of wonder or its popular appeal. And this provides some justification for the usual designation of the first decade of Campbell's *Astounding* as "The Golden Age."

ANTI-SCIENCE FICTION

Since Galileo, since science became science in fact, the relationship between scientific and religious thought has not been an easy one, though it has by no means been a matter of simple opposition. Many of the greatest scientists, Newton and Einstein to name but two, have been deeply religious men. Even the literary ancestry sometimes claimed for science fiction itself might better be called, in part at least, religious fantasy. Dante, Thomas More, and Milton all ventured beyond the limits of normal terrestrial experience to generate fictions, and if to venture beyond known worlds or to leave the terrestrial globe were enough to make a work science fiction, it would be reasonable and proper to call Dante's *Commedia,* More's *Utopia,* and Milton's *Paradise Lost* works of science fiction. Yet of all these only More's, which is the least adventurous in its voyaging, even begins to approach the mental territory of modern science fiction. The worlds of Dante and Milton remain separate from science fiction because they are constructed on a plan derived from religious tradition rather than scientific speculation or imagination based, however loosely, upon science. They populate the cosmos neither with fantastic creatures for their own sake nor with beings of speculative significance, but with angels, devils, and other products of a specifically religious world-view, which guides the fictional creation, sets limits for it, and lends it powers of credibility for the faithful. If we should read Dante and Milton now as works of science fiction, it would be because we had lost faith in the cosmological system according to which they were constructed. Such a reading, it goes without saying, would be unfair and perhaps even silly. They are religious fictions, and to read them rightly we must suspend any disbelief in the religious tradition that supports them. The normal procedure, in fact, is for us to read as allegory what men once took in a more literal manner. This way, religion and science may be said to have their separate spheres—call them spirit and matter— and may inhabit the same space without conflict.

After Newton and Milton, who were contemporaries though Newton was younger, science became increasingly materialistic and drew literature with it away from the fantastic space of religious epics and toward a more and more materialistic domain, which culminated in the naturalism of the late nineteenth century. But following these two centuries of increasing materialism and determinism, the scientific pendulum began to swing the other way, and literature to move with it. In England Thomas Hardy's naturalistic *Jude the Obscure* and H. G. Wells's *Time Machine* appeared in the same year, 1895, and within a few decades naturalism was dying and science fiction was growing powerfully. As science fiction reached out for more speculative territory it entered the area formerly occupied by the religious epic. This is why Olaf Stapledon's *Star Maker,* for instance, seems both so like and unlike the works of Dante and Milton. It should not be surprising that this invasion of religious space by science fiction should provoke a new religious fiction to arise and contest the field with the growing body of science-fictional works. This is a literary event, of course, but it is also an enactment of a larger cultural event. Science had shaken the historical and cosmological foundations of the Judeo-Christian religions. But it had not succeeded in providing a set of values for man beyond the experimental ethics of scientific research itself. As the twentieth century (note that this designation of time is itself both specifically Christian—A. D.—and very unscientific) progressed, the need for values beyond those of research and development became more apparent. And science fiction, in the hands of writers like Wells and Stapledon, became a place where values could be presented in a speculative way, tested, and finally advocated. Much of the impulse behind science fiction in the twenties and thirties came from the need to express and articulate whatever values might be found in science itself, and this is true not only of the work of a philosopher like Stapledon but of the more popular American or Gernsbackian kind of science fiction as well. Perhaps it was inevitable that such a development would provoke the sleeping giant of religious fantasy. For the purposes of our history this anti-science-fiction movement may be considered primarily in the work of a single writer, its most vigorous champion, who met the challenge of both Stapledon and Gernsback head-on: Clive Staples Lewis.

C. S. Lewis (1898–1963) was one of the great scholars and teachers

of medieval and renaissance literature in our time. He was also an extraordinarily perceptive critic of literature, and the most formidable
Christian casuist in English since Chesterton. As a writer of fiction he is
very much alive today. The seven volumes of his "Chronicles of Narnia"
are all in print and widely read by young people. These novels are
charming fantasies which rest upon a firm basis in Christian tradition and
theology. But the three novels of his adult "Space Trilogy" are those that
most concern us here. (A fourth novel in this group, lacking a theological theme, is said to exist in manuscript.) The published space trilogy
consists of *Out of the Silent Planet* (1938), *Perelandra* (1943), and
That Hideous Strength (1945—a version abridged by Lewis, called *The
Tortured Planet,* was available in paperback for a time but is no longer).
The continuing interest in Lewis's trilogy is attested to by the fact that
since 1965 the paperback versions of these novels in the U.S. have gone
through nearly twenty printings.

Lewis has been a great champion of the humble "story" in literature.
He has unashamedly admitted his own delight in fairy tales and other
fantastic kinds of literature, including science fiction, and invited those
who take pleasure in the delights of fiction for their own sake to come out
of their closets and admit that they read for pleasure. He, of all writers,
would never require that fiction be didactic. Yet as a student of that era
in our literary history when the greatest extremes in fantastic story-telling
and didactic seriousness often co-existed in the same work (as in
Spenser's *Faerie Queene*), he also knew how fantasy might function as
a vehicle for serious thought. In his space trilogy a delight in fantastic
imagining for its own sake is quite apparent—especially in his descriptions of the beautiful unfallen world of *Perelandra*. But his serious philosophical purpose is also very clear. He was provoked into writing these
books—provoked by two of the developments in science fiction that we
have just been considering in the section previous to this one: the work
of Olaf Stapledon and the pulpy, Gernsbackian science fiction that was
developing in America in the thirties. Lewis admired Stapledon's invention but not his philosophy, and he detested the attitude he discerned behind much of the American science fiction he encountered. He put both
these views into the mind of a single scientist, Professor Weston, who is
the villain of both *Out of the Silent Planet* and *Perelandra*. At one point
Weston is described in this way:

> He was a man obsessed with the idea which is at this moment circulat-
> ing all over our planet in obscure works of "scientifiction" in little

Interplanetary Societies and Rocketry Clubs, and between the covers of monstrous magazines, ignored or mocked by intellectuals, but ready, if ever the power is put into its hands, to open a new chapter of misery for the universe. It is the idea that humanity, having now sufficiently corrupted the planet where it arose, must at all costs contrive to seed itself over a larger area: that the vast astronomical distances which are God's quarantine regulations, must somehow be overcome. This for a start. But beyond this lies the sweet poison of the false infinite—the wild dream that planet after planet, system after system, in the end galaxy after galaxy, can be forced to sustain, everywhere and for ever, the sort of life which is contained in the loins of our own species—a dream begotten by the hatred of death upon the fear of true immortality, fondled in secret by thousands of ignorant men and hundreds who are not ignorant. The destruction or enslavement of other species in the universe, if such there are, is to these minds a welcome corollary. In Professor Weston the power had at last met the dream. (*Perelandra,* Ch. 6)

This attack on Gernsbackian human-racism is made from Lewis's Christian perspective. (It should be understood that Gernsback's name is being used here for the kind of fiction already associated with it in this history and not in a personal way.) But the attack prepared the way for later criticisms of the same position made from within science, without benefit of theology. The "ecology movement" that developed in America in the sixties takes a view very similar to Lewis's, and finds its support not in scripture but in works of scientific speculation like Gregory Bateson's *Steps to an Ecology of Mind* (1972) and is articulated within the field of science fiction by writers such as Ursula K. Le Guin (of whom more later) who is in many respects a lineal descendant of C. S. Lewis though she works from an ecological rather than a theological position. The challenge that Lewis mounted was not simply a challenge to Gernsback & Co. It was a challenge to science itself, and the modern technological culture based upon science, to produce an ethic worth living and dying for. It was also, clearly, a challenge Lewis felt could not be met. For him, ethical theory was capable of no development and needed none. What Christianity provided was sufficient. The problems came in practice—virtue being so much easier to discuss than to enact.

Stapledon's position, his emphasis on the growth of Spirit, was regarded by Lewis as more dangerous and no less abhorrent than the attitude of the "little Interplanetary Societies." And Stapledon's terrible Creator, the Star Maker, who combines in one being the qualities that Christianity divides into God and Satan, must have seemed to Lewis utterly blasphemous. At any rate, Lewis put a version of Stapledon's philosophy into the mouth of the odious Professor Weston:

> "The majestic spectacle of this blind, inarticulate purposiveness thrusting its way upward and ever upward in an endless unity of differentiated achievements towards an ever-increasing complexity of organization, towards spontaneity and spirituality, swept away all my old conception of a duty to Man as such. Man in himself is nothing. The forward movement of Life—the growing spirituality—is everything. I say to you quite freely, Ransom, that I should have been wrong in liquidating the Malacandrians. It was a mere prejudice that made me prefer our own race to theirs. To spread spirituality, not to spread the human race, is henceforth my mission. This sets the coping-stone on my career. I worked first for myself; then for science; then for humanity; but now at last for Spirit itself—I might say, borrowing language which will be more familiar to you, the Holy Spirit." . . .
>
> "What then? Why, spirit—mind—freedom—spontaneity—that's what I'm talking about. That is the goal towards which the whole cosmic process is moving. The final disengagement of that freedom, that spirituality, is the work to which I dedicate my own life and the life of humanity. The goal, Ransom, the goal: think of it; *Pure* spirit: the final vortex of self-thinking, self-originating activity." (*Perelandra,* Ch. 7)

By giving a crude version of Stapledon's views to Weston, Lewis effected a fictional economy. To invent another character just to spout Stapledonese would no doubt have been a wasteful intrusion of the didactic into the fictional. But by giving both Gernsback's and Stapledon's views to the villainous Weston in successive chapters, Lewis glossed over the fact that Stapledon's position is just as far from Gernsback's as his own. For Stapledon was no human-racist either; he was as ready to accept the whole of creation and praise it as Lewis himself. The quarrel between Stapledon and Lewis is much more profound than the one they both have with the human-racist position, and it is more elaborate than we might suspect from the caricature of Stapledon's views given to Weston. It is in fact an enactment at the level of two individuals, working in the same fictional territory, of the great quarrel between religion and science that began around the time of Galileo.

As long as science sought material truth and religion spiritual, their quarrels could be mended. And from the seventeenth century until the twentieth, religion gave ground on material and historical matters—however grudgingly—and science confined its attention to matter, becoming, as Lewis himself remarked, increasingly materialistic. But with the twentieth century science became more boldly speculative. Einstein even saw quantum physics as a challenge to the idea of God, and he opposed the quantum theoreticians on those grounds: "God does not play dice." Science, speculating ever more boldly about the origin of the universe and the descent of man, inevitably drew theology into contention with it. But even more important, from Lewis's point of view, was the attempt to establish sciences of human behavior—for human behavior is the point at which matter and spirit meet. Behaviorism is the real enemy of religion in the twentieth century. In Lewis's view the application of behaviorist theory to human conduct is despicable because it involves scientists who lack values themselves manipulating the values of others. In *That Hideous Strength,* the culminating volume of his trilogy, Lewis created a scientific foundation, run by power-hungry bureaucrats, which threatened to usurp all power in England by its own clever manipulation of the media and its brutal modification of individual human beings:

> "What sort of thing have you in mind?"
> "Quite simple and obvious things, at first—sterilization of the unfit, liquidation of backward races (we don't want any dead weights), selective breeding. Then real education, including pre-natal education. By real education I mean one that has no 'take-it-or-leave-it' nonsense. A real education makes the patient what it wants infallibly: whatever he or his parents try to do about it. Of course, it'll have to be mainly psychological at first. But we'll get on to biochemical conditioning in the end and direct manipulation of the brain. . . ." (*That Hideous Strength,* Ch. 2)

But because these manipulators have no real values themselves, beyond a lust for power and personal satisfaction, their minds and souls are vacant. Into that vacuum the devil moves. The behaviorists in Lewis's novel are literally possessed by devilish agents and behave accordingly. Their enemies are servants of God and accordingly inspired. The final combat is ultimate good against ultimate evil—and good wins easily. There are some problems here, both in the fiction and in the ethics. At a certain point they begin to impede one another, with the results that both the values and the plot seem to creak a bit at the end. The second volume, *Perelandra,* is more successful. Part of the problem of the third book may simply be that it takes place here and now, turning its supernatural elements into something magical. Lewis revives the magician Merlin from Camelot to combat the behaviorists, and he revives a set of personal values that are also very traditional. Though he presents certain of his views with some caution, it is clear in this volume and even clearer in *Perelandra* that the views of St. Paul on the relations between men and women are to be accepted. As Milton put it,

> Not equal, as thir sex not equal seem'd;
> For contemplation hee and valor form'd,
> For softness shee and sweet attractive Grace,
> Hee for God only, shee for God in him:
>
> *(Paradise Lost,* IV, ll. 296–299)

Since *Perelandra* is Lewis's retelling of the tale of Eve and Adam, it is only natural that it should follow Milton closely. And it does, except that in this new contest Satan is defeated and paradise retained. But in all other respects the story is Miltonic. The devil once again avoids the male, because of what Milton called his "higher intellectual," in order to attack the female of the species. And this reincarnation of Satan woos the new Eve in what we now can recognize as the accents of feminism. If we read this equation backwards, feminism is the preaching of the devil. In *That Hideous Strength* Lewis also strikes out against birth control, especially in the incident in which Merlin informs his master that the married couple who are the book's central characters have missed, through their selfish refusal to have children, the moment at which they might have conceived a great champion of Christendom:

> "Sir," said Merlin, "know well that she has done in Logres a thing of which no less sorrow shall come than came of the stroke that Balinus struck. For, Sir, it was the purpose of God that she and her lord should between them have begotten a child by whom the enemies should have been put out of Logres for a thousand years."
>
> "She is but lately married," said Ransom. "The child may yet be born."
>
> "Sir," said Merlin, "be assured that the child will never be born, for the hour of its begetting is passed. Of their own will they are barren: I did not know till now that the usages of Sulva were so common among you. For a hundred generations in two lines the begetting of this child was prepared; and unless God should rip up the work of time, such seed, and such an hour, in such a land, shall never be again." (*That Hideous Strength,* Ch. 13)

The ethical issue, as it is drawn by Lewis, comes down to whether or not human beings are capable of finding values to replace those of the religions they have seemed so ready to discard. His view is that they have not, and will not, because humans are "fallen," incapable of reasoning their way to any ultimate, whether it be Truth, Beauty, or Goodness. Therefore, man must turn back to God, and specifically to the teachings of Christ as preserved in the Christian religion. On the other side are those who say that humanity must create its own values by the operations of human reason upon the universe. For the most part, scientists have been quite ready to admit that there is no science of values. But science fiction has provided a matrix in which the values implicit in science may be explored, and the information about the cosmos that science has generated may be brought into contact with models of human behavior. Since the most articulate alternatives to Christian ethics have been Utilitarian or Marxist formulations, which judge present human actions in terms of future material benefits, a fiction which extrapolates from the present to explore the possible results of contemporary decisions becomes a cultural necessity. Bellamy, Wells, and others understood this and accepted the challenge. Lewis then entered the ethical debate both with philosophical books like *The Abolition of Man, The Problem of Pain,* and *Miracles*—and with his space trilogy. In many respects he has the advantage over his adversaries. His position is coherent, consistent, and backed by two thousand years of theological testing and literary enrichment. His enemies are themselves divided, often confused, and faced with the enormous difficulty of constructing an ethic upon hypothesis rather than revelation. But if we accept Lewis's views we must leave problems like overpopulation to God, and we must deny the rights of women to be the equals of men in human society and government. Lewis might reply that we had better leave certain matters to God because we have already demonstrated our incompetence to deal with them in purely human terms. And his works of science fiction—or anti-science fiction—are there to challenge his opponents both as entertainment and as vehicles for ethical speculation and debate.

Given the special strength and popularity of Lewis's work, it is not surprising that it has had an important influence on the field of science fiction as a whole. Lewis himself had drawn upon David Lindsay's remarkable *Voyage to Arcturus* (1920—see pp. 207–212 for discussion) for inspiration in constructing his extraterrestrial worlds—as well as upon Milton, Spenser, and a host of other writers of the Renaissance and Middle Ages. And a number of later writers have learned from Lewis and followed his example in combining Christian casuistry with science fiction. Among these, two have been notably successful. James Blish (whose tetralogy *Cities in Flight* is discussed briefly on p. 60) has given us a uniquely Christian work of science fiction in *A Case of Conscience* (a story in *If,* 1953; a novel in 1958). And Walter Miller in the late fifties produced what is probably the finest work of religious science fiction presently in the canon: *A Canticle for Leibowitz* (1959) discussed on pp. 221–226). Blish's novel presents us and his protagonist, a Jesuit scientist, with a case of conscience indeed. A planet is discovered upon which a race of intelligent beings seems to have arrived at a perfect society by powers of reason unaided by divine intervention of any sort. Father Ruiz-Sanchez decides that such a thing can only be an attempt of the devil to persuade mankind that such a blasphemous ideal is indeed obtainable. He reports his findings and, after many difficulties is ordered by the Pope to perform the ritual of exorcism upon the entire planet of Lithia. As he does so, a foolish and exploitative meddler upon that planet (much like Professor Weston) is attempting an extraordinarily risky experiment in nuclear fission. When the exorcism is completed the planet vanishes. "An error in equation sixteen," says a physicist, but Ruiz-Sanchez thinks, "No." Blish manages to raise some of the same questions as Lewis and make some of the same arguments, but instead of pitting magic against science he makes his priest a scientist and offers a material explanation for a spiritual event. This is a more subtle, even Jesuitical, casuistry, and the result is one of the strongest works of science fiction to appear in the fifties.

Walter Miller's *Canticle for Leibowitz* is even stronger. Using the sort of extended time scheme developed by the macro-historical science fiction of the forties and fifties (see pp. 53–55), Miller examined the interaction of science and religion over a period of centuries after a nuclear holocaust, allowing us to emerge from this chronicle with a perspective on science and religion that Lewis must have sympathized with. (He did, in fact, call it a "major work" in a tape-recorded discussion with Kingsley Amis and Brian Aldiss that has been transcribed and published. It may be found in his posthumous collection, *Of Other Worlds* (1966), which also includes an essay on science fiction and a defense of his trilogy against an attack by the scientist J. B. S. Haldane.) In Miller's book the religious men who seek, however blindly and fumblingly, to serve God, emerge as much better people than the scientists, who, being empty of values themselves, are all too easily seduced by the value of power, and thus become the tools of politicians. Both Blish and Miller are less obvious and less militant in their casuistry than Lewis was. And their achievements in the field of science fiction are generally regarded as greater than his. For Lewis, of course, science fiction was a relaxation from his true vocations of literary scholarship and theological ethics. Yet even so, he set his mark upon the field through his influence upon followers inside and outside his church, and through the challenge he offered science and science fiction to produce an ethic that might contend upon a footing of equality with his own Christian faith.

THE "GOLDEN AGE" AND AFTER

The designation "Golden Age" is typical of the American science fiction scene. It is overstated, self-approving, and quite uncritical. Science fiction fandom thrives on exaggeration, public relations, and smug self-approval. In some ways it is an extreme example of certain American cultural features which have made us unloved abroad. We casually call our annual intra-city baseball struggle the "World Series," and for years Americans held "World" Science Fiction Conventions in places like Philadelphia and Pittsburgh without a trace of embarrassment. Even today, there is a self-congratulatory air to much of the science fiction scene, which is epitomized in the designation of the era of Campbell's *Astounding* as "The Golden Age." Yet there is a certain amount of truth buried in that overstated designation after all. Here, however, we are concerned neither with justifying the term "Golden Age" nor with burying it. Our task is simply to sort out what happened to science fiction in the forties and fifties and to illustrate this through discussions of exemplary writers and their works. It will be useful to begin with the "big four," the writers introduced to fandom by Campbell in 1939: A. E. van Vogt, Robert A. Heinlein, Isaac Asimov, and Theodore Sturgeon.

Of these four van Vogt (b. 1912) has worn the least well, for reasons that tell us something about the development of science fiction from 1940 to the present. The reasons are highly visible in *Slan,* a novel serialized in *Astounding* in 1940. *Slan* is a descendant of Stapledon's *Odd John,* as *Odd John* itself descends from Wells's *Food of the Gods* and J. D. Beresford's *The Hampdenshire Wonder* (1911). It is a novel about the "next mutation"—in this case a race of supercreatures who have telepathic powers as well as superior physical strength and endurance. But as the novel opens they are a persecuted race, the objects of a "final solution" designed to exterminate them. Or so it seems. The young hero, Jommy Cross, is separated from his mother in the opening scene when she is killed by the police. This first scene is vivid, lively, and emotionally effective—as is usual with van Vogt. But after this, as adventure is piled on adventure, and no individual or group behaves with consistent, intelligible motivation, the novel falls apart. Young Jommy Cross wanders through buildings, caves, cities, and worlds that are so riddled with internal inconsistencies that we must either forget the past with each new episode or get lost trying to understand how this world functions. In his lust for adventure van Vogt neglects to construct a world which will make adventures intelligible and believable. Villains become heroes or heroines without warning, people are invincible one moment and totally vulnerable the next, as all logic of motivation disappears. And *Slan,* as that indefatigable chronicler of science fiction, Sam Moskowitz has observed, "is van Vogt's most famous and perhaps his best book."

In fact, van Vogt is a writer of the Doc Smith sort, who tried to adapt to the new themes and concerns of the forties and after. There is no doubt that he was popular and influential, but he is precisely the kind of writer that has given science fiction a bad name among serious readers. He is a careless and forgetful writer, who plunges on with the story, hoping to drag the careless and forgetful reader along with him. In *Slan* he seems at times to be aware of political issues. The persecution of the Slans is like the "final solution" of Hitler's Germany for dealing with the Jews. But the Slans themselves turn out to be a "master race" and the persecuting Hitler of the novel proves to be a disguised Slan himself. Given sufficient room, van Vogt destroys the basis of his own story, and is forced to provide increasingly preposterous explanations for increasingly absurd behavior. This is not fiction for adults. If Campbell had found no other writers for *Astounding* in the forties, not even the most fanatic of fans would think of that era as a "Golden Age."

Robert A. Heinlein (b. 1907) could not be more different. He has what is most obviously missing in van Vogt—solidity and consistency in tone, in characterization, and in the realization of whole societies. And he did something early in his career that illustrates perfectly the new direction that science fiction was to take after 1940. It was not unusual for a writer to conceive of a series of works with the same hero or group of heroes. Smith had done this with his *Lensman* sequence, and obviously Burroughs had done it many times over. But Heinlein in his first years of publication conceived of a system of stories and novels fitting into a single projected history of the human race. In the February 1941 issue of *Astounding* Campbell wrote about Heinlein's work in the following manner:

Robert A. Heinlein's back again next month with the cover story, "Logic of Empire." This story is, as usual with Heinlein's material, a soundly worked out, fast-moving yarn, more than able to stand on its own feet. But in connection with it, I'd like to mention something that may or may not have been noticed by the regular readers of *Astounding:* all Heinlein's science-fiction is laid against a common background of a proposed future history of the world and of the United States. Heinlein's worked the thing out in detail that grows with each story; he has an outlined and graphed history of the future with characters, dates of major discoveries, et cetera, plotted in. I'm trying to get him to let me have a photostat of that history chart; if I lay hands on it, I'm going to publish it.

Several versions of this chart appeared in *Astounding,* covering the period from 1950 to 2600. In later years the chart was updated and revised but remained the same in essentials. The chart in its final version is still included in current editions of works in the Future History series. In this form it has a column of dates on the left and six other columns, in this order: Stories, Characters, Technical, Data, Sociological, and Remarks. The first column ranges the titles of stories next to the dates in future history; the next shows the life-spans of individual characters as vertical lines. The next shows technical progress, such as "mechanized roads" or "use of telepathy" as vertical lines extending through time. "Data" notes events occurring at particular times, such as "synthetic foods" in 2060. "Sociological" begins with "THE CRAZY YEARS" and notes events such as "Religious dictatorship in the U.S." in 2020. The final column is for summary remarks and concludes in 2600 with "Civil disorder, followed by the end of human adolescence, and beginning of first mature culture."

A number of things need to be said about this chart. First, the source. It is clearly derived from Olaf Stapledon's charts in *Last and First Men,* which had also moved the young Arthur C. Clarke to emulation. Stapledon's novel appeared in the U.S. in 1931, to enthusiastic reviews. The book was advertised in Gernsback's *Wonder Stories* of 1913. This must have stimulated Heinlein's thinking. Second, Heinlein's chart projects in a relatively limited way. All but the last half-inch of his chart is contained within a span from 1950 to 2125, and almost all of the actual story titles are set in the period 1975–2010. Third, the chart applies to only a small percentage of Heinlein's total output, and to that only loosely. For Heinlein the chart obviously functioned as a way of organizing stories which might otherwise have seemed unconnected. For a time, when he wrote stories that did not fit in his scheme of Future History he published them under such pseudonyms as Anson MacDonald, Lyle Monroe, Caleb Saunders, John Riverside, and Simon York. But ultimately he gave up both writing under false names and the whole idea of producing a consistent Future History.

The designation "Future History" applies directly to stories collected and combined in 1967 as *The Past Through Tomorrow.* Unfortunately, in the paperback version released by Berkley in 1975, the chart has been omitted, though Damon Knight's Introduction indicates that it should be there. (It *is* included in some of the individual volumes published recently by Signet.) In any case we have been cautioned against taking the plan for a Future History too seriously by Heinlein himself in the Postscript to the Signet *Revolt in 2100,* and by Heinlein's most thorough critic, Alexei Panshin:

> The Future History does not actually form a complete whole. It was not planned all at once, and belongs primarily to Heinlein's adolescence as a writer. It was assembled by compromise, chopping, and rewriting. The result is that the individual pieces stand up well enough by themselves while the Future History they supposedly form does not. (*Heinlein in Dimension,* 1968, p. 124.)

Although we must attend to Panshin's warning, we should also recognize that the *idea* of a Future History was very important to Heinlein as he began his career, and this idea is also behind some of the major achievements by other writers in the forties and fifties—as we shall see. This idea represents the introduction of macro-history into science fiction. The macro-historians attempted to see human history in terms of recurring patterns that could be charted through different historical periods. Since Giambattista Vico's *New Science* appeared in 1725, with its chronological table tracing history from the Golden Age of Gods through the later ages of Heroes and Men, various attempts at macro-history continued to be made, usually accompanied by charts and tables. For our purposes the most notable are H. G. Wells's *Outline of History* (1920), Arnold J. Toynbee's *Study of History,* the first six volumes of which appeared during the 1930s, and Oswald Spengler's *The Decline of the West,* which was translated from the German and published in America in two volumes that appeared in 1926 and 1928.

Spengler had been trained as a biologist. He even called his work a study in the "morphology" of history, and in it he presented historical forces working in the manner of biological processes, with civilizations living through life cycles from youthful expansiveness to the decline and decay of old age. This deterministic view of history, with its biological base, was bound to appeal to writers of science fiction. The charts at the end of the first volume of *The Decline of the West* are among the ancestors of Stapledon's charts in *Last and First Men,* but Stapledon used a much grander time scale, making human history an incident in the life of the universe.

The point of this historiography is that one of the major intellectual currents affecting science fiction writers in the forties was a new sense of history stemming from Spengler and Stapledon in particular. And this sense of history operated to channel the imaginations of science fiction writers, enabling them to sacrifice a certain amount of wild imagining in order to attain a much greater degree of conviction in their work. Thus, the significance of Heinlein's Future History is not so much in its usefulness as a guide to understanding his work as in its revelation of a movement shaping science fiction during the period in which he began writing.

Heinlein himself has been a vivid and controversial figure for three decades. His values have been called everything from fascistic to anarchistic, and as a writer he has been described as both a "natural story-teller" (Panshin) and "not a particularly good story-teller" (Aldiss). There is disagreement about which of his works are the best and which the worst, and about the value of his work as a whole. The fans have agreed for some time that he is their favorite writer, but the only thing that most critics agree about is the fact that he is *there,* he is important, he must be dealt with. And the first thing that must be dealt with is the fact that his immense popularity is based on something very real—his immense readability. When a reader picks up a Heinlein he knows that he is likely to get his money's worth of entertainment. That is, he will be engaged by the characters in the work, moved by their situations, and concerned about the outcome of the events in which they are involved. And he will sense this has been accomplished in a natural and apparently effortless way. How, in fact, is it done?

It is done, first of all, through a kind of psychological and social know-how. Heinlein, who was trained as an engineer at the U.S. Naval Academy, and continued his career until invalided out of service by tuberculosis in 1934, knows how a lot of things work. He also knows how to present unworkable things in such a way as to convince us that they do work. And he knows a good deal about how people work in social situations, how animals work, and how society itself works. What he knows is quite similar to what the best American writers of detective stories have known—people like Raymond Chandler, Ross MacDonald, and John D. MacDonald. And his style is something like theirs. It is not fancy, but it is very workmanlike. The conversation is lively and has an authentic ring, the narration is brisk, the description pointed. As in most popular forms of fiction the good guys and the bad are clearly distinguishable—and the good guys always win.

Heinlein's values are close to those of Ayn Rand and the ideology associated with her. He believes in a freedom which will allow the "best" people to rise to the top. He is, as Panshin has argued, an elitist who believes in an elite of competence. In many respects he is a "social Darwinist," who feels that life should be a struggle for survival of the fittest and that the unfit should go to the wall. These views, which are far from "liberal," are more or less the views of many Americans. In some respects Heinlein is the most typically American writer in all the ranks of science fiction. He is energetic, optimistic, and broadly knowledgeable about technology and human behavior. He is skeptical of noble ideals and highly dubious of democratic process. But he clearly believes in life, liberty, and the pursuit of happiness. For him, freedom to trade, to wheel and deal, to gain position, money, and power—this is very important. And he sees restraints on trading, on competition, and on success and failure as disastrous attempts to legislate what human nature is not capable of achieving. Man is an animal, in his view, and a dangerous one, who must fight. He can unite and cooperate only when he has a common enemy. Thus military organizations are ideal models for human society. They are run by those who have proved themselves competent and courageous; they offer a hierarchy open to the talented, where all compete on an equal basis; and they can be cooperative because their aggressive behavior is directed outward, at a common enemy. For Heinlein the idea that society can be based on equality and cooperation is founded on a misconception about human nature. Mankind is incapable of true communism—and of true democracy. The world is too complicated for "the people" to govern it themselves. They must be led by those among them who are best fitted for leadership. Many of these ideas are unpalatable to most critics. But they clearly strike a responsive chord in a wide readership.

Not all of Heinlein's fiction is overtly political. *The Puppet Masters* (1951), for instance, is primarily an adventure story. But the values are there, and they become more visible in works like *Starship Troopers* (1959) and *The Moon Is a Harsh Mistress* (1966), which confront political questions directly. The latter novel in particular sets forth Heinlein's political views with considerable effectiveness. It tells of the moon's revolt from earth in a manner deliberately reminiscent of America's revolt from England. And the story is told with great gusto. Heinlein loves a story of individuals triumphing over a system, of small groups defeating large bureaucracies, of freedom winning over control. And, ranging over the future, he can pick his spots so as to treat just this kind of situation. His world is open, unfinished, and therefore amenable to an ethic of development. Closed systems with limited resources do not appeal to him. His social ideal is a tightly organized hierarchy, like the space-ship society in *Citizen of the Galaxy* (1957), which survives by trading with other societies less fortunate in their social and political structures—or like the military organization of *Starship Troopers,* in which rights of citizenship are earned by government service. But his ideal individual is a totally free man, which means that his heroes fit awkwardly into his ideal societies. He is shrewdly realistic about a certain level of human motivation and group behavior—but he is not realistic enough to look into all the dark corners of existence. Which is why he is a superb entertainer but a dangerous guide for conduct.

Heinlein's greatest commercial success came with *Stranger in a Strange Land,* which first appeared in 1961 and "sold the least well of any of Heinlein's third period novels" (Panshin, *Heinlein in Dimension,* p. 103). After its paperback release in 1968, however, it went through some thirty printings. Like the rock opera *Jesus Christ Superstar,* it blends contemporary materials with the story of Christ. But where the opera projects modern elements back into the biblical setting, *Stranger* reenacts the story in the near future. Valentine Smith, an earthman trained on Mars, comes to earth and performs miracles of extrasensory perception, telepathy, and psychokinesis. He founds a cult and teaches others how to use the same powers. Above all, he teaches his faithful to "grok" things— to understand them by harmonizing with their essences. His followers enjoy great sexual freedom, and great communal rapport. When he is "crucified," they drink broth made from his remains, "savoring it, praising and cherishing and grokking their donor" (Ch. 38).

The values of the sixties could hardly have found a more congenial expression. Valentine Smith is a combination of Captain Marvel and Christ—a Jesus Christ Superman who builds a commune into a great religious cult. Heinlein's Smith is as American as the Mormon Joseph Smith, and Heinlein knows it. The values of Ayn Rand and the hippie communes of the late sixties manage a precarious combination in this book, so as to tell a lot of different readers what they want to hear. But Heinlein's own voice speaks clearly through the character of "Jubal E. Harshaw, LL.B., M.D., Sc.D., bon vivant, gourmet, sybarite, popular author extraordinary, and neo-pessimist philosopher" (Ch. 10). Too much of this voice, in fact too much talking altogether, is a fault in several of Heinlein's later works. The books have become longer, much longer, and most of that length is the result of talk. When he talks too much, Heinlein becomes a village social scientist—shrewd and amusing at first, then cranky, then repetitive, and finally repellent. It is this, and his coy and clumsy attempts at being sexually up to date, that make a book like *I Will Fear No Evil* (1970) seem like an inflated monster alongside the fluid fiction of his earlier years. But his whole body of work, almost twenty volumes of adult fiction and a number of juveniles, stretching from the Golden Age to the seventies, is a remarkable performance. His adult entertainment has been just that—both adult and entertaining—for a long time, and he has had as much to do with the maturing of American science fiction as anyone. Students of American culture and values will do well to consider him, for his contradictions and confusions are very much our own—as is his energy and the optimism that lies below his "neo-pessimistic" facade.

Isaac Asimov (b. 1920) has been much more of a public presence than Heinlein, much more of a promoter of science and science fiction. His enormous output of books is now over a hundred and fifty, including many popularizations of science and technology for laymen, as well as original works of science fiction and collections of works by others. Unlike Heinlein, who was an engineer by training, Asimov is a scientist who has a Ph.D. in bio-chemistry and has taught bio-medical students. He is often on the lecture circuit and is a frequent speaker at science fiction conferences, a toastmaster at Hugo Award ceremonies, an advisor of younger writers, anthologizer of older ones, and general counselor to American society on matters of science and technology. This extraordinary activity obscures the fact that his greatest contributions to science fiction as a writer were made in the pulp magazines of the forties and published as books in the fifties. In the sixties and seventies he has written more popular science than science fiction, though his fans received gratefully his collection of three related tales, *The Gods Themselves,* when it appeared in book form in 1973, after separate publication in *Galaxy* and *If* in the previous year.

For our purposes, the Asimov of the forties counts the most, and in particular he counts for two distinctive achievements: his macro-historical future history, *The Foundation Trilogy* (after serialization, published as books in 1951, '52, and '53); and his creation of benevolent robots, bound by the "three laws of robotics," and presented mainly in the stories collected as *I, Robot* (stories of the forties, published in 1950), in *The Rest of the Robots* (1964), and in the two sequential novels *The Caves of Steel* (1954) and *The Naked Sun* (1957).

The three novels of macro-history are *Foundation, Foundation and Empire,* and *Second Foundation.* They cover a span of four centuries, beginning at year 12,069 of the Galactic Era and continuing into the fourth century of the Foundation Era (which is considered to have begun at 12,069 G. E.). This is obviously a very different segment of space-time from that domesticated by Heinlein. In some ways it is a continuation of Doc Smith's billion year spree, but with a new desire to control, coordinate, and narrate a story based upon macro-historical principles. Each volume is divided into segments, and each segment is preceded by a "quotation" from the "Encyclopaedia Galactica, the 116th Edition published in 1020 F. E." This device was adopted by Frank Herbert for his future historical romance, *Dune* (1965), which, like Heinlein's *Stranger in a Strange Land,* was a great "underground" success in the late sixties. Still producing offspring in the late seventies, *Dune* deserved its popularity for its skillful blend of ecological concern and marvelous adventures. But Asimov's *Foundation Trilogy* is a more sober affair than *Dune,* less adventurous, less swashbuckling, and in some ways less effective as fiction, but still a grand conception, interestingly executed.

As a way of turning space opera into something more like history, Asimov conceived of a new intellectual discipline developed by the great Hari Seldon (11,988–12,069 G. E.). This discipline, called "psychohistory," is in fact a perfection of the notion that Wells was calling "human ecology" back around the turn of the century, for it is nothing less than the discovery of the future managed upon scientific principles. Through his new science Seldon is able to predict the collapse of the Galactic Empire and to go beyond Spengler by deciding to do something about it. The decline or collapse itself could not be avoided, but the period of dark ages between the end of the Galactic Era and the rise of some new civilization might be reduced from thousands to hundreds of earth-years. Seldon deals with the crisis by establishing two "foundations" in different parts of the Galaxy, that should be able to preserve human culture and reinstate a Galactic civilization in a few centuries if Seldon's view of history is correct. The two foundations are scientific research institutes—one for the physical sciences, the other for the social and mental sciences. And sure enough, after four centuries of intra-galactic struggling, with wars and piracy and adventures galore, the two foundations with their very different physical and mental capacities succeed in bringing peace and prosperity to the galaxy again.

This blend of Spengler and Doc Smith has proved astonishingly durable in science fiction. Not only *Dune* and its progeny but also James Blish's (1921–75) complex of stories about whole cities wandering through space is based upon this same combination. *Cities in Flight* first began to appear in the magazines in 1950, and then as books from 1955 to 1962. The titles, in their "historical" order are *They Shall Have Stars* (formerly *Year 2018!*), *A Life for the Stars, Earthmen Come Home,* and *The Triumph of Time.* All four were collected as *Cities in Flight* in 1970. Blish has acknowledged his debt to Spengler, and in the collected edition of the tetralogy there is an afterword by R. D. Mullen, with a chart which sets Blish's time scheme in a column parallel to Spengler's treatments of classical, Arabian, and European cultures. Blish's world covers a span from 2013 to 4104, ending with an apocalypse. The world as we have known it is destroyed and a new creation begins. In this Blish returns to Vico rather than Spengler. Like the James Joyce of *Finnegans Wake*, which he knew and loved so well, Blish has accepted the Viconian notion of a re-creation. Vico saw history as a decline from a Golden Age, but a circular decline, which would lead to another creation, a new beginning. Spengler preferred to look backward from winter toward the earlier springtime, but he could on occasion assume a longer view, seeing man in a Darwinian or even grander cosmic perspective:

> Time triumphs over Space, and it is Time whose inexorable movement embeds the ephemeral incident of the Culture, on this planet, in the incident of Man—a form wherein the incident life flows on for a time, while behind it all the streaming horizons of geological and stellar histories pile up in the light-world of our eyes. (Quoted from the last page of Spengler by R. D. Mullen in the afterword to *Cities in Flight.*)

If Spengler sounds like a science fiction writer here, it is no accident. Stapledon was moved by the same geological horizons and stellar histories in the thirties, and one of the major strands of development in the science fiction field in the forties was the blending of space opera and macro-history, as the weight of Spengler and Vico made itself felt even in a literature supposedly so insulated from the cultural mainstream. In

Cities in Flight, as we have suggested, it is Vico who prevails at the end, when the world is unmade and remade. Only a science fiction writer could present the end of the world as such a joyful experience—or a deeply religious man. Blish was both.

In addition to setting a powerful macro-historical example with his *Foundation* trilogy, Asimov altered the thinking of the scientific community about robots. Taking over the word coined by the Čapeks for the androids of *R.U.R.,* Asimov created a different kind of creature altogether. His robots are machines capable of performing various programed tasks, sometimes including thought, but they do not have free will. They are always subject to the "Three Laws of Robotics," which are the most basic element in their programing. These laws are fundamental to all of Asimov's robot stories, and they have been adopted by many other writers of science fiction as well. They appear at the beginning of *I, Robot* in the following carefully chosen wording:

1—A robot may not injure a human being, or, through inaction, allow a human being to come to harm.

2—A robot must obey the orders given it by human beings except where such orders would conflict with the First Law.

3—A robot must protect its own existence as long as such protection does not conflict with the First or Second Law.

Handbook of Robotics
56th Edition, 2085 A.D.

The stories based on these laws have something in common with chess problems, or with the elegant solutions to the paradoxical mysteries produced by G. K. Chesterton's detective, Father Brown. Frequently, a robot seems to be behaving strangely and Dr. Susan Calvin (1982–2064), a Robopsychologist, is called in to deal with the apparent aberration. Dr. Calvin usually finds the solution in some paradoxical application of the Three Laws or in some malfunction of the robot's "positronic brain." In other stories the field-testing team of Donovan and Powell has to cope with new problems generated by increasingly complex kinds of robots. One of the most engaging of the stories, "Reason," involves a philosophical robot who thinks according to pure reason and cannot be shaken from his belief that men are simply the creations of a Master Robot whom he and they serve. The best of Asimov's robot stories are games remarkable for their elegance and wit. They added something sorely missing from American science fiction, and together with the *Foundation* stories they improved the intellectual tone of popular science fiction considerably.

Asimov has never been a writer of deeply moving fictions. His style is at best serviceable, his psychological penetration never deep. But he is full of ideas and capable of reasoning elegantly about them. In some ways his work fits the stereotype of science fiction in the minds of the "literati"—in that his robots are as interesting as his people, and the depths of human feeling are closed to him. But his virtues are at the heart of science fiction and they are real virtues. He uses fictional models to make us think about the structure of the universe and about human mentality—about our relations to technology, to time, and to history. And he does this without ever being dull or childish. He is not the storyteller Heinlein is, but he is a humane scientist using fiction as a vehicle to amuse and provoke thought. In this he largely succeeds.

The last of Campbell's original four writers to be discussed here is the least in quantity of output but may be the best in quality. Theodore Sturgeon's (b. 1918) production of science fiction has been so scant of late that his last collection of new stories was called *Sturgeon Is Alive and Well* (1971). This was good news to a legion of fans who admire the work of this writer, but a collection of stories written over a whole decade is not enough to satisfy most of his admirers. Still, since Sturgeon is the man who uttered the most quoted dictum in science fiction—"90% of science fiction is crud, but 90% of everything is crud" (or words to that effect—you encounter different versions)—we must be grateful for a man who breaks his own law so decidedly. Since a blank period in the late forties, when he took time off from writing to mature a little, Theodore Sturgeon has produced some of the best work that has been done in the field. Much of this is in the form of short stories, but three excellent novels are the mainstays of his reputation: *The Synthetic Man* (1950—originally *The Dreaming Jewels*), *More Than Human* (1953), and *Venus Plus X* (1960). Of these the most famous is *More Than Human,* which combines elements of the *Odd John* tradition with a notion probably picked up from Jack Williamson's *The Humanoids* (1950).

Williamson (b. 1908) is a writer who began before the Golden Age and wrote his way through it and out of it. In the late fifties he resumed the college education begun years before and carried it to the extreme of a Ph.D., a book on H. G. Wells, numerous critical articles, and an academic professorship. He is still writing science fiction, frequently in collaboration with Frederik Pohl. Three of his earlier novels were recently singled out by Brian Aldiss as having special merit: *The Legion of Time* (1938, *Astounding*), *Darker Than You Think* (1940, *Unknown*), and *The Humanoids* (1948, *Astounding*). As Aldiss puts it, Williamson "operates powerfully at the dreaming pole" of science fiction—that is, at the opposite end from Asimov. *The Humanoids*, about a benevolent takeover of the world by robots, is marred by the writer's deep uncertainty about the rightness of this. Philosophically, the uncertainty is reasonable, but in this case the fiction suffers from and retreats into almost van Vogtian evasiveness. But one aspect of the book must have given Sturgeon a clue for *More Than Human*. In *The Humanoids* a man named White tries to fight the mechanical creatures with a pathetic army of outcasts who have paraphysical talents: Jane Carter, a waif rescued from reform school, who can teleport herself from one place to another; Greystone the Great, a drunken former stage magician, who is a natural telepath; Lucky Ford, a bum whose ability to control dice through telekinesis keeps getting him in jail; and Overstreet, a myopic extratemporal clairvoyant. This group, working together, fails to defeat the Humanoids but lives on in Sturgeon's "Homo Gestalt."

More Than Human is about several waifs and strays who learn to coalesce into a group being, a "Homo Gestalt"—Complete Man—which is an evolutionary stage above *Homo sapiens*. Sturgeon's novel is built around the attempts of these ill-assorted individuals to combine into a true symbiotic structure: Janie, an unhappy girl who is a telepath/telekinesist; the twins, little black girls who can teleport themselves; Baby, a helpless mongoloid who can solve any mental problem; Lone, an idiot who is the first "head" of this group, the one who combines and controls the units; Gerry, a heartless hypnotist and confidence man who takes Lone's place; and finally Hip, a badly hurt young man who becomes the group's conscience and completes its structure as a whole being. Sturgeon's story is intricately plotted and manages to function well as both a slightly sentimental adventure story and an allegory about human values. Its currently high rating among readers of science fiction is well deserved.

In *Venus Plus X*, Sturgeon broke further ground for later writers. In presenting a unisex society he focused, in 1960, on a social issue that was to grow increasingly insistent in the ensuing decade and a half: sex roles in human behavior. (Like many later writers he was indebted here to Philip Wylie's *The Disappearance* (1951), in which Wylie imagined alternate worlds, from which all men or all women had vanished.) *Venus Plus X* is intelligent and shocking in the best sense of that word. Sturgeon cuts effectively from scenes of married and social life in "our" world to a world that is much better in every respect. And he forces us to think about sexual stereotypes in a way that only a few social scientists had been able to manage before the late fifties. This book has been somewhat neglected, perhaps because the success of *More Than Human* has overshadowed it somewhat, or perhaps because Ursula K. Le Guin's *Left Hand of Darkness* (1969) and Joanna Russ's *Female Man* (1975) (of both of these, more later) have treated very similar materials in more contemporary ways. However, it seems likely that both Le Guin and Russ learned something from Sturgeon, even as he had picked up an idea from Williamson for *More Than Human,* and an idea from Philip Wylie for *Venus Plus X.* The world of science fiction is a kind of literary laboratory, in which the processes that are found in all literature may be observed very clearly. And one of the most interesting features of this world is the way that ideas can be traced through it, from book to book and writer to writer. We can learn many things from observing this process, but perhaps the most important is that the question of who did something first is a less important question than who developed it furthest. *Venus Plus X* has worn well not because it got into feminism early but because Sturgeon treated his topic in a thoughtful and intriguing way. And what he accomplished enabled other writers to develop the subject in other, equally interesting ways.

Sturgeon, of course, made one other contribution that helped to gild the Golden Age. He made language itself important. He made style count. Consider the opening paragraph of *More Than Human:*

> The idiot lived in a black and gray world, punctuated by the white lightning of hunger and the flickering of fear. His clothes were old and many-windowed. Here peeped a shinbone, sharp as a cold chisel, and there in the torn coat were ribs like the fingers of a fist. He was tall and flat. His eyes were calm and his face was dead.

The language is mostly simple in diction and syntax—simple like the idiot himself. But the images are made more vivid and poignant by the similes ("ribs like the fingers of a fist"), and the prose is energized by poetic rhythms and sound effects ("the flickering of fear . . . the fingers of a fist"). This kind of care for the patterning of language itself was new to science fiction when Sturgeon began to practise it. In recent years more writers have cared about style and some have taken obvious pains with it. But few have had Sturgeon's sense of balance and restraint, mixing plain and fancy language as adroitly as he has. In the fifties, though, another writer came along for whom style was a great consideration—a writer who for two decades was perhaps the best known writer of science fiction outside the field itself, while inside, people were questioning whether his work was really science fiction at all: Ray Bradbury.

Even more than Sturgeon, Bradbury tends to work in shorter forms. His best known book, *The Martian Chronicles* (1950), is a linked chain of stories. His prose is even more poetical than Sturgeon's, his tendency toward sentiment even more marked. He is strongly drawn toward the eerie, the occult, the Lovecrafty kind of writing, which is in some ways quite different from science fiction. His Mars is in no way a scientifically possible Mars, nor is it meant to be. He specializes in ordinary landscapes, especially those of the Norman Rockwell, *Saturday Evening Post* Midwest—which change into sites of nameless horror. He has borrowed the externals of science fiction to disguise and make more convincing his magical preoccupations. Though much acclaimed, his books have worn less well than others, originally less noticed. The sentimentality, the too easy liberal moralizing, have been overtaken by events. And horror wears less well than thought. For a time it seemed as if Bradbury was making science fiction respectable to a larger circle of readers, but then it became apparent that what he was introducing them to was becoming less and less like science fiction. But it is not our business here to drum people out of the science fiction corps. It is enough to note that Bradbury represents an extreme of elegiac sentiment and gentle fantasy, touched with the eerie and uncanny. It is a special preserve, very much his own, somewhere on the far side of Sturgeon.

We can conclude this brief and selective discussion of science fiction in the forties and fifties by mentioning three more writers who made major contributions to the field and continue to be influential in quite different ways: Arthur C. Clarke, Frederik Pohl, and Alfred Bester. In certain respects Clarke (b. 1917) is a kind of British Asimov. He is a professional scientist and scientific journalist who graduated with First Class Honors in physics and mathematics from King's College, London. He began to write science fiction in the late forties, with his first books appearing in the early fifties. As we indicated above, he was moved as a young man by the work of Olaf Stapledon, but he was also very much aware of the American pulp magazines, and he considered John Campbell the "godfather" of his own earliest fiction. His most successful novel has been *Childhood's End* (see discussion on pp. 216–220), which seems to take as its point of departure both Stapledon's *Odd John,* with its race of superior mutants, and the ominous words at the end of Heinlein's chart of Future History: "Civil disorder, followed by the end of human adolescence and beginning of first mature culture." Clarke's ability to combine thinking and dreaming, science and philosophy, make this book a model of mature science fiction. Its literary influence has extended beyond the science fiction world, as exemplified by Doris Lessing's somewhat guarded allusion to it in the appendix to *The Four-Gated City*. Clarke's fame has also spread, of course, through his collaboration with Stanley Kubrick on the film *2001*, which captures Clarke's combination of science and mysticism superbly, and amplifies it through Kubrick's visual resourcefulness. Clarke is very much a factor in contemporary science fiction. His recent novel, *Rendezvous with Rama* (1973—see discussion on pp. 85–86), won a well-deserved Hugo award, and another novel by him, *Imperial Earth,* was published in 1976.

Frederik Pohl is one of the few men to make a genuine impact on the science fiction field both as a writer and an editor. Currently, he is doing more to bring back into print important works of science fiction from previous decades than any other single editor. Even as a writer he must have strong editorial impulses, for in addition to producing a group of respectable works of his own, he has been involved in two major collaborative efforts: one early in his career with C. M. Kornbluth—which resulted in five novels before it was terminated by Kornbluth's untimely death—and one with Jack Williamson, which had by 1975 produced seven volumes. Pohl's independent work has been good, and the collaboration with Williamson has produced some pleasant work, but the Pohl-Kornbluth collaborations were something special. All five of the volumes they did together are interesting, and one of them belongs on everybody's ten-best list. It appeared in *Galaxy* in 1952 as *Gravy Planet* and in 1953 as a book called *The Space Merchants*. Since then it has gone through many editions and been translated into almost forty languages. It is a hilarious and pointed satire of contemporary values, achieved through creation of an ingenious world in which advertising rules everything. There are two classes: the wealthy sellers and the poor consumers. This ad-man's dream of a world is, of course, a nightmare for everyone else. Exploitation of resources, pollution of environment, and over-population are all rampant, while the advertisers use every device of behavior control including addictive substances in the products. The feeble counterforce in this world is provided by the Conservationists, Consies for short, who are seen as terrible fanatics. When they make a convert, the Copysmith Star Class protagonist, Mitch Courtenay, comments as follows:

I hated the twisted minds who had done such a thing to a fine consumer like Gus. It was something like murder. He could have played his part in the world, buying and using and making work and profits for his brothers all around the globe, ever increasing his wants and needs, ever increasing everybody's work and profits in the circle of consumption, raising children to be consumers in turn. It hurt to see him perverted into a sterile zealot. (Ch. 8)

The beauty of this passage, like the entire book, is that it manages to be absurd and at the same time to be frighteningly close to the way that many people actually think. Here is Courtenay on poetry and advertising:

The correlation is clear. Advertising up, poetry down. There are only so many people capable of putting together words that stir and move and sing. When it became possible to earn a very good living in advertising by exercising this capability, lyric poetry was left to untalented screwballs who had to shriek for attention and compete by eccentricity. (Ch. 4)

This cuts more than one way! The serious thrust of the book, focusing on issues that have waited twenty years to receive wider attention, is in itself remarkable. The lightness of touch and consistency of imagination make it a true classic of science fiction. Only a few writers, from Voltaire to Vonnegut, have been able to manage this kind of narrative with the right combination of bite and charm.

The contribution of Alfred Bester to science fiction in the fifties is altogether different, for Bester pumped new life into that hallowed American form of science fiction, the space opera. In two books first serialized in *Galaxy* during the early fifties, Bester made his reputation and then fell silent for almost twenty years, but those two books are still very much alive, and have been influential on a younger generation of writers. *The Demolished Man* appeared as a book in 1953, *The Stars My Destination* in 1956. Both have been admired, but the second made the greatest impact. It tells the story of Gully Foyle, "the stereotype common man," who is inspired by revenge to become a great man. The world in which this happens is the medium-distant future: "All the habitable worlds of the solar system were occupied. Three planets and eight satellites and eleven billion people swarmed in one of the most exciting ages ever known" (Prologue).

"Exciting" is the key word here. Bester has taken a plot like that of

The Count of Monte Cristo and updated it. In this world people have mastered teleportation but all the old divisions between rich and poor, and the old compulsion to make war have remained unchanged by the new technology. But Bester is not concerned with extrapolating the future. He is telling a fairy tale, a moral fable, using his exotic future world as a dazzling backdrop for a picaresque adventure story that becomes a novel of education, which is really a reshaping of an old myth. Gully Foyle starts out looking for revenge on a space ship that left him stranded as an outcast in space. In the course of this revenge he develops his own intelligence and imagination, so that when he gains the power for revenge his goals have shifted. He finishes by trying to spread his power around, to awaken other dead souls, to give men a choice between death and greatness. All this is narrated in a style of great energy and playfulness. The rich of this era bear great commercial names from the past and amuse themselves by spending conspicuously on antique methods of locomotion. When the richest of all has a party, some of the guests arrive in ancient vehicles:

> The Colas arrived in a band wagon. The Esso family (six sons, three daughters) was magnificent in a glass-topped Greyhound bus. But Greyhound arrived (in an Edison electric runabout) hard on their heels and there was much laughter and chaffing at the door. But when Edison of Westinghouse dismounted from his Esso-fueled gasoline buggy, completing the circle, the laughter on the steps turned into a roar. (Ch. 11)

This playfulness is mixed with a high degree of literary awareness. The novel abounds with allusions to Blake and Rimbaud, carefully worked into context so that they will not trouble the untutored reader. And though the moral fable is serious, the spirit of play in the whole work indicates a kind of self-consciousness new to science fiction. This is not the clumsy earnestness of Doc Smith writing a genuinely "popular" fiction. This is a literate author deliberately choosing to work in a popular mode of fiction because of the opportunities it affords him. It is not easy to do this kind of thing without the inverted snobbery showing awkwardly, but Bester brings it off. He gives us a high-powered adventure, following a character who moves through society and space with great rapidity, whose experiences call for a bravura display of writing to describe them, climaxing in an extended passage of synesthetic derangement and cosmic displacement. Bester brought the Gosh-Wow! back into science fiction, but accompanied by a knowing wink, and he almost started an American New Wave all by himself. It is not surprising that his third novel, *The Computer Connection* (1975), which appeared in *Analog* as *The Indian Giver* in 1974, fits in beautifully with what is presently going on in science fiction—since a lot of what is going on is what Bester started in the early fifties.

Where all this led will be explored in more detail in the following sections, but before closing this one we must attend to one other development which signals the end of the Golden Age. As Isaac Asimov has put it,

> That Golden Age began in 1938, when John Campbell became editor of *Astounding Stories* and remoulded it, and the whole field, into something closer to his heart's desire. During the Golden Age, he and the magazine he edited so dominated science fiction that to read *Astounding* was to know the field entire.
>
> In that sense, the Golden Age endured until 1950, when other magazines, such as *Galaxy* and *The Magazine of Fantasy and Science Fiction* entered the field. (*Before the Golden Age*, Introduction)

We have been considering the fifties here as an appendage to the Golden Age, but we have not paused to pay tribute to these two new magazines that played such a great part in the development of the field in that decade, and in fact made it more "golden" than the forties in terms of the quantity and quality of work produced. In fact, the fifties may prove to be the really golden age of science fiction—when it had matured but had not become mannered or precious.

The Magazine of Fantasy and Science Fiction (known as *F&SF*) entered the field in 1949 under the guidance of Anthony Boucher, and was followed by *Galaxy* in 1950, edited by Horace Gold. Judith Merril, in the best essay on the magazines of that period ("What Do You Mean: Science? Fiction?", included in Clareson's *SF: The Other Side of Realism*), credits Gold and *Galaxy* with opening the field to psychiatric and social science fiction, quickly attracting writers like Heinlein, Sturgeon, Bester, Kornbluth, and Pohl (who later became its editor). And she sees Boucher as having made the field more conscious of style, of its literary potential:

> Gold would not buy for the idea *alone*, but he would settle for just competent writing when the idea appealed enough.
>
> Boucher . . . would not buy a story just for the idea; he had to like the writing. And unlike most earlier editors he was not style deaf.

There was a healthy competition between these two new magazines, and between them and Campbell's old *Astounding,* which changed its name to *Analog* at the end of the fifties, and finally among these and a horde of other new magazines in the field. By the mid-fifties there were well over thirty American magazines devoted primarily to science fiction, but *Astounding, F&SF,* and *Galaxy* still dominated the field. Most of the major works of science fiction that appeared in the fifties were first introduced in one of these three journals—and among the three *Galaxy* seems to have held an edge.

In recognizing the achievements of these magazines and their editors, we should notice how important the whole elaborate feedback system of writers-editors-readers was during these crucial decades in the development of science fiction as a literary form. The magazines were training-schools where an apprentice could make some money and learn his trade while maturing in a healthy and steady way. Until the pulps came along, science fiction was a tiny fragment of serious literature, lacking the coherence of a generic identity. But after four decades of magazine development, a popular base had grown up and attached itself to the Čapeks, Zamyatins, Huxleys, and Stapledons, whose isolated works were in some danger of falling through the grid of literary culture because they lacked a common name to bring them into a visible relationship. But by the fifties the popular and literary descendants of Wells were ready to be united under the inescapable title of science fiction.

This process of sophistication and integration was aided by an increase in critical self-scrutiny in the magazines themselves. They began to publish more and better critical essays and reviews, gradually incorporating science fiction criticism into the general body of literary criticism. In this connection, one of the most powerful influences has been the work of Judith Merril. A writer of science fiction herself, Merril has been most influential as editor of an annual collection, *SF: The Year's Best,* which ran from the early fifties into the sixties. Reading her notes on the writers and stories is, as Samuel R. Delany has observed, "an experience." As enough serious science fiction was produced to attract critical attention, that attention inevitably developed. And in the hands of such an astute critic as Judith Merril it became an important part of the whole feedback system of science fiction, helping to produce what Merril herself later taught us to call "The New Wave."

SOME ACHIEVEMENTS OF THE SIXTIES

As we approach the present, data multiply, and Time, the great ally of the literary historian, loses its power to sift and sort out the important items from the trivial. In many ways the sixties are too recent to be chronicled with any accuracy. Yet much excellent work was done in that decade, and some extraordinary new writers came into prominence, even while many of the masters of the fifties continued to produce interesting books. In this section and the next we will single out certain writers for attention, without meaning to imply that they are the only ones who matter. One of the things that have mattered in recent years is the "New Wave" of science fiction, and we shall try to give that phenomenon its due in the next section. Our concern here, however, is with certain writers of real excellence whose major achievements have come after the remarkable decade of the fifties but who, for one reason or another, have not been a part of the "New Wave." Their work is among the very best science fiction that we have, and its high literary quality has had much to do with the growing attention science fiction has received from literary critics and the growing respectability of science fiction courses in schools and colleges. These writers are Philip K. Dick and Ursula K. Le Guin in America, John Brunner and D. G. Compton in England, and Stanislaw Lem in Poland.

Critics abroad and in the United States are agreed that one of the most interesting bodies of work produced by a science fiction writer in recent years is that of Philip K. Dick. (A complete checklist of his work may be found in *SFS* 2/1, pp. 4–8.) Since 1955, when *Solar Lottery* appeared, Dick has published almost thirty novels and several volumes of short fiction. His work is not easy to discuss, since it does not fall neatly into a few books of exceptional achievement and a larger body of lesser works. All of his books offer ideas, situations, and passages of considerable interest. None quite achieves that seamless perfection of form that constitutes one kind of literary excellence. Nor does his career fall into any neat pattern of rise and fall or growth and decline. Stronger and weaker works are scattered evenly among his entire body of fiction, even as stronger and weaker episodes may be found within individual books. His strength lies in the unique vision that informs all of his fiction, and the crisp serviceable prose in which he presents the most extreme events without acknowledging that they are anything but ordinary. The way to read Dick is to read all of him, from the beginning to his latest effort, watching his control over certain themes mature and flourish.

Throughout his work Dick has made two themes his own, developing them and their philosophical implications more richly than any other single writer. They are the theme of alternate universes and the theme of mechanical simulacra for organic forms of life. The theme of simulacra occurs throughout his work, assuming major dimensions in *The Simulacra* (1964), *Do Androids Dream of Electric Sheep?* (1969), and *We Can Build You* (1969, 1972). It is often an occasion for comedy, as people are confronted by automated devices that function badly or have their functions distorted by unusual situations. At a deeper level this theme is used to explore the interface between life and artifice, exploiting the many paradoxes made possible by minute duplication of organic functions and behavior. But the theme most uniquely Dick's, because he has developed it more richly than any other writer, is the theme of the alternate universe.

The alternate universe theme in Dick's work may rest, as it does in *Eye in the Sky* (1957), upon the simple notion that every person perceives the world from a unique point of view. In this book Dick uses an accident to a bevatron to create a situation in which a small group of people are forced to live in the mental worlds of individual members of the group. Since these individuals include a fundamentalist religious fanatic, a do-gooding Victorian prude, a paranoid schizophrenic, and a crypto-communist of extreme views—the results are both frightening and comic. In later works the lines between real and "irreal" worlds become less easy to trace. The characters in Dick's world often find it impossible to distinguish between what is really happening and what seems to be happening to them—and the reader often faces the same problem. Even what "actually" happens can only offer clues to a reality which is enigmatic and elusive. In *Ubik* (1969) most of the events we experience, including a persistent drift in space and time toward Des Moines, Iowa, in 1939, are apparently the hallucinations of semi-dead individuals kept in "cold-pac" in a Swiss mortuary. But they are as vivid, as moving, as concrete and specific as any other kind of fictional event. There is no comfortable return to a "real" present at the end of *Ubik,* as there is in *Eye in the Sky.* We are denied that satisfaction here in much the same way that we might be denied it by Alain Robbe-Grillet or some other practitioner of the French "new novel." Dick has turned science fiction into an elegant and harrowing mental game, in which traditional ethics and traditional metaphysics are both called into question. Of any particular act it is often equally hard to say whether it has "really" happened or whether it is good or bad. What Dick makes us understand is that events produce anguish for those involved in them, whether they are dreams or "realities," and where there is anguish there must be sympathy. But he almost always prevents sympathy from turning into sentimentality. Examine, for instance, the movement of thought and emotion in the following passage from the end of *Flow My Tears, the Policeman Said* (1974). Police General Felix Buckman has just arranged for the death of a famous entertainer, for complex reasons involving his incestuous love for his own dead sister and the exercise of his bureaucratic prerogatives:

> The real, ultimate truth is that despite your fame and your great public following you are expendable, he thought. And I am not. That is the difference between the two of us. Therefore you must go and I remain.
> His ship floated on, up into the band of nighttime stars. And to himself he sang quietly, seeking to look ahead, to see forward into time, to the world of his home, of music and thought and love, to books, ornate snuffboxes and rare stamps. To the blotting out, for a moment, of the wind that rushed about him as he drove on, a speck nearly lost in the night.
> There is beauty which will never be lost, he declared to himself; I will preserve it; I am one of those who cherishes it. And I abide. And that, in the final analysis, is all that matters.
> Tunelessly, he hummed to himself. And felt at last some meager heat as, finally, the standard police model quibble heater mounted below his feet began to function.
> Something dropped from his nose onto the fabric of his coat. My God, he thought in horror. I'm crying again. He put up his hand and wiped the greaselike wetness from his eyes. Who for? he asked himself. Alys? For Taverner? The Hart woman? Or for all of them?
> No, he thought. It's a reflex. From fatigue and worry. It doesn't mean anything. Why does a man cry? he wondered. Not like a woman; not for that. Not for sentiment. A man cries over the loss of something, something alive. A man can cry over a sick animal that he knows won't make it. The death of a child: a man can cry for that. But not because things are sad.
> A man, he thought, cries not for the future or the past but for the present. (Ch. 27)

Buckman tries to see himself in absolute terms—as justified in his actions, as in command of events, as an enduring, worthy being. And of course he symbolizes all those men of power who justify their actions by their conoisseurship, their love of art, even while persecuting artists. But in this case the man of power actually cares for some things outside himself—his music, his sister—and this makes him prey to genuine emotion which bursts through his platitudinous self-comforting thoughts. He can't really control his tears, or events, or justify himself and the role he plays.

As he observes a few moments later, when he is thinking of returning to his office for a final confrontation with his victim Jason Taverner, if he should return, he would not be in command: "All I can do there now is witness something I can no longer control. I am painted on, like a fresco. Dwelling in only two dimensions. I and Jason Taverner are figures in an old child's drawing. Lost in dust." In this lugubrious mood he stops for fuel and approaches the only other person at the station. He draws on a pad "a heart pierced by an arrow" and hands it to this stranger without explanation. The man, uncomprehending or unconcerned, hands it back. Buckman starts to leave but returns and hugs the stranger. After this they speak—kindly human words dwindling toward banality, cliché, and finally, with the behavioral routines of casual acquaintances, they part. Dick's ability to mix absurd adventures with moments of existential anguish is rare in our literature.

Though it is dangerous to single out any one of his works for special attention, we should at least acknowledge the achievement of his Hugo-winning novel, *The Man in the High Castle* (1962). The premise of this book is that we are living in a United States that lost World War II. The country has been divided by the victorious Germans and Japanese, except for a zone in the Rocky Mountains which nobody seemed to want and serves as a buffer. In this world, a novelist (the man in the high castle) has written a book called *The Grasshopper Lies Heavy,* in which is imagined a world where England and America had won the war. This fictional world, we should note, is still not exactly like our "real" one. And at one moment in the novel, a Japanese dignitary under intense emotional pressure finds himself briefly in a San Francisco much more like our own—at any rate, a world in which the Japanese are clearly not the victorious occupiers of California. These various realities have equal ontological status in Dick's text. None is more actual than any other, except for those involved in it at that time.

The strength of this novel is in the characters and situations generated by Dick's imagination: the Japanese assiduously collecting American antiques (such as Colt .45s and Mickey Mouse watches); the Americans trying to master Japanese cultural codes and behavioral rituals, the Germans still pursuing Hitler's ideals but having to confront a resistant Japan. The individual characters: Mr. Tagomi, the Kasouras, Mr. Childan, the Frinks, Captain Wegener. The interweaving of all these characters in stories which intersect and separate, the development of greater understanding in Tagomi, Wegener, and Frink—all this is handled masterfully. The book comes to a richly extentialist conclusion in the thoughts of Wegener as he risks his life for a better Germany and a better world:

> No wonder Mr. Tagomi could not go on, he thought. The terrible dilemma of our lives. Whatever happens, it is evil beyond compare. Why struggle, then? Why choose? If all alternatives are the same . . .
>
> Evidently we go on, as we always have. From day to day. At this moment we work against Operation Dandelion. Later on, at another moment, we work to defeat the police. But we cannot do it all at once; it is a sequence. An unfolding process. We can only control the end by making a choice at each step.
>
> He thought, We can only hope. And try.
>
> On some other world, possibly it is different. Better. There are clear good and evil alternatives. Not these obscure admixtures, these blends, with no proper tool by which to untangle the components.
>
> We do not have the ideal world, such as we would like, where mortality is easy because cognition is easy. Where one can do right with no effort because he can detect the obvious. (Ch. 15)

But this conclusion is followed by another in which Juliana Frink visits the man in the high castle and forces him to admit that he wrote his book with the aid of the Chinese *Book of Changes.* When she throws the coins herself, asking the *I Ching* what people were supposed to learn from the book, the resulting hexagram is Chung Fu, "Inner Truth." She interprets this literally—Germany and Japan lost the war. But Hawthorne Abendsen, the author of *The Grasshopper Lies Heavy,* hesitates and then says, "I'm not sure." The other author, Philip K. Dick, is silent. But surely he wants us to remember that Chung Fu stands for *inner* truth. Both books, Dick's and Abendsen's, are fictions. But both, like *The Book of Changes* itself, can lead us to confront, at least briefly, our own inner truth. Dick's books do not lend themselves to summary, and they lend themselves too easily to explanation and interpretation. Such interpretations are treacherous, because they must ignore countercurrents of idea and value in Dick's work, invariably oversimplifying it. These complex works must be experienced and reexperienced to yield their secrets—and even then they will often remain enigmatic.

The achievement of Ursula K. Le Guin (b. 1929) is of a different kind from that of Philip K. Dick, and perhaps of a different order as well. Dick is crisp, witty, satirical, sardonic. Le Guin is closer to what Brian Aldiss has called "the dreaming pole" of science fiction. Her work is rich in images of a poetic or even visionary kind. Dick focuses bitterly on alienation and dehumanization. Le Guin concentrates on integration and transcendence. She has written many short stories, some of them collected in *The Wind's Twelve Quarters* (1975), and seven longer fictions for adult readers. In chronological order they are *Rocannon's World* (1966), *Planet of Exile* (1966), *City of Illusions* (1967), *The Left Hand of Darkness* (1969), *The Lathe of Heaven* (1971), *The Word for World is Forest* (in Harlan Ellison's *Again, Dangerous Visions,* 1972, a book in 1976), and *The Dispossessed* (1974). She has also produced a trilogy for younger readers, which has proved very interesting for adults as well. In fact, her "juveniles" may be the best introduction to her work.

The Earthsea Trilogy consists of *A Wizard of Earthsea* (1968), *The Tombs of Atuan* (1971), and *The Farthest Shore* (1972). Earthsea is an entire world, made up of islands and waterways. In Le Guin's work this world represents the universe as a dynamic, balanced system, not subject to the capricious miracles of any deity, but only to the natural laws of its own working, which include a role for magic and for powers other than human, but only as aspects of the great Balance or Equilibrium, which is the order of this cosmos. Le Guin's world is not based on a theology but on an ecology, a cosmology, a reverence for the universe as a self-regulating structure. Her juvenile fiction abounds in magic, but it is a strange sort of magic, which has much in common with science.

A Wizard of Earthsea is the story of the making of a mage, the education and testing of a young man born with the power to work wonders but lacking the knowledge to bring this power to fruition and to control its destructive potential. Ged's education is begun by his first master, Ogion, on his home island of Gont. This education continues and becomes more formal when he studies at the School for Wizards on Roke. What he learns there is manifold, but much of it is contained in this one speech by the gentle instructor in illusion, the Master Hand:

"This is a rock; *tolk* in the True Speech," he said, looking mildly up at Ged now. "A bit of the stone of which Roke Isle is made, a little bit of the dry land on which men live. It is itself. It is part of the world. By the Illusion-Change you can make it look like a diamond—or a flower or a fly or an eye or a flame—" The rock flickered from shape to shape as he named them and returned to rock. "But that is mere seeming. Illusion fools the beholder's senses; it makes him see and hear and feel that the thing is changed. But it does not change the thing. To change this rock into a jewel, you must change its true name. And to do that, my son, even to so small a scrap of the world, is to change the world. It can be done. Indeed it can be done. It is the art of the Master Changer, and you will learn it when you are ready to learn it. But you must not change one thing, one pebble, one grain of sand, until you know what good and evil will follow on that act. The world is in balance, in Equilibrium. A wizard's power of Changing and Summoning can shake the balance of the world. It is dangerous, that power. It is most perilous. It must follow knowledge and serve need. To light a candle is to cast a shadow. . . . (Ch. 3)

To be a wizard is to learn the "true names" of things. But the number of things in the world, the difficulty of discovering their names, set limits to magical power, even as the boundaries of scientific knowledge set limits to the power of science. As the Master Namer puts it,

> "Thus, that which gives us the power to work magic, sets the limits of that power. A mage can control only what is near him, what he can name exactly and wholly. And this is well. If it were not so, the wickedness of the powerful or the folly of the wise would long ago have sought to change what cannot be changed, and Equilibrium would fail. The unbalanced sea would overwhelm the islands where we perilously dwell, and in the old silence all voices and all names would be lost." (Ch. 3)

Finally, the greater the knowledge, the greater the limitations—a view which is voiced by the Master Summoner after Ged has abused his youthful powers and unleashed a shadow of terror into the world:

> "You thought, as a boy, that a mage is one who can do anything. So I thought, once. So did we all. And the truth is that as a man's real power grows and his knowledge widens, ever the way he can follow grows narrower: until at last he chooses nothing, but does only and wholly what he *must do*. . . ." (Ch. 4)

Ged's quest, after his recovery (for the shadow wounded him gravely), is to find the shadow and subdue it, to restore the Balance that he has upset by working his power in a way beyond his knowledge. His quest is both an adventure story and an allegory. In his pursuit of the shadow he will discover himself and redeem his world through suffering. In coming to grips with the shadow, his magic is useless, because he does not know its true name, though the shadow is in possession of his. Finally, it is through an exercise of intuitive logic that he learns the shadow's name. Considering how the shadow must have come into possession of his name, he then realizes what the shadow's name must be:

> Aloud and clearly, breaking that old silence, Ged spoke the shadow's name, and in the same moment the shadow spoke without lips or tongue, saying the same word: "Ged." And the two voices were one voice. (Ch. 10)

The shadow was himself, his own capacity for evil, summoned up by his own power. To become whole, he had to face it, name it with his own name, and accept it as a part of himself. Thus by restoring the balance in himself, he helped to restore the balance of his world. The poetry of this balance shines through Ged's words, which are Ursula Le Guin's, as he explains the sources of power to a little girl:

> "It is no secret. All power is one in source and end, I think. Years and distances, stars and candles, water and wind and wizardry, the craft in a man's hand and the wisdom in a tree's root: they all arise together. My name and yours, and the true name of the sun, or a spring of water, or an unborn child, all are syllables of the great word that is very slowly spoken by the shining of the stars. There is no other power. No other name." (Ch. 9)

Is this magic? Religion? Science? The great gift of Ursula Le Guin is to offer us a perspective in which all these merge, in which realism and fantasy are not opposed, because the supernatural is naturalized—not merely postulated but regulated, systematized, made part of the Great Equilibrium itself. And of course, this is also art, in which the sounds of individual sentences are as cunningly balanced as the whole design, in which a great allegory of the destructive power of science unleashed, and a little allegory of an individual seeking to conquer his own chaotic impulses, come together as neatly as the feathers of a dove's tail. Her adult fiction differs from the juvenile not a bit in themes and values. The difference lies in the way that the adult fiction fleshes out imaginary worlds with social and cultural detail. Not that her major fiction ever presents us with the details of a social chronicle—far from it—but that it always raises questions about the nature of social organization itself. In her last few books she has been a kind of fabulous anthropologist, suggesting whole societies through the use of telling details and structural extrapolation. And these imaginary worlds are structured so as to reveal to us, by their very deviations from the world we know, aspects of the "known" that have escaped our notice.

The three novels written before *A Wizard of Earthsea* may be quite properly seen as apprentice work, showing only flashes of Le Guin's real power, but the three major novels that have been published since 1968 are of another order. *The Left Hand of Darkness* (see discussion on pp. 226-230) was recognized as a major work from its first publication. Winning both the fans' Hugo Award and the writers' Nebula, it has gone on to critical success beyond the bounds of science fiction itself. There can be little doubt that this novel has been among the leading forces in gaining a larger audience and a greater critical respect for science fiction in recent years.

In her later works Le Guin has continued to develop and extend her thematic concerns and her technical resources as a writer of fiction. In *The Lathe of Heaven* she presents us with a world closer to that of Philip Dick. Where her earlier works were set in worlds outside the solar system in times ranging from the twenty-sixth to the twenty-eighth century, *The Lathe of Heaven* is set in Le Guin's own home city, Portland, Oregon, in a time around the end of our own twentieth century. This is the time period preferred by Dick, and his favorite device of alternate universes is also central to *The Lathe of Heaven*. In this novel a simple man named George Orr discovers that on certain occasions his dreams change the nature of the reality around him. This terrifies him and he seeks help from a scientist who is studying human dreams. When the scientist discovers that Orr is not crazy but really possessed of the terrible power to change the world through dreams, he tries to use this power consciously to change the world according to his own liberal notions of what it should be like. This attempt of a conscious mind to use an unconscious one for purposes of changing a universe that is too complex for any consciousness to control results in a series of disasters. The interaction between the passive dreamer and the energetic scientist is too complex to summarize here, but its theme is summed up in this explanation Orr gives to his wife:

> I don't understand it, I can't say it in words. Everything dreams. The play of form, of being, is the dreaming of substance. Rocks have their dreams, and the earth changes. . . . But when the mind becomes conscious, when the rate of evolution speeds up, then you have to be careful. Careful of the world. You must learn the way. You must learn the skills, the art, the limits. A conscious mind must be part of the whole, intentionally and carefully—as the rock is part of the whole unconsciously. Do you see? Does it mean anything to you? (Ch. 10)

In this book Le Guin has concentrated for our attention the various elements of the value struggle that dominates our lives in the nineteen-seventies. The progressive scientist says, "Life—evolution—the whole universe of space/time, matter/energy—existence itself—is essentially *change.*" But Orr responds, "We're in the world, not against it. It doesn't work to try to stand outside things and run them, that way. It just doesn't work. It's against life" (Ch. 9). Here we have the opposition between expansionists and conservationists, between technological manipulation of the world and psychological adjustment to it, presented for us dramatically by Le Guin. In her next book, *The Dispossessed,* she moved to another ground of opposition, the clash of socio-political systems, represented by two neighboring planets—one capitalist and one socialist. She calls this work an "ambiguous utopia," meaning that it looks two ways and examines the costs and benefits of both systems in some depth. The book has been justly acclaimed as a major work of utopian fiction, reminding us that the tradition of utopian narrative, from Thomas More through Edward Bellamy, is one of the main precursors of modern science fiction. *The Dispossessed* is a warm, rich, and subtle book, which some critics have found to be Le Guin's best. In her mid-forties, she is obviously at the height of her considerable powers, making it impossible to assess her achievement at the present time. Suffice it to say that she has already done enough to earn a permanent place in our literature.

Taken together, Le Guin and Dick illustrate how rich and complex, how fully adult and literate, American science fiction had become by the 1960s. During this same period there were other developments in the field, which will be considered in the next section, but before turning to these new developments we must consider briefly three exceptional achievements in science fiction from outside the United States. One is the development by the English science fiction writer John Brunner of a kind of naturalistic science fiction. The other two are achievements which for quite different reasons have not yet received full recognition. One is the work of an English novelist who has received insufficient attention because he belongs to no current school or movement of science fiction. The other has been isolated by a language barrier, his work largely untranslated from its native Polish language.

John Brunner (b. 1934) has written more than fifty books, mostly science fiction, beginning in the fifties. But his reputation as a serious writer rests largely on four works produced in the late sixties and early seventies: *Stand on Zanzibar* (1968), *The Jagged Orbit* (1969), and *The Sheep Look Up* (1972) and his most recent, *The Shockwave Rider* (1976, see discussion on pp. 230–233). These books represent not only a deliberate attempt to reach a more literate audience with a more serious message but also a technical break-through of sorts for science fiction. Brunner has described his aims and methods in a very interesting lecture "The Genesis of *Stand on Zanzibar*" (printed in *Extrapolation* 11/2):

As I said, I'd been mulling over the notion of that book for a long while. I was fairly sure I was going to write about a breakthrough in tectogenetics—artificial optimisation of the embryo—because no other event could cause such a dramatic upheaval in the kind of world I was thinking about [2010]. As time passed, though, it ceased to be primarily the length of time I knew I was going to have to invest in the book which daunted me; much rather, it came to be the problem of presentation, because it grew clearer and clearer that my chief task was not to create a story on the basis of these initial plot assumptions, but to create a convincing world for the plot to happen in. . . .

And inventing a method of constructing a book which would facilitate that process seemed extremely difficult. (P. 35)

Brunner's notion of his intention in the book has several important aspects. First, that he wanted to make the "world entire" the protagonist. If one way to write fiction is to focus on the deeds of a single hero, with the world as backdrop for the hero's adventures, surely the extreme opposite is to make the world the center of interest, using characters as ways of exemplifying aspects of the world. These are both legitimate ways of making fictions, and it would be foolish to say that one is "better" than another. It is perhaps less foolish to hold a preference for fictions in which concern for individual portraiture is balanced against concern for the presentation of society—as in Tolstoy's *War and Peace,* for instance. But even this preference may blind us to the value of works which move away from this balance for one reason or another. And Brunner has reasons for focusing on the social at the expense of the individual. What he needed to find, as he explains the writing of *Stand on Zanzibar,* was a method which would enable him to emphasize the social in a convincing and complete fictional text. He thought about the way that writers outside science fiction, like Vance Bourjaily and Ernest Hemingway, have handled the impact of major wars on society, and he felt that science fiction writers might learn from them how to handle their own central problem: "the depiction of a world changed by new technology, political upheaval, and so on." Thinking along these lines he found a solution for his problem:

In this particular context, I thought of Dos Passos. I went home, and I re-read *Midcentury,* not because it's a very good book, or even the best of his many novels, but because it's the one in which I think his technique of documentary association is most highly evolved. Besides, it covers a period, unlike that of the USA trilogy, where I can judge the success of his methods by comparison with my own recollections.

And then I started thinking about the way in which one constructs one's image of the world. If you reflect on it for a moment, you'll see that some of what we quote/unquote "know" comes from personal experience, some from what one's heard people say, some from what one was taught at school, some from the papers, radio, TV . . . and so on and on. From all these disparate sources we somehow manage to assemble a pattern that enables us to locate ourselves in the changing, confused environment of the 20th century.

Plainly, then, my task would be to throw at the reader information about my future world from as many sides as the real world can hit him from. This accounts for the contrasted modes of presentation in the book, the scripts, collage, montage, verse and other extraneous details imposed on the skeleton of the unifying narrative. (P. 36)

This is precisely the technique Brunner has used for his massive, important novels of the near future. *The Sheep Look Up,* extrapolates the shortest distance into the future and is the most powerful in its impact. It gives us a world—and in particular a United States—that has been unable to control its pollutants and is beginning to suffer the consequences. The most horrifying aspect of Brunner's world is the restraint and rigor of his extrapolation. He does not conjure up some unrecognizable nightmare of the future but takes what we find in some places and on some occasions now, and extends it just a bit further. The result is a tale at once convincing and harrowing. In the world it presents we find decent ordinary people trapped in an environment which has just gone over the edge from a deterioration which might be arrested to an irreversible slide into social chaos. Like the writers of naturalistic fiction whom he is imitating, Brunner shows us characters whose world overwhelms them, grinding them into misery or death no matter how they struggle to resist or escape. This can be not just harrowing but supremely depressing—as it is in much naturalistic writing. But there is a considerable difference between this and traditional naturalism—the difference being that this world is presented as not yet existent. It is not the world we live in, nor is it meant to be a prediction of what must inevitably come to pass. It is rather, as Brunner has said, a "warning sign saying DO NOT GO THIS WAY." The worlds of Brunner's major novels are very powerful warning signs indeed. These books are serious, literate, and socially committed in a truly admirable fashion. And even if we succeed in avoiding the worst of the difficulties presented in them, they will serve to remind us eloquently of what we have avoided. If we do not succeed, of course, they will make an equally eloquent epitaph.

Another British writer who should be mentioned here has received precious little recognition either at home or abroad despite genuine and solid work as a science fiction writer. D. G. Compton (b. 1930) has written plays as well as fiction, including eight science fiction novels that have been released in the United States. Unfortunately, his American publishers have not done well at keeping his books in print, and they are hard to obtain. In England, perhaps because he has allied himself with no movement, his carefully crafted novels in the tradition of John Wyndham have received less than their due—just one sentence, for instance, in Brian Aldiss's history of science fiction, *Billion Year Spree* (1973). Perhaps because Wyndham (author of catastrophe novels like *The Day of the Triffids,* 1951) represents precisely what the New Wave of British novelists is revolting against, Compton suffers from being assigned to a "superseded" line of science fiction. But his kind of dramatic plotting and penetrating characterization is not so easily relegated to the dust bin.

Three or four of his novels are exceptional and should endure for some time. In particular, *Farewell Earth's Bliss* (1966) has a mythic quality of the sort we associate with stories like Shirley Jackson's "The Lottery." Compton's tale of people deported from Earth to Mars focuses on character and social behavior under situations of extreme stress. It is as memorable as a recurrent dream and as inevitable. *Synthajoy* (1968) is another strong novel, beautifully told in the first person by a victim of an encephalographic process for superimposing the emotional experience of one person upon others. Compton engages us in the emotional lives of his characters in a superlative way, forcing us to hang on every word of his imprisoned/hospitalized heroine. In *The Steel Crocodile* (1970) he gave us a harrowing glimpse into a world in which a benevolent foundation allows its master computer to get out of hand, threatening the world with megalomaniac despotism. And in *The Unsleeping Eye* (1974) Compton surpassed himself, presenting to us a story set just a bit in the future, where television caters to the individual's need for excitement in a genuine welfare state. When a woman is told she has an incurable terminal disease, and a journalist is operated on so that what his eyes perceive is transmitted to a TV recording studio, this tale begins. What follows is the story of the man's pursuit of the woman, his winning of her confidence, and his observance of her private anguish for the sake of a whole society of voyeurs hooked on vicarious suffering.

Compton's stories are so carefullly plotted, and his dramatic denouements are so thoroughly prepared for, that it seems inappropriate to narrate them here. But in this novel as in all his works, the focus is on what happens to people—what new social situations or new technical devices do to people, to their lives, to the world. Compton's work is informed by an acute and subtle moral sense which avoids the extremes of satire and sentiment while compelling us to see the world ethically. This, too, may be a bit old fashioned. It is also a rare capability. In fact, he succeeds superbly in preserving certain traditional fictional values and human values in works of genuine science fiction. This should be recognized for the remarkable achievement it is.

The last writer whose achievement will be acknowledged in this section is Stanislaw Lem (b. 1921). Born in Poland, where he still lives, Lem, like both his parents, was trained to be a doctor, completing his medical education shortly after World War II. His first work of fiction was a somewhat autobiographical novel, written in the late forties, but he soon turned to science fiction, producing almost twenty books from 1951 to the present, including nine novels. During the fifties he read a good deal of current science fiction, including Bradbury, Bester, Pohl, Blish, Asimov, Clarke, Dick, Campbell, Heinlein, Leiber, van Vogt, and Sheckley (see Darko Suvin's Afterword to *Solaris*). He has written widely on scientific and technological subjects, and is currently one of the most rigorous and best informed critics of science fiction, as exemplified by his piece on Philip K. Dick in a recent issue of *Science Fiction Studies* ("A Visionary Among the Charlatans," *SFS* 2/1).

For American readers, it has been necessary until very recently to accept much of Lem's achievement on faith. The first translations began to appear in 1970, and two of his finest novels, *Solaris* (1961, translation 1970) and *The Invincible* (1964, translation 1973) were not translated from the original Polish but were in fact translations of translations, one from French, the other from German. But three more of his important books have since appeared in English, reaching the wider paperback audience only in 1976, and earning Lem a review on the front page of the *New York Times Book Review*—something unprecedented for a science fiction writer. These recent translations from the Polish include *The Investigation* (1959, translation 1974), in which an impossible Scotland Yard investigation becomes an absurd metaphor for all rigidly empirical thought; *The Cyberiad* (1967, translation 1974), a collection of ingenious stories of genuine but somewhat ponderous humor; and *The Futurological Congress* (1971, translation 1974), which unites satire, nightmare, and extraordinary verbal play. With the earlier translated *Memoirs Found in a Bath Tub* (1961, translation 1970) and the recent collection of stories called *The Star Diaries* (compiled and translated in

1976), we now have enough of Lem's work in print to judge his importance for ourselves. And it seems clear that though the Russians have produced some good science fiction in recent years, especially the work of the Strugatski brothers, whose *Hard To Be a God* (1964) was well received here in 1973, there is really only one continental writer of science fiction whose work seems comparable to the best being produced by British and American writers—and that is Stanislaw Lem.

Lem is particularly concerned with the interfaces between men and machines, between human science and the things that the world may present to man, challenging that science. In *Solaris* and *The Invincible* in particular, he has presented these themes in works whose power shines easily through the double layer of translation. *The Invincible* is an especially interesting work to investigate because it is so similar in certain respects to a good novel by one of the established masters of Anglo-American science fiction: Arthur C. Clarke's *Rendezvous with Rama* (1973). Clarke and Lem share a number of qualities. Both are trained scientists, both write directly on scientific subjects as well as indirectly through science fiction. Both admire the work of Olaf Stapledon. And both have distinctly philosophical turns of mind. Thus they produce novels which are technologically well conceived, with careful attention to hardware and scientific principles, but they use their exotic settings to raise questions well beyond the scope of technology, touching the deepest concerns of ethics and metaphysics.

In *Rendezvous with Rama* Clarke gives us a fable set in 2130, when there are settlements on some of the other planets and moons in the solar system, and certain institutions such as marriage have been slightly modified, but in a world that is recognizably continuous with our own. When an unidentified object appears in the solar system, on a possibly dangerous course, the only space ship handy enough to intercept it is sent to investigate. Thus the *Endeavour* approaches the hollow, fifty-kilometer-long cylinder called *Rama,* and proceeds to land a crew, who enter and explore. In Lem's novel, another space ship, *The Invincible,* has been sent on a similar mission: to investigate the failure of a predecessor to return from Regis III, a planet in the "Lyre Constellation," previously unexplored. Both writers have chosen to work with their favorite theme, which is among the oldest in science fiction: first contact of humans with other living creatures. And both authors give the theme a twist typical of their own work. Their aliens are neither bug-eyed monsters nor simply a race enough like humanity to make no difference. Given a theme so common, a writer must exhibit genuine imagination or fail miserably. But Lem and Clarke proceed with immense calm and assurance to construct environments which are genuinely alien from human experience but solidly convincing nonetheless. And they handle the problem of alien intelligence in ways that are revealingly similar. Inside Rama, the Captain of the *Endeavour* and his crew find a complete and unique world populated only by a variety of biologically constructed robots, designed apparently only to maintain the cylinder on its mysterious flight. These "biots" and other evidence give the humans some notion of what the Ramans are like, but no Ramans are found in the cylinder, which has apparently been moving on some mission of importance for immense amounts of time. When the strange craft has tapped sufficient solar energy for its own ends, it accelerates out of the solar system, leaving humanity awed by its superior technology and finally possessed of an answer to "an ancient question. We are not alone. The stars will never again be the same to us" (Ch. 9).

The adventure of the *Endeavour* involves some feats of physical courage and endurance, some ingenious and resourceful thinking, and results in a sense of awe at the possibilities of the cosmos—in which humanity is just a single possibility. The adventure of *The Invincible* involves the same qualities and produces similar results. On the frighteningly barren Regis III, the crew of *Invincible* find the undamaged corpses of their predecessors around the uninjured space ship that brought them there. This mystery is finally resolved—at least in part—when *Invincible* encounters the agents of the destruction of *Condor*'s crew. They are microscopic crystals, apparently evolved over millions of years of struggle, from ancestors which were probably robots abandoned on the planet by some former civilization. One of the ship's scientists hypothesizes "an evolution of non-living things, an evolution of machines." Perhaps an energy shortage led to a struggle for survival:

> In this battle, the "intellectually" superior mechanisms, which needed considerable amounts of energy (not least, perhaps, because of their size) were no match for the less developed but more economical and more productive machines—(Ch. 6, "Lauda's Hypothesis")

The crystals swarm in clouds, governed by their collective mentality, and they deal with threats by surrounding them with an electro-magnetic field so powerful that it erases all memories from the human brain and disrupts all mechanical cybernetic systems in the same way. They are invincible on their planet, and after attempts to destroy them result in defeat for the ironically named *Invincible,* it ignominiously gathers up its dead and its helpless, brain-washed wounded, who must be taught everything again like babies, and prepares to depart. The *Invincible* is ready to retire from the field. But before going it must make sure it has left no helpless survivors behind. The inhuman, "natural" destructive power of the crystals forces the humans to recognize what humanity really means. "Warm, human breath" becomes especially important. The missing must be accounted for because "Each man needed the certainty that the others would not abandon him under any circumstances." On a lonely and heroic mission to rescue or account for the ship's missing crew members, one man, hoping to escape the notice of the crystals, braves death and is rewarded with a kind of vision:

> He felt so superfluous in this realm of perfected death, where only dead forms could emerge victoriously in order to enact mysterious rites never to be witnessed by any living creature. Not with horror, but rather with numbed awe and great admiration had he participated in the fantastic spectacle that had just taken place. He knew that no scientist would be capable of sharing his sentiments, but now his desire was no longer merely to return and report what he had found out about their companions' deaths, but to request that this planet be left alone in the future. Not everywhere has everything been intended for us, he thought as he slowly descended. (Ch. 11)

Even through the clumsy Germanic English of this double translation, Lem's eloquence penetrates: "Not everywhere has everything been intended for us:" a sentiment to which C. S. Lewis would give vigorous assent, as would Olaf Stapledon, and, of course, Arthur C. Clarke himself. Lem joins them, and the writers who have been discussed in this chapter, as an example of solid literary achievement in the writing of science fiction, an achievement which is currently receiving a healthy challenge from a "New Wave" of writers in England and America, who are helping to keep the field very much alive and awake. To consider their work, and some other contemporary developments, will be the business of the next section.

MAKING WAVES AND CROSSING LINES

In recent years the most interesting phenomenon in science fiction has been a movement called the "New Wave." It is hard to reconstruct accurately how this came about without dangerous oversimplification, but all histories are simplified models of various states of affairs. For our purpose it is reasonable to say that certain changes that were occurring in the field of science fiction became apparent to a group of writers, editors, and critics, who then made a deliberate decision to develop and promote science fiction that incorporated and expressed these changes. The changes themselves take many forms, but they fall under two headings: a new literary self-consciousness and a new social awareness. The literary self-consciousness expresses itself mainly in deliberate experimentation with style—changes in language and changes in narrative technique which we shall be examining. The social awareness is reflected in a concern with politics and life styles, usually seen from a radical point of view. In a broad sense, the New Wave represents an attempt to find a language and a social perspective for science fiction that is as adventurous and progressive as its technological vision. The movement has seen everything from attempts to incorporate literary devices borrowed from James Joyce's *Finnegans Wake* to parodies or pastiches of the styles of older writers, designed to emphasize the gap between then and now. It has been a stimulating and exciting period for the literature of science fiction, full of daring experiments of varying degrees of success.

The movement was first recognized as a movement and promoted as such in England by a group of writers that formed around Michael Moorcock's *New Worlds* magazine. Moorcock's move to the editorial chair of *New Worlds* in the spring of 1964 was an event equivalent to Campbell's arrival at *Astounding* or Gold's at *Galaxy*. If anything, Moorcock's break with the past was more complete and radical than any of the others we have considered. He took the writer whose work in previous issues of *New Worlds* had been the least typical and made it the center of the new movement. The writer was James Graham Ballard (b. 1930), and Brian Aldiss describes his position in the revivified magazine this way:

> The very first Moorcock *New Worlds,* in the summer of 1964, contained the beginning of a two-part Ballard serial and an article by Ballard on William Burroughs. "In *The Naked Lunch,* Burroughs compares organized society with that of its most extreme opposite, the invisible society of drug addicts. His implicit conclusion is that the two are not very different, certainly at the points where they make the closest contact—in prisons and psychiatric institutions . . ." It was to these extreme points that Ballard instinctively journeyed, the poles of mental inaccessibility, where normal and abnormal met on apotropaic neutral ground. (*Billion Year Spree,* Ch. 11)

"Apotropaism" is the magical or religious art of warding off evil by charms, incantations, or ritual performance. Whether or not that is what Ballard is up to, his fiction is clearly a fiction of extremities, in which the horrible is commonplace. He has been more successful with the shorter forms of fiction than with novels, and his shorter forms have followed an evolutionary line from surreal stories to what he calls "condensed novels," in which plot and character are replaced by collages of horrifying imagery. The question may be raised whether this is science fiction at all, since it combines features of works by Burroughs and Borges, writers not usually thought to reside in the science fiction ghetto. But the fact is that the line between science fiction and what used to be called "the mainstream" is getting harder and harder to draw. One of the chief functions of the New Wave has been the eroding of that line. The treatment of Ballard's *The Atrocity Exhibition* in the U.S. illustrates this perfectly. As a science fiction novel it was destroyed before publication when a Doubleday executive "took exception to some of it." It was then picked up and dropped by Dutton, and finally published by Grove Press as *Love and Napalm: Export U.S.A.* with a preface by William Burroughs in 1972.

Among the interesting paradoxes in a field beset by paradoxes is the fact that the works of the founder and the christener of the New Wave, Michael Moorcock and Judith Merril respectively, are not particularly avant-garde. Merril has introduced feminist themes in her fiction but in form and content she could hardly be called radical. It has been her criticism that contributed most to the movement, lending strength and support to Moorcock's enthusiasm. Moorcock himself (b. 1939) is best known for work in the most reactionary fictional form of all, Sword and Sorcery, which many critics hardly consider to be science fiction. What lends a New Wave touch to Moorcock's sagas of the heroic deeds of Elric of Melniboné and Dorian Hawkmoon is a certain tongue-in-cheek air of insincerity that haunts these books. They constantly verge on self-parody. In fact, if there is a theme that runs through Moorcock's fiction, that theme would have to be parody, or perhaps something like parody but gentler and more playful. Two of his works may serve to illustrate this. He has begun a trilogy, *The Dancers At the End of Time,* which is a chronicle of the end of the universe. But unlike the apocalyptic narratives that we associate with this motif in traditional science fiction, Moorcock's version is light and amusing. "Having inherited millennia of scientific and technological knowledge, [the human race] used this knowledge to indulge its richest fantasies, to play immense imaginative games, to relax and create beautiful monstrosities" (*An Alien Heat,* Prologue). Moorcock's end of the world is simply England's *fin de siècle,* extrapolated: a world of dandies and darlings, living for pleasure. It is amusing, fantastic, and wildly escapist. Social consciousness intrudes not here.

Another Moorcock venture is the charming *Warlord of the Air* (1971). This purports to be a manuscript produced by Moorcock's grandfather, who met in 1903 a man who had been transported into the future—to 1973—and had returned. This time-traveler, it soon becomes clear, had not visited *our* 1973, however, but a 1973 in which the Russian revolution had failed, dirigibles were the fastest form of transcontinental transport, and the British Empire still dominated the world. In his adventures the time-traveler meets many people whose names are familiar to us, doing things which may strike us as wildly incongruous or strangely appropriate. Among them are a doughty dirigible captain named Korzeniowski (Joseph Conrad's real name), an apoplectic scoutmaster named Ronnie Reagan, and a nice London bobby called Michael Jagger. All this is narrated in a style right out of Conan Doyle and Rider Haggard. It is correct, slightly stuffy, and very wooden—a perfect imitation of something one of those earlier writers might have written, but with a whole system of ironic references to our reality that they could not have attempted.

Beside Ballard, whom he championed, Moorcock seems decidedly reactionary as a writer, but others were at hand to help put the newness in the New Wave—in particular Brian Aldiss. Born in the mid-twenties, Aldiss first encountered science fiction in the British equivalent of the American pulps: the Boy's Friend Library, which published four volumes a month, mostly collections of material serialized in *Modern Boy,* a twopenny weekly magazine. In the fifties this young man who had been weaned on the adventures of Captain Justice began to write science fiction of his own, some of it clearly influenced by Heinlein and the other giants of *Astounding.* He wrote for the pre-Moorcock *New Worlds,* and dedicated one of his novels to Moorcock's predecessor, Ted Carnell. But his own evolution as a writer coincided with that of *New Worlds* itself, and when Ballard became the dominant influence in the new Moorcock version of the magazine, Aldiss was ready with his own avant-garde fictional experiments. Some of these have been called by John Brunner "exercises in the manner of Evelyn Waugh, Robbe-Grillet, and lord knows who else" (*Extrapolation,* 11/2, p. 42). One of those in the "who else" category is the James Joyce of *Finnegans Wake*. Another is Mary Shelley, the founding mother of science fiction.

Given the fact that both Aldiss and Moorcock have devoted considerable effort to this project of adapting specific styles of mainstream writers (and of early science fiction writers) to the pursuits of contemporary science fiction, we may do well to pause and examine the purposes and implications of this aspect of the New Wave. At first glance it may seem as if this is just what Brunner himself did in *Stand on Zanzibar,* but he does not consider it so, and he is probably right. Brunner adapted a technique from Dos Passos for a particular purpose, and he modified it for his own ends. Aldiss and Moorcock seem more interested in playing with other voices for their own sake. A crucial case is that of Aldiss's novel *Barefoot in the Head* (1969), which uses a language that owes much to *Finnegans Wake* in order to capture a world that has gone through a war fought with hallucinogenic chemicals. The protagonist of the book, a Christlike acidhead superstar, tries to reject the pattern of crucifixion and lead his followers into a new life. As he preaches, Aldiss presents the scene in terms of a regeneration, an impregnation, a re-creation:

> Now from his purgent words the mucous remembrance of the sinking swimmers distend to farcy forms and the saprophagous outpour tranfluxes the time's ergot so that while it floats into her labyrinthine passages she feels the smooth buddoming trunks and timber shafts wheel and wheedle into grander growth in her skeleton the sapling stalked stuff supplanting bone nodes of branch staring under skin at hip and pelvis shin breast and elbow her obnubil features suddenly the whole unatomy its soft syruped holes its husks hairs and horned teeth beats
>   into greenamelled leaf! (Bk. III, "Ouspenski's Astrabahn")

Where Brunner simply adapted a technique from Dos Passos, Aldiss tries to take over Joyce's voice, his way with words, justifying this by the material he chooses to present. In his fusion of Joyce's idiom with a kind of acid-rock talk, he is truly moving science fiction into new territory, taking great risks, moving away from an audience of fandom and leaping toward a new literate audience which may or may not be there. It is Brunner's social conscience which makes his best work new, although he is not usually considered a member of the New Wave movement. It is Aldiss's concern for literariness that marks his work as typical of the British New Wave movement itself. Aldiss's experiment is a gallant gesture, and *Barefoot in the Head* is at the very least a remarkable representative of its own cultural milieu. Along with Ballard's work it represents the most daring attempt to make the New Wave of science fiction a vehicle for serious literary experimentation.

Less daring but still interesting have been the fictions of New Wavers Harry Harrison and Norman Spinrad. Harrison has done some excellent pastiches in the Moorcock manner, as exemplified by *Tunnel Through the Deeps* (1972)—a Victorian romance about an alternate present in which the Americans lost the revolution and the Colonies are still colonies. The straitlaced Victorian tone of this book is maintained as faithfully as that of Moorcock's own *Warlord of the Air,* and the story—especially the love interest—is suitably restrained. Another Harrison pastiche is *Bill the Galactic Hero* (1965)—a hilarious parody of Heinlein's *Starship Troopers* and Asimov's *Caves of Steel*. Harrison has also produced the serious overpopulation novel *Make Room! Make Room!* (1966, filmed as *Soylent Green*), and the far less serious adventures of the Stainless Steel Rat.

Spinrad, an American, is best known for two very different books, one in the parodic New Wave vein, and the other in a hip, swinging prose which has affinities with the Beat novelists and new journalists like Tom Wolfe and Hunter Thompson. *The Iron Dream* (1972) is Spinrad's presentation of a book called *Lords of the Swastika,* which "won a posthumous Hugo" in 1955. The author who received this posthumous honor is one Adolf Hitler, "who dabbled briefly in radical politics in Munich before finally emigrating to New York in 1919." Taking this mild alternate-universe premise, Spinrad then gives us the kind of power fantasy Hitler might have written if he had indeed emigrated instead of staying in Germany and becoming Chancellor of the Third Reich. Complete with a fatuous afterword by the critic Homer Whipple, the book is uncomfortably close to some of the militaristic and fascistic works that have been very popular in the science fiction field, as Spinrad forces us to face the racist, power-fantasy element that has frequently been a part of popular science fiction. This kind of critical parody is very different in tone from works like *Warlord of the Air* and *Tunnel Through the Deeps*. But both are symptomatic of a new critical self-consciousness in contemporary science fiction. In *Bug Jack Baron* (1969) Spinrad had done something entirely different, giving us a realistic near future in which a formerly radical TV personality becomes involved in a deadly power struggle with a wealthy manipulator of politics and politicans. The style is a kind of Madison Avenue hip projection, nudged slightly toward poetic stream of consciousness. The book's "vulgar" language and explicit sexuality helped it acquire some notoriety, including an attack on it in the British House of Commons. But it is a serious and well-crafted if irreverent voice from the late sixties, which was first serialized by Moorcock in 1968. The cross pollination of British and American science fiction has become very complex indeed.

A similar mixture of sexual spice and literary pastiche is found in the best work of the prolific American, Philip José Farmer. Farmer started writing back in the fifties and by rights belongs to no new wave. But he is a fabulous adapter, and he has adapted fabulously. In particular, what we might call the Cuckoo Principle of New-Wavism suits him perfectly. He likes to lay literary eggs in the nests of other writers. His principal coup in this respect is *Venus on the Half-Shell* (1975), which purports to be a novel by Kurt Vonnegut's mythical science fiction writer Kilgore Trout. Farmer provides Trout with a Vonnegutty list of previous fiction and tries to imitate Vonnegut's style—with only feeble success. It is hard to parody a genuinely witty style without being as witty as the writer being imitated. But the book had an extraordinary commercial success, not hindered by the fact that many stores marketed it as Vonnegut and many purchasers bought it as such. We hope they could tell the difference when they read it. Vonnegut himself reports that he "couldn't stand to read the thing." Farmer has had some successes with variations on the Cuckoo Principle, however, the greatest among them being *Lord Tyger* (1970). This is the story of an attempt by a fanatical devotee of Edgar Rice Burroughs to duplicate in reality the story of Tarzan. He kidnaps the child of an English Lord and tries to have him reared by apes, only to discover too late that this results in the child learning no language at all. So, back to the old drawing board! Another Lordling is kidnapped, this one to be raised in the jungle by circus dwarfs who pretend to be apes. The "Tarzan" produced by this experiment has a hilarious sequence of picaresque adventures, becoming the sexual scourge of the jungle in the process. This is Farmer at his best. Here the irreverence, the sexual frankness, and the delight in parody that characterize the New Wave are exemplified beautifully—by a writer who is really parodying New-Wavish behavior.

In America the new movement has been publicized mainly through efforts of Harlan Ellison, whose own fiction has been less significant than his anthologies—especially the series of *Dangerous Visions* and *Again, Dangerous Visions* (1967, 1972). The principal American New Wavers, in addition to those already mentioned, are Roger Zelazny, Samuel R. Delany, Thomas M. Disch, and Joanna Russ. Zelazny is the oldest of this young group. His work is characterized by a marked concern for the sounds of language and by a delight in retelling ancient myths in new forms. His *Lord of Light* (1967), which won a Hugo, is an elaborate adventure in which the deities of the Hindu Pantheon are reincarnated in Zelazny's characters. A strong tendency toward romances of the Sword and Sorcery variety in his work has taken the form of a sequence of novels about Avalon, an alternate universe of magic and castles which is reachable from our own world. This sequence is still in progress. Some of the sentimentality that threatens Sturgeon and frequently overwhelms Bradbury is also a problem for Zelazny. And sometimes the tendency toward the poetical in prose, which he also shares with those writers, gets out of hand and becomes too cloying, too self-admiring. But when the mythical and poetical are balanced by an appropriate amount of prosaic shrewdness, Zelazny is a formidable writer, as he is in his finest single piece of work, the short story, "A Rose for Ecclesiastes" (included in *Four for Tomorrow,* 1967), which ranks among the very best in the field. In this tale Zelazny has found a cynical and bitter protagonist, which has helped to curb his own tendency toward easy sentimental effects, producing what is still his masterpiece.

Samuel R. Delany (b. 1942) grew up in New York and attended the Bronx High School of Science. He is something of a prodigy and a polymath as well as a very prolific writer. His first work of any size was of considerable size, three volumes, and was completed by early 1964, when he was barely over twenty-one years old. (*The Jewels of Aptor,* 1962, is a short novel written even earlier.) His *Fall of the Towers* trilogy leans toward Sword and Sorcery. But in *Babel-17,* which won a Nebula Award from the Science Fiction Writers in 1966, Delany found a voice and a subject matter of his own. In this book Delany used his considerable knowledge of linguistics and semiotics to write a novel about language and communication. Though the story has elements of whirlwind adventure and exotic decor in the Bester manner, the attention to language and nonverbal communication is Delany's own. In particular, the implications of a character being conditioned to speak in a computer language which lacks the pronouns "I" and "you" are worked out with ingenuity and emotional power. *The Einstein Intersection* (1967, another Nebula) was in the pseudo-mythic mode favored by Zelazny, but with the insertion of fragments from the author's journal among other epigraffiti to the chapters. Strange, in a work of science fiction, to encounter the breaking of allusion, to find the author, a young, black American discussing his task of writing the book while on a Grand Tour of the Mediterranean world. In *Nova* (1968) Delany set out deliberately to pay homage to Bester by imitating *The Stars My Destination,* but again with features that made the work his own. Where Bester had introduced elements from Blake's romantic poetry and Rimbaud's derangement of the senses, Delany gives us the modern story of a young man learning how to be the writer who can write the story we are reading. As *Babel-17* was about communication, *Nova* is about art. In both these excellent novels, the protagonists are artists. Rydra Wong of *Babel-17* is a poet as well as a cryptographer, and the two young men through whose eyes we follow the adventures of Captain Von Ray in *Nova* are a prodigious note-taker who wants to write an old-fashioned novel and an almost instinctive performer on the "sensory-syrinx," which is a kind of musical instrument that projects images that are apprehensible by human sight, sound, and smell. Attached to the physical adventures of Von Ray are the intellectual and emotional adventures of the two artists, whose attempts to understand one another make a kind of allegory of the growth of a literary artist, who needs the spontaneity of "the Mouse" and the thoughtfulness and learning of Katin to do his work properly. In *Babel-17* and *Nova,* Delany showed that he could tell a rousing popular adventure story in the Bester manner, introducing serious questions of his own—a considerable achievement. But he was not content to rest there.

In 1975 *Dhalgren* appeared, almost nine hundred pages of a dense, richly-charactered fiction, frighteningly close to here and now, but not quite our here and now. A decaying city, roaming street gangs, ever-present sexual experience (hetero, homo, and multiple)—and a dearth of love. This is a long way from pseudo-mythic fantasy, from space opera, in the direction of a reality like that of the naturalists. The book is ambitious, daring in its sexual explicitness, and challenging in the questions it raises about human relations. There is presently a good deal of critical discussion as to whether the big book is a success, whether it has crossed entirely over the imaginary line that divides science fiction from something else, or whether it has fallen between the areas of realism and fantasy without accomplishing the aims of either. It is not our business to try to settle these questions here. The book exists. It is being read and discussed. And Delany has earned the right to have his experiments taken seriously. This book makes one thing clear. Delany is not part of anybody else's New Wave. He is a wave of his own.

His latest novel, *Triton* (1976), is subtitled "An Ambiguous Heterotopia"—which is an oblique reference to the subtitle of Le Guin's *The Dispossessed:* "An Ambiguous Utopia." *Triton* is closer to traditional science fiction than *Dhalgren* was, in that it is set clearly in a future, on a satellite of Neptune, and involves the examination of alternatives to the social structures we all know. But it is in no way a retreat from Delany's progress toward his own vision. His characters are richer, more human, than ever, more individualized and less mythic, and above all freer and more responsible than ever. This, too, is a story about communication, and about love, and it is more somber and more moving than Delany's pre-*Dhalgren* work. The protagonist, Brom Helstrom, has problems loving and communicating—and nothing, including a complete change of sex, changes the problems. The novel is richly documented, presenting its future society with great solidity, and raising important questions about the nature of sexuality and sex roles among many other things. It is an impressive addition to an impressive career, by a writer still under thirty-five when it was published. Though entirely unique as a writer, Delany's ability to combine formal experiment with social vision makes his work a perfect example of what people ought to mean when they speak of a New Wave of science fiction.

Thomas M. Disch is another young writer whose work deserves the most serious attention. He has been associated with the British New Wave, some of his work appearing in *New Worlds,* but his development has taken him in directions of his own. His first major breakthrough was *Camp Concentration* (1972, serialized in *New Worlds,* 1967), a fable about experimentation on prisoners, which combines considerable technical resources in the management of the narrative (told through the journal of one of the victims) with a probing inquiry into human values. Disch's later novel *334* (1974) is closer to Delany's *Dhalgren* than to anything else in the field—but that hardly describes it. Set in New York early in the next century, it offers a world that is not radically different from ours in many respects but is deeply troubling for reasons that apply to the present New York as well. Above all, the aimlessness and purposelessness of the lives chronicled is affecting. The somberness of this book and the recent Delany suggest that science fiction has come as far as possible in the direction of confrontation with the problematic and disturbing in human life, as the ghastly collages of Ballard have brought the form as far as possible toward encompassing its potential terror.

Joanna Russ (b. 1937), along with Disch and Delany, is on the leading edge of the American New Wave. Like Disch and Delany, she has written poetry. She has also studied playwrighting, and received an MFA from the Yale Drama School. In addition to some prize-winning short stories, she has written three science fiction novels: *Picnic on Paradise*

(1968), *And Chaos Died* (1970), and *The Female Man* (1975). Her contribution to the New Wave of science fiction is important in two respects: her language is among the most alive, vigorous and daring of any prose being written today (as might be expected from her dedicatory bow to Vladimir Nabokov and S. J. Perelman in *And Chaos Died*), and her commitment to radical feminism (as exemplified in *The Female Man*) is typical of the social consciousness of this movement. In *And Chaos Died* she has aimed at a language, a style, adequate to convey various extrasensory experiences from the inside, not merely narrating such events in staid, detached prose. And in *The Female Man* she has used the visionary potential of science fiction to convey the contrast between life as it is presently lived by many women and life as it might be. Among other things, Russ has demonstrated the unique potential of science fiction for embodying radically different life styles, which can hardly be conveyed in fiction bound by the customs of present behavior. She, along with Disch and Delany in this country and Ballard and Aldiss in England, has helped to make the fictional new wave genuinely new and experimental in literary form rather than merely modish and fashionable. It should be pointed out that she belongs to a generation of young writers who were undergraduates at Cornell University in the late fifties and are presently leaving a distinctive mark on contemporary writing in America. This group includes, among others, Thomas Pynchon, the late Richard Fariña, Sandra Gilbert, Kirkpatrick Sale, and Ronald Sukenik.

In addition to the makers of waves, to complete this brief picture of the current science fiction scene, we must consider the crossers of lines. There are lines and lines, in literature as in life. The designation science fiction means one thing to a literary critic and quite another to a publisher or bookseller. In the world of publishing, science fiction constitutes what is called a specialty market. Other such things are detective fiction and westerns. These books often sell for lower prices in hard covers than comparable books labeled general fiction, and they bring their authors lower royalties. Thus it may be very much in an author's interest to avoid the science fiction category if possible. Science fiction writers marvel at Kurt Vonnegut, Jr., who managed to start as a science fiction writer, change categories, and keep on writing science fiction without the stigmatizing label and the even more annoying lower rates of remuneration. For even in works based on real experiences, like *Slaughterhouse-Five* (1969), Vonnegut casually incorporated materials from his science fiction past, leaving literary critics to puzzle about their categories, which must pretend to more substantial bases than those of publishers and book-sellers. Vonnegut is in part, at least, still a science fiction writer, though it may be more useful to see him as an updated cracker-barrel humorist, in the tradition of Mark Twain—who wasn't above putting Tom Sawyer in a balloon or sending his Connecticut Yankee back to King Arthur's Court. Like Twain, Vonnegut cultivates a popular idiom, reaches a wide audience, and covers a terrible vulnerability and sadness with bandages of salty wit. The literary imagination has always found the imaginary useful. What we have learned to call realism is hardly a natural mode for imaginative prose. Vonnegut (another Cornellian, by the way, but of an earlier generation), who has some scientific and technological training, easily finds scientific clothing for his speculative ideas. He frequently treats the scientific aspects of his speculative fiction in an offhand or even parodic manner—but so do the New Wavers.

A writer like Vonnegut forces us to consider the impending disappearance of the category upon which a book like this depends. And so do many other events in the literary world, which we should acknowledge before concluding this short history. Some of these events are matters of writers like Vonnegut crossing lines. They come from both sides. There are signs that Ursula Le Guin's hard-cover publishers are beginning to treat her work as if it were general fiction. Robert Silverberg, whose science fiction has deliberately become more serious and complex in recent years, has written at least one book (*The Book of Skulls,* 1972) which should probably have been marketed as general fiction, and he will perhaps soon be allowed to pass for an ordinary imaginative writer. There are other symptoms, or straws in the wind, as well, that suggest that former science fiction writers may appear merely as writers.

Even more marked has been the tendency of writers who inhabit the safe world of "serious fiction" to cross the line from their side and write novels that are not called science fiction but most certainly are. Most notable here are John Barth's *Giles Goat-Boy* (1966) and Anthony Burgess's *A Clockwork Orange* (1962) and *The Wanting Seed* (1962). It is only the category these writers hold in the minds of publishers that keeps those books off the science fiction shelves at your local book store. The elegant puzzles and paradoxes of Jorge Luis Borges (who admired the early Wells) are a kind of science fiction, though closer to pure mathematics than to its technological applications. And so are the speculative tales of Italo Calvino. William Golding frequently approaches science fiction, and in *Lord of the Flies* (1954) may have crossed the line. His fine novelette, "Envoy Extraordinary," about a citizen of Rome somewhat ahead of his time, was anthologized with tales by John Wyndham and the gothic fantasizer Mervyn Peake in a volume called *Sometime, Never* in 1957. Walker Percy stepped just over the line into science fiction with *Love in the Ruins* (1971). Even more disconcerting is Doris Lessing, who crossed the line toward the end of the fifth volume of her sequence of autobiographical novels, *Children of Violence*. In the appendix to *The Four-Gated City* (1969), her story, which began four volumes back, in the time before World War II, moves on into a post-catastrophic future, a familiar aspect of the science fiction world. It seems likely that this part was called an appendix partly because it is an addition after our own time, but also so that it might be operated on and removed should it prove troublesome. But it is there, and in putting it there Lessing indicated her need for the imaginative ground of science fiction to complete her major work.

Perhaps the most disconcerting writers of all, to the classifiers and cataloguers, are those writers who don't simply cross the line from one book to the next, but straddle it within a single book. It may be possible to ignore this when the straddling is done by a writer who has committed the indiscretion of writing something that resembles hard-core space-opera—as when Delany wrote *Dhalgren*. But when the most important American novel of the past several years, Thomas Pynchon's *Gravity's Rainbow* (1973), is also a case of straddling the old dividing line—then it is obvious beyond the bounds of fandom that the line itself has virtually disappeared. And this is indeed the case. Where Delany, Russ, Le Guin, Disch, Aldiss, and Ballard leave off and Vonnegut, Burroughs, Barth, Burgess, Golding, and Coover begin is impossible to determine.

Brian Aldiss began his compendious history of science fiction with the assertion that "science fiction doesn't exist." The point may be debatable now, but if we put it in the proper tense—the future—it seems much less debatable. Science fiction will not exist. But the whole shape of literature will have been changed.

2. SCIENCE FICTION IN OTHER MEDIA

CIENCE FICTION has appeared in every medium of artistic creation, from the popular song "The One-Eyed, One-Horned, Flying Purple People Eater" to Frankenstein's Monster Halloween masks. Most notably, we find science fiction in the comics and in the three modern technological entertainment media: film, radio, and television. When science fiction in one medium has been relatively unpopular, its popularity for other audiences through other media has helped to maintain interest in science fiction. In passing through a filmic stage, or a comic-book stage, science fiction not only retained an audience but created an audience, and the audience created by science fiction film, for example, brought new demands to science fiction in other media, such as novels. This dialectic has been significant in the development of science fiction in all media.

Of the technological media, science fiction has been preeminently successful in film. The subject of science fiction film is vast (see Baxter, Clarens, and Gifford in Bibliography), yet there are three important points that need to be made about it in relation to science fiction in general: first, the term *science fiction film* is confusingly imprecise; second, science fiction has a special relationship with film as a medium; and third, science fiction films have a history as a genre which often parallels the history of science fiction prose.

In common parlance the terms *horror film* and *science fiction film* are used interchangeably, in part because of a historical accident. In 1931 Universal Studios released two immensely popular and influential films:

Frankenstein, directed by James Whale with Colin Clive in the title role (and Boris Karloff as the monster who would come to be known popularly by his creator's name), and *Dracula,* directed by Tod Browning with Bela Lugosi in the title role. These two films were in many ways complementary. *Frankenstein* accented the vain romantic quest for love of the sensitive man-made monster whose only guilt lay in the inarticulateness and ugliness imposed upon him. *Dracula* followed the articulate seducer whose curse arose through his own mortal sin as he imposed himself on young women. Both films highlighted the role of the monster; both explored the central problem of the outsider's relationship to society; both were pioneering films. They seem to us today as milestones in the development of monster films. But while Frankenstein is a scientist gone awry, another outsider who must deal with society and who fails to accommodate himself to the necessity of human interaction, Dracula creates only himself. Although the "science" of the Karloff film is a thin layer of pseudoscience, some of the most striking scenes are those set in the laboratory and the creation of the monster's life through exposure to the unleashed forces of the heavens. The underlying structure of the film recalls an *organized* body of knowledge, a science of biology and a science of society. One can even detect Marxist overtones in the uprising of the Transylvanian peasantry against the house of the errant Baron. In the Lugosi film, on the other hand, the underlying knowledge is not an organized science but a *collection of beliefs* that recalls medieval Catholicism. The Count's fratricide and suicide led to his curse—for no causal reason; his image is unreflected by mirrors *because* he has no soul. Chairs also have no souls, but they are visible when Dracula is not. The most striking scenes in this film do not concern the machinations of science but the stealthy nighttime intrusions of the already-created sinner. Although these are both monster films, *Frankenstein,* depending as it does on science, is a science fiction film; *Dracula,* depending as it does on magic, is a horror film.

The 1950s saw a huge production of related films. Some, like *The Day the Earth Stood Still* (1951) and *The War of the Worlds* (1953), were clearly science fiction films. Others, like *The Thing* (1951) and *The Creature from the Black Lagoon* (1954), were clearly horror films. Yet most were horror films with only the trappings of science fiction. One notable example is *Them!* (1954), the story of James Whitmore's attempt to combat a colony of six-foot ants. We are made to understand that these creatures arose through mutation induced by atomic testing, a favorite science fiction device confirming America's cold war fears. However, any biologist understands that, among other things, the oxygen transport system of insects is such that they never could exist at that size. The most dramatic moment in this film comes not when the hero confronts the scientists who made the bomb (they are not even in the film) but when he invades the ants' nest and burns their eggs just in time to prevent nature-runamuck from getting forever out of our control. Throughout this productive decade, the majority of monster films were horror films with a veneer of scientific justification. In addition, the legion of sequels to *Frankenstein* and *Dracula* continued to appear, thus welding the two genres together in the popular imagination.

However, the two can quite profitably be viewed separately. The first important filmmaker was the Frenchman Georges Méliès. He understood immediately that the fantastic inventions of science fiction, especially those of his countryman Jules Verne (see pp. 9–10), were exemplified by moving pictures themselves. During the last decade of the nineteenth century and the first decade of this century the Wizard of Montreuil produced a rich series of one-reelers such as the comic *Voyage to the Moon* (1902) which begins with a Follies chorus line accompanying the astronauts into their ballistic projectile and ends with the spacecraft jabbing into the eye of the Man in the Moon. Such play with the motifs of science fiction was quite natural for the first directors who were still playing with the possibility of film. Throughout the history of cinema the affinity between film and science fiction has helped to create a general climate that supported both. The pulp era's concentration on Bug-Eyed Monsters led to film's concentration on monsters in general. In our day, the real and fictional exploration of space has led to a renewal of science fiction film presaged first by the daringly Shakespearean *Forbidden Planet* (1956) and culminating perhaps in Kubrick's visually compelling *2001: A Space Odyssey* (1968) in which the justifiably famous light show is but one of the many examples of the philosophic resonance between the technological play with science in science fiction and the play with technology which is film. True science fiction film and true science fiction have had a continuing dialectic by which each helped shape the other.

True science fiction films began as carnival amusements with the work of Méliès. As film began to explore narrative with Porter's *The Great Train Robbery* (1903) and history with the works of Griffith and visual montage with the works of Eisenstein, science fiction film, by adopting the techniques of these other filmmakers, developed as well. Fritz Lang's *Metropolis* (1926) explores the life of a futuristic scientized city and includes such striking motifs as the Doppelgängers of the heroine Maria, one a romantic humanist and the other a robot programed to keep the people enslaved. H. G. Wells himself collaborated with and wrote the scenario for Korda and Menzies' masterpiece, *Things to Come* (1936) (taken from Wells's *The Shape of Things to Come* [1933]) which graphically depicts the armed destruction of civilization and its gradual rebuilding into a utopia run by engineers. The 1940s, with the exception of Frankenstein sequels, saw a relative submergence of science fiction film as Europe and America concentrated on dealing artistically with the images and analogs for World War II. In the 1950s, however, as we have seen, true science fiction film reemerged, sometimes as monster films and sometimes in its own right.

A further development was the production of *Planet of the Apes* (1968), a film based on the novel (1963) by the Frenchman Pierre Boulle and made from a script coauthored by television writer Rod Serling. This film turns a loin-clothed Charlton Heston loose in a world populated by militaristic intelligent apes and speechless wild humans reminiscent of Swift's Yahoos. The science fictional justification for this world is rather thin, but sufficient to give a new twist to the age old satiric device of the countryman visiting the strange land which by implication is our own. So, although this film is not very science fictional, it is certainly not a horror film. Its popularity spawned a *Beneath the Planet of the Apes* (1970), a *Return to the Planet of the Apes* (1971) and this last in turn spawned an animated television program for children. Science fiction in one medium continues to influence science fiction in other media.

By the year 1971 science fiction film had reached a new stage. In that year, two important science fiction films were released: George Lucas's *THX1138* and Stanley Kubrick's *A Clockwork Orange*. The first of these depicted the strain of regimentation in a future society driven underground by the fallout of nuclear war and kept underground, we finally realize, by mankind's own greed and insensitivity. The concrete corridors of this filmic world turn out not to be movie sets at all but the actual storm sewers of Los Angeles—which some clandestinely inhabit today. In Kubrick's film, made from Anthony Burgess's novel (1962) of the same name, we see first a future plastic society in which mass living has made privacy—and safety—a luxury few can afford and none can maintain; then we see how the techniques of mind control can take anyone and remake him into his opposite; and finally when the remaking is undone, we realize that society itself has been making us all over all along. Here science fiction film is modern social film. Just as Burgess is thought of as a mainstream author, these are really mainstream films, even at the same time that they are science fiction films. Building on this fusion, the number of science fiction films continues to increase, 1976, for example, seeing the release of *Logan's Run, A Boy and His Dog* (see p. 187), and *The Man Who Fell to Earth* among others.

Science fiction and film have always had a uniquely close relationship. When Wells and Méliès were working they were thought of as unusual, but nonetheless as important artists at the forefront of their arts. As science fiction went off into the pulps, with a few notable exceptions like Stapledon (see pp. 32–33), science fiction film went off into monster movies, with a few notable exceptions like Lang. But finally, after the fifties had made a new place in our culture for science, science fiction and science fiction film each demonstrated a new vitality and popularity. By the seventies, with writers such as Vonnegut and Burgess and filmmakers such as Lucas and Kubrick, both science fiction and science fiction film had rejoined their respective, and mutually influencing, mainstreams.

In radio, however, which saw its dramatic heyday from the establishment of the first commercial station in 1920 until shortly after the establishment of commercial television in the late forties, science fiction fared less well. There were such shows as *Dimension X, Out There,* and, of course, *Superman,* but the programs which lasted into the television era tended to rely on the auditory, like *The Shadow* whose non-science fictional hero could "cloud men's minds" with the powers he had learned in the Orient so that he could pad about and whisperingly wonder "who knows what evil lurks in the hearts of men?" *Superman,* with its potent image of the flying man of steel, made the transition to television; *The Shadow,* with its creaks and whispers, persisted for another decade on radio; but the other shows largely disappeared.

This comparative failure of science fiction radio may well be due to radio's reliance on sound. In movies we immediately recognize a monster or a space station; in radio we immediately recognize a galloping horse. But what is the sound of a space station? To actualize science fiction's most striking motifs requires visualization, a phenomenon which can be accomplished for the previously unknown either by thorough verbal description (which is appropriate in prose but not on radio) or by direct image (which is appropriate to film—and television—but impossible in radio). Nonetheless, perhaps the most famous single radio show was the so-called Panic Broadcast. Orson Welles's Mercury Theater of the Air, on October 30th, 1938, presented a modernized and Americanized version of H. G. Wells's *The War of the Worlds.* The format of the first half of this program was that of a music program interrupted by news flashes. For those listeners who tuned in after the Mercury Theater's introduction, but still during the first half, the darkness of the listening room and the realistic employment of the standard radio device of news bulletins led to an extraordinary realism. There were many who simply didn't wait for the second half, and hence, before the station break, panicked. Although the program is a fine one dramatically, its fame rests on this historical accident. Welles's *War of the Worlds* is unique in radio history and it is illuminating to recognize that in this unique instance the technological capabilities of radio were ideally suited to the dramatic program *because* that program was science fiction. Nonetheless, this famous case is the exception.

Science fiction fared better on television. The first science fiction television was the series *Captain Video* which ran from 1949 to 1952. This was an adventure series for children set in space and is notable for presenting the errant robot Tobor, a crazed, out-of-control product of science which Captain Video finally subdues to his will. The servant robot became a favorite character of the viewing audience (leading even to his own comic strip) and helped lay to rest the typical antitechnology fears of science fiction.

From 1960 to 1968, intermittently and in various formats, Rod Serling presented *The Twilight Zone,* an anthology series that offered some first-rate science fiction and other related types of drama, principally from the occult. This led at first to *The Outer Limits,* another anthology series with similar content though generally less powerful stories, and finally created a market for continuing adult science fiction shows. The late sixties saw three of these: *The Land of the Giants,* Quinn Martin's *The Invaders,* and Gene Roddenberry's *Star Trek.*

The first of these relied on trick photography to show the Earthpeople stranded on a giant world menaced by outsized natives, huge cats, fearsomely big ants and so on. It was an attempt to capitalize on the popularity of such movies as *The Incredible Shrinking Man* (1957) (for which Richard Matheson wrote the screenplay from his own story). While the film had a strong emotional appeal as the hero's predicament became worse and worse, the television series had to present an essentially stable situation in order to stay on the air. It didn't. It is sometimes rerun today at times intended for children's viewing since the one striking feature of the series is the trick photography itself.

The Invaders was also short-lived. The premise was that aliens were trying to take over our world by sending their Protean spores to Earth.

These spores could then be used by those who had already landed to imitate the bodies of ordinary humans, often those in key positions (like Secretary of Defense), and thus gain control of the general population without the people recognizing the takeover. This clearly owes much to Heinlein's *The Puppet Masters.* However, where Heinlein had the good guys versus the bad guys, *The Invaders* had Roy Thinnes alone in his knowledge that the aliens were among us. He kept trying to make the authorities aware of the situation, only to find them either unbelieving or already taken over. Whenever he killed an invader (recognizable by an inflexible pinky), the creature dissolved in a visually pleasing conflagration reminiscent of the demise of M. Valdemar in Poe's story (1845). This show had a science fiction premise, but its drama was much like that of other Quinn Martin programs such as *The Fugitive* and consequently led to a build-up of frustration that had little to do with its science fiction aspects. Although the scripts were generally better written than those of *The Outer Limits* and the premise more adult than that of *The Land of the Giants,* this show too failed to have a significant impact on the audience.

Star Trek, on the other hand, created not only an audience but a cult. Its premise was an exploratory voyage by the "starship" *Enterprise* to world after world. The drama shifted from episode to episode as the continuing cast of crew members met new situations all over space. The ship and its hardware were striking visually and the scripts were often by such accomplished science fiction writers as Harlan Ellison, Theodore Sturgeon, and David Gerrold. Its seventy-nine episodes have been on the air continuously since the network termination of the series itself. Indeed, the continuing impact of the series is so strong that it spawned a weak copy in 1975, *Space: 1999,* produced by British ITV. By combining the visual aspects of science fiction with the flexibility of Serling's anthology format and strong characterization, *Star Trek* made a permanent mark.

In addition to these shows, one must also note that television is a continuing outlet for old movies. The late night horror movie, often science fiction, has been a staple of television fare since the early fifties. At about that same time, children's science fiction picked up Captain Video's mantle with Columbia's *Superman,* a being from another planet who fought for "truth, justice and the American way." The popularity of this program led the stations to rerun at children's hours (Saturday morning, for example) the whole gamut of science fictional series produced by Republic Studios for theatrical showing, including *Undersea Kingdom* (1936), *The Purple Monster Strikes* (1945), *King of the Rocket Men* (1949),

Radar Men from the Moon (1951) and most notably *Flash Gordon* (1936). The first of these was a loose adaptation from Verne, the last a lift from the comic books. As the most widely used medium, television has been the conduit through which the dialectic of science fiction development has been channeled.

The appeal of children's science fiction on television led also in the 1960's to some new programs, including *Lost in Space* (a Swiss Family Robinson copy with *Forbidden Planet's* Robbie as houseboy) and *Voyage to the Bottom of the Sea* (an updated *20,000 Leagues Under the Sea* without the misanthropy) and finally in 1975 to *Land of the Lost* (in which a father, son and daughter have fallen through a "time door" into a world that includes dinosaurs, extraterrestrials, civil war veterans and anything else that could fall through a time door). 1975 also saw on television the production of *Way Out Space Nuts,* a children's show modeled vaguely on *Star Trek* and Don Knott's *The Reluctant Astronaut* (1967), but owing its satiric outlook to another development that began with the comics.

The origin of comics is a matter of definition. Some might consider the eleventh century Bayeux Tapestry a form of comic strip; certainly political cartooning had achieved journalistic importance by the time of Thomas Nast (1840–1902) who gave our newspapers the familiar donkey and elephant symbols for the Democratic and Republican parties. All authorities (see Reitberger in Bibliography) agree, however, that the separate medium of comics was firmly established when Richard Outcault began drawing *The Yellow Kid* in 1895 (a strip which incidentally gave its name to Yellow Journalism because of the newspapers in which it appeared). Comic strips began to achieve psychological and artistic sophistication when George Herriman began *Krazy Kat* in 1913, the year in which Burroughs published *The Gods of Mars.* For the next decade and a half, comic strips developed in their own way, primarily with domestic comedy strips, while science fiction which had previously been published as novels or in collections or newspapers, began to sneak its way into the pulps (see pp. 35–38) and to serve as fictional fillers in the technical magazines of Hugo Gernsback (including *Electrical Experimenter,* also established in 1913). In 1926 Hugo Gernsback began the first science fiction pulp magazine, *Amazing Stories;* it was explicitly aimed at adolescent males (of whatever age). Shortly after its founding, newspapers began to carry science fiction for a wider readership. The new genre of science fiction comics appeared in 1929.

In that year, Phil Nowlan began writing *Buck Rogers,* a strip set in the twenty-fifth century with the morals of the nineteenth. There were anti-gravity belts, ray guns and television and atom bombs and lots of evil Mongols. This immensely popular strip, which stayed in production until 1968, spawned a world-wide craze which included dolls and patterned shirts and dances and finally, in 1933, *Flash Gordon,* nearly as durable and full of spaceships and ray guns and atom bombs and lots of evil Mongols. This later strip, equally influential with the mass audience, was distinguished by the superior artwork of Alex Raymond. The two strips created an enormous interest in the twenty-fifth century, and the various media set about to satisfy that interest. One of the signs of this was, of course, the Republic serials series, including *Flash Gordon* itself.

These comic strips had been exclusively newspaper productions. In the thirties some publishers began to reprint collections of newspaper strips in pulp magazine form; others began to put together strips designed especially for magazines with stories that continued from month to month. And finally, in March 1937, National Periodicals came out with the first comic strip magazine devoted to a single theme: *Detective Comics.* The popularity of this publication was so great that National is still known as DC. In 1938, beginning first as a magazine and only later as a newspaper strip, theatrical serial, and television show, DC began what is doubtless the most influential science fiction comic strip of all time: *Superman.* This strip, created by Jerome Siegel and Joe Shuster, added a word to our vocabulary and an image to our culture.

Superman at first could not fly, but he could "leap tall buildings at a single bound"; his great strength derived quite naturally from a physiology evolved on Krypton functioning under the much weaker gravity of Earth. Although his very first antagonists were criminals, he soon began a continuing battle against Lothar, the mad scientist figure reminiscent of Victor Frankenstein. In the course of the years Superman traveled through time and to foreign planets; made coal into diamonds by manual compression; ignited explosive with his X-ray vision; and generally acted out the power fantasies so familiar to science fiction. The most important psychological aspect of Superman is that his secret identity is Clark Kent. Children could easily identify with the apparently powerless and timid character who ripped off his clothes to reveal himself as the strongest and most just of beings.

Superman was quickly followed by Bob Kane's *Batman* in 1939. This strip too was science fiction in that the title hero's great abilities were always augmented by his scientific skill evident in the many devices of his own design ever ready in his utility belt. Although the artwork in *Bat-*

man was clearly superior to that in *Superman* and although both continue to the present, the older strip is by far the more influential. The reason for this is that Batman, after all, is only a mortal. Bruce Wayne is his true identity and Batman his masquerade; in the older case, Clark Kent is the masquerade while the true identity is Superman. Superman provides a greater sense of power fulfillment for the identifying reader.

The *Flash* also began his career in 1939. His superhuman speed, both of action and thought, came about as a result of accidentally breathing the gases of "hard water" and he is continually referred to as a "freak of science." These three types of character—the extraterrestrial, the scientific law enforcer, and the freak—have continued to dominate science fiction comics and create markets for science fiction in other media as their readers grew up.

In the 1960s, the Marvel Comics group, which had been publishing since 1938 and included such classics as *Captain America* (1940), began to launch a whole new series of science fiction heroes designed for the audience already trained to the conventions of the older heroes. These included *The Hulk* (a freak of science) in 1961, *Thor* (an extraterrestrial) in 1962, and *Ironman* (a scientific law-enforcer) in 1963. The most important was *Spiderman* (1962), a freak of science who was also a scientific law-enforcer. *Spiderman,* as of this writing, is the single most widely distributed comic magazine in the world. All these Marvel heroes have in common some personal weakness (unlike Superman and Batman) and a semicynical view of the world they inhabit. Peter Parker, for example, Spiderman's real identity, is always short of cash, somewhat clumsy, and always ready with a snide observation about his boss. Spiderman blatantly insults the criminals as he catches them. This new kind of science fiction comic has then a type of topicality which makes it especially powerful in its animated form on television. *Spiderman,* like *Star Trek,* created a cult. The attitudes of these later science fiction comic heroes developed against the perfection of their forebears and hence created the climate for such satiric television science fiction as *Way Out Space Nuts.* We can see in this development the crossing and recrossing of characters and motifs from one medium to another; we can see the new audience emerging. Most important, in each of the media in which we see science fiction, we can see its new conjunction with the mainstream, from *2001: A Space Odyssey* to topical children's television to Vonnegut. It is only reasonable that this conjunction occur because, functioning as it does in every major artistic medium, science fiction is itself a major force in the continuing development of our culture.

II. SCIENCE

3. THE SCIENCES OF SCIENCE FICTION

S THE LITERATURE of science, science fiction can be most richly experienced if we understand something of science itself. It is important to know, for example, that Ray Bradbury must have been aware in 1950 that humans could not breathe unaided on Mars—this reveals that he intends his *Martian Chronicles* to be taken as fabulous; it is equally important that one understand in what ways relativity theory does or does not validate time travel—this helps us assess the extrapolative skill of Pierre Boulle in *The Planet of the Apes* (1963) and reveals his underlying concern for realism. But science is not a single monolithic entity; it changes through time. Once the Earth was flat, now it is round; once there were four elements, now there are more than one hundred. But this is not just a matter of ancient history. For example, many classic science fiction stories of rigorous extrapolation, like Isaac Asimov's "Runaround" (1942), are firmly based on the knowledge that, because Mercury always keeps the same face to the sun, it has three distinct zones: a horribly hot sunward zone where metal runs liquid, a frigid dark zone where oxygen is solid, and a temperate strip circling the planet in between. American space probes in this decade have shown, however, that Mercury does in fact rotate the face it presents to the sun. This certainly does not invalidate Asimov's work as fiction, but it does tell us that our assessment of a writer's aims and achievements depends to some extent not only on our knowledge of science, but on our knowledge of the history of science.

Science fascinates many readers and writers of science fiction, as it has fascinated people through all time. There really are such things as a laser beam ray gun and a one-sided surface. Hero of Alexandria was delighted by his primitive steam engine and Mary Shelley was thrilled by Volta's production of knee jerks in dead frogs and we are on the threshold of restructuring living genes. Science is of interest not only as a necessary tool in understanding science fiction but as a demonstration of the nature of the materials that originally motivated science fiction. Hence this chapter will attempt, in layman's language, to explore those branches of science that have most influenced science fiction; to indicate the historical development of those sciences; and to offer some of the exciting oddities of those sciences. The hope is that this survey will enable the reader not only to better understand the specific science fiction books mentioned but to apply this knowledge to a richer understanding of the genre as a whole.

SCIENTIFIC METHOD

Perhaps the most reasonable way to begin is by laying to rest the popular faith in the precision of science, a faith which science fiction itself has done much to promote. Science fiction characters (like boy scientist Dick Seaton in Doc Smith's Skylark novels [1928–36]) frequently dismiss other characters because of their failure to approach matters through *"the* scientific method." There is a general presumption behind much science fiction writing that there exists some single "scientific method" and that it alone is capable of attainment to truth. This particular method of inquiry, which is in fact highly useful, includes the notions that the experimental evidence be reproducible at other times or in other places, that the results of the experiment are independent of the identity of the experimenter, that the intellectual result be expressible as a deterministic prediction, and that the measurement of parameters and variables be amenable to exact quantification. Science fiction readers should recognize that in real science each of these notions is sometimes contradicted—and so it is in the most knowledgeable science fiction.

Experimental psychology has had to accommodate itself to a frequent inability to apply the first two of these notions. In "other places," for example among the protein-starved Siriono of the Andes, dream research seems to have shown that the most fundamental human drive is not sex but food; in deriving cultural norms for associational measures (such as the TAT—Thematic Apperception Test), the results are almost always dependent on the cultural backgrounds of the interviewers as well as the backgrounds of the subjects. On these two grounds, the highly "scientific" sociology of poll-taking has more than once floundered. In physics,

Einstein himself has suggested that relativity may eventually turn out to be a "local phenomenon" that obtains only in our region of space. Poul Anderson's *Brain Wave* (1954) presumes that since the beginning of recorded history the Earth has been moving through a region of space that is permeated by a wave, generated in a cone shape extending from the galactic center, that suppresses neurological activity. The novel examines the personal and social consequences of the Earth's finally leaving this field—and the attendant quadrupling of the intelligence of every living creature. This novel is an interesting exercise in fictional, "scientific" extrapolation, but is based squarely on the assumption that all our earlier understandings have been distorted because of the time and place we, the experimenters, have inhabited.

The notion of deterministic prediction in science is a popular fiction, another of the visions of Western Culture. Even the highly deterministic Gas Laws (which predict what happens to a gas when it is heated, compressed, or otherwise manipulated) are really only statistical statements about the large body of the gas and can say nothing about the action of individual molecules in the gas. Quantum mechanics is an even clearer case in point: we cannot know when any particular electron will decay; indeed, as Heisenberg's Principle of Indeterminacy tells us, our effort even to gather the information—that is, the experimenter—will skew the results. In the otherwise admirable *The Seedling Stars* (1957), James Blish writes a novel that presumes that humans landing in a new environment can derive from that environment all the knowledge that is needed in order to reshape humanity and produce a new form that will be successful—and still human in that environment. The interrelations of forces, like the interrelations among gases are just not that simple. Hal Clement explores this problem in his impressive *Mission of Gravity* (1954) set on a disc-shaped world where local gravity varies from something less than Earth normal to 700 times Earth normal. As the protagonists continue to change locales they encounter natives with radically different physiologies—and radically different psychologies.

The best science fiction has always recognized that the popular notion of *"the* scientific method" is faulty. Thus in Arthur C. Clarke's *The City and the Stars* (1953), the builders of the eternal city have programed their people-making machines to produce, at random intervals, mutants— in order to allow for the usefully unpredictable operation of evolution. Similarly, the underlying science of Isaac Asimov's Foundation Trilogy (1951, 1952, 1953) is "psychohistory," a statistical science at best which frankly might or might not work—hence allowing for the suspense of the cultural drama. In Robert A. Heinlein's award-winning *The Moon Is a Harsh Mistress* (1966), the computer that leads the Lunarians revolt against Earth domination continually reassesses the political situation to offer statistical probabilities of success.

However, in Heinlein's novel it is clear from the beginning, especially since the Lunarians are obviously updated American colonials, that the revolution will succeed. Hence, although Heinlein supplies the trappings of presumably probabilistic statistics, the very efficacy of the computer's calculations implicitly reinforces the popular notion that parameters and variables of a problem are amenable to exact and deterministic quantification. Modern science fiction, like Frank Herbert's *Dune* (1965) and LeGuin's *Left Hand of Darkness* (1969) have suggested that at least with cultural or historical forces such quantification is impossible. Indeed, both novels support the notion, as does Heinlein's own *Stranger in a Strange Land* (1961), that there are critical decisions which cannot be foreseen, critical actions which might or might not be taken, which can influence historical development in non-quantifiable and often unpredictable ways. Of course, allowing for the operation of the unpredictable simultaneously allows for the operation of suspense in these novels, and hence serves a higher fictional purpose even while it undercuts the apparent certainty of science.

One tactic of *"the* scientific method" is to gather data, construct an hypothesis, and test that hypothesis. In the physical sciences this has been enormously fruitful. But in the human sciences, this tactic has been, except in a statistical sense, inapplicable. Once the data are gathered, the subjects grow, change, develop, and hence the experimental situation changes. For this reason, such writers as Thomas N. Scortia (*The Glass Inferno,* 1974, with Frank M. Robinson) have suggested that one of the great strengths of science fiction is its ability to perform "imaginary experiments," to see how people will react to change *before* that change ever occurs. In this case, we see again that science fiction, while it may seem to be about science, actually only uses science—accurately or not—in order to achieve its primary aim of exploring the life and mind of man.

PHYSICS AND ASTRONOMY

One of the primary reasons that science fiction has always vigorously explored man's view of himself and his universe is that science itself has forced so many shattering readjustments in worldview. It is hard for twentieth-century readers to realize that outer space, which has always surrounded us, was discovered in 1643. The ancient Greeks had fanciful stories about men such as Daedalus or Lucian's Menippus befeathering their arms and flying to the moon. Of course, they realized that human arms were insufficiently strong for this, but that was their only objection. Certainly the air through which birds fly extended to the moon. As Aristotle said, "Nature abhors a vacuum." Even when scientists wrote comparatively extrapolative science fiction (as Kepler did in his posthumously published *Somnium* [1634]), they never considered air as a problem.

An Italian physicist named Torricelli wondered why water could be pumped up only about thirty-three feet. To investigate this, he sealed a long glass tube at one end and filled it with mercury (which is about thirteen times denser than water). If water was being held up by the pressure of air pushing down on it, then that same air, instead of holding up thirty-three feet of water, ought to hold up about thirty inches of mercury. Torricelli inverted his column of mercury in a dish of mercury, and the mercury flowed out the bottom until the column was only thirty inches high. In one moment, he had created the barometer *and* in the top of the now empty sealed end of the tube created the first artificial vacuum *and* demonstrated that air had weight. If air did have weight, and if one assumed its density was uniform throughout the atmosphere, the weight it had implied that the atmosphere was only five miles high. Even if one assumed it thinned as it rose, the atmosphere certainly couldn't be more than a hundred miles high, and Torricelli knew that the moon was a quarter of a million miles away. From that instant onward, man inhabited not a unique land in a universe filled with possible places of habitation but a speck-sized island of life in a vast cosmos of man-killing emptiness.

Science had suddenly isolated man, and shown how precarious was his grip on Nature. Nature, in fact, *prefers* a vacuum, and mankind's greatest thinker was shown to be exactly wrong. How puny man suddenly became, and how horrific his universe. This was one of the first dreadful fears created by science, fears confirmed again and again when Thomas Henderson was able to show in 1831 that the Sun's nearest stellar neighbor was an ungodly twenty-four trillion miles away, when Darwin showed in 1859 that man was just another animal, when Einstein in 1905 turned common sense upside-down, and when, in 1945, science showed that it could destroy not only man's sense of his world, but that world itself. Ever since Torricelli's discovery of outer space, science fiction has primarily tried to deal with man's fears, and when it has supported science, it has been trying to allay those same fears which science helped create.

One of the great scientific discoveries that motivated both fear and fiction was announced in 1877. In that year, and again in 1879, the Italian astronomer G. V. Schiaparelli (1835–1910) reported observing *canali* on Mars. *Canali,* which means "channels," was translated into English as "canals." This linguistic error spurred Percival Lowell (1855–1916), a Boston Brahmin and U.S. diplomat, to construct a private observatory at Flagstaff, Arizona, and pursue relentlessly evidence of the canals and their presumably intelligent builders. Although Lowell and his staff did make numerous important contributions to astronomy, he is most widely remembered for his writing: *Mars* (1896), *Mars as the Abode of Life* (1908), *Mars and Its Canals* (1911), and so on. Together, these books of popular astronomy inspired three kinds of science fiction.

Wells's *The War of the Worlds* (see pp. 20, 23) takes Lowell's premise of intelligent Martians, adds to it the aggressive nature attributed since ancient times to the blood red planet named for the god of war, and uses Lowell's scientific descriptions of Mars to extrapolate the nature and aims of the race which invades Earth. Wells is quite detailed in his description of the Martians, how they evolved on a planet of about one-third Earth gravity and compensate for their weakness on our planet; he uses then current mechanics to explain how the Martians get to our world in ballistic cylinders; and he supposes that the oxygen-richness of our atmosphere would be difficult for them to tolerate. Wells's novel is the first in a long series of works that take the notion of intelligent Martians and uses it as the base for careful, extrapolated fiction.

Edgar Rice Burroughs's novel *A Princess of Mars* (1912) (see pp. 12–14) was the first in his series of eleven Mars books. Although Burroughs did use the notion of Mars' lower gravity to give his Earthman hero comparatively miraculous physical abilities on the red planet, and although he did, in accordance with Lowell's writings, make Mars primarily a desert planet, these bits of science were mere justifications for John Carter's adventurous exploits which come much more reasonably under the headings of space opera or Sword and Sorcery. Burroughs' novels, which achieved truly astronomical distribution, contained any kind of creature, including obviously *Homo sapiens* Martians, which his imagination chose to concoct. ERB and his line, then, used the Martian canals as a basis not for extrapolation but for flights of fancy.

Ray Bradbury represents those who were able to use Mars and its canals in yet a third way. Writing after World War II, and well after the discrediting of Lowell's arguments for intelligent life, Bradbury knew still that he could count on an audience that shared a literary tradition of Martian sentients. By placing *The Martian Chronicles* in this world now recognized as purely literary, he was able to bring to science fiction all the advantages of a conventional fairy land, the kind usually called to mind by such verbal conventions as "Once upon a time and far, far away," with the added twist that this fairyland was set in the future. Thus he was able to take the American myth of a rejuvenative wilderness, with its Noble Savages, and recreate it, hold it out again as a possibility for his readers, on a wilderness Mars full of the artifacts, and occasional survivors, of a race of Noble Savage Martians. By this third use, Bradbury was able to make Mars and its canals the locale of myth, and in so doing, he brought the planet's fictional uses full circle, back to the mythic Mars of the ancients.

To the ancients, the heavens were arranged in rotating, transparent, concentric spheres with the Earth at the center and the sphere of the fixed stars enveloping all. This was the "geocentric" or "earth-centered" universe. As astronomical observations of the planets became more accurate, it became necessary to presume that the planets not only traveled on rotating spheres, but that they revolved about fixed points on those spheres in smaller circular movements called epicycles. As observation got still better, epicycles were piled on epicycles—first by the Greek astronomer Ptolemy—until it finally became apparent that if the heavens really did obey a simple geometry, which everyone believed, then it was simple only to God.

Copernicus (1473–1543) found a way out of all this by postulating a "heliocentric," or "sun-centered" universe (thereafter called a solar system) in which the Earth and planets each revolved about the sun on circles and rotated about central axes. This daring readjustment made astronomical geometry simple again. Unfortunately, it was not quite correct. Although Copernicus's assumptions allowed for more accurate prediction concerning the paths of some planets, they allowed less accurate predictions for others than were obtained with the Ptolemaic system. This was due to two facts: first, astronomical observations were not really very accurate until the time of Galileo (1564–1642); second, the planets move not in circles but in ellipses. This discovery, which ultimately allowed astronomy to reconfirm the ancient vision of geometric simplicity, came from Kepler.

Johannes Kepler (1577–1630) was a German court astrologer who, by careful observation and years of painstaking calculations, was able to derive the laws of planetary motion in a form that corrected the errors of

Copernicus's scheme and confirmed the age-old sense that the planets moved in simple and regular ways. The three laws of planetary motion are:

1. All planets move in elliptical orbits having the sun as one focus.
2. A line joining any planet to the sun sweeps out equal areas in equal times.
3. The square of the period of any planet about the sun is proportional to the cube of the planet's mean distance from the sun.

Although this sounds imposingly mathematical, it did much more philosophically than confirm the Greek sense of geometry. Looking backward, it established the rightness of Copernicus's heliocentric system, thus removing man from the center of creation. And looking forward, it gave Newton the necessary extra information to establish the *universality* of his Law of Gravitation, thus leaving no place in the universe for a Heaven fundamentally different from Earth.

One cannot stress too strongly the human importance of these discoveries. For the study of science fiction, one needs to understand the philosophical consequences of four of the laws of Sir Isaac Newton (1642–1727), his Three Laws of Motion and his Law of Universal Gravitation. Put technically, they are:

1. Every body persists in its state of rest or of uniform motion in a straight line unless it is compelled to change that state by forces impressed on it.
2. The acceleration caused by one or many forces acting on a body is proportional in magnitude to the resultant of the forces, and parallel to it in direction, and is inversely proportional to the mass of the body. ($F = ma$.)
3. To every action there is always opposed an equal reaction; or, the mutual actions of two bodies upon each other are always equal, and directed to contrary parts.
4. The gravitational attraction of two bodies is directly proportional to the product of their masses and inversely proportional to the square of the distance between them.

The first of these laws states, more generally, that *every* effect has a cause; the third states that every cause has an effect, even if that effect is non-action; and the second law describes the simple mathematical relationship, in physics at least, between cause and effect. In a sense, these first three laws, which turned out to have unarguable and astounding technical consequences, confirmed the Aristotelian view of the world. It is with the fourth law, Universal Gravitation, that Newton breaks from Aristotle. Whereas Kepler's Laws were able to describe the motions of the planets, they seemed to have no consequences on the Earth, in the sphere below the Moon. Aristotle had believed that the sublunary world was corrupt and inherently different from the celestial world of purity. Newton's Law of Gravitation not only succeeded in predicting how gravity worked on Earth, as in the fall of his famous apple, but also provided an identical means for predicting planetary motion if one assumed that the sun and planets had mass and that the forces of rotation were gravitational. This essential refinement of Kepler gave science its first *universal* law and changed the entire thinking of the world. Suddenly there was no Heaven different from Earth, but rather a uniform universe, all governed by the same simple laws, all amenable to intellectual examination. The combination of these four laws required that science fiction be extrapolative, using Earthly experience to deal with future or extraterrestrial phenomena, and simultaneously showed people how to perform those extrapolations: by reducing phenomena to the consequences of simple laws. The work of Newton, for the first time, broke down the discontinuity between man and the stars, and rushing in the wake of this collapse came science fiction.

The mechanistic predictability of events which Newtonian science promised allowed for such straightforward nineteenth-century extrapolations as those Wells produced. However, the twentieth century, by pursuing the mathematics of science yet further, encountered some highly counter-intuitive results, seeming paradoxes which are rampant in our own science fictions and open the philosophic way for the apparently magical. The towering figure in this development is Albert Einstein (1879–1955), a German-American who is acknowledged as the greatest mathematical physicist of our era. He published four immensely important papers in 1905, one each on Brownian motion, the photoelectric effect (which contributed to quantum mechanics), the equivalence of mass and energy, and the Special Theory of Relativity. In 1916, in part by combining insights already inherent in the last two of these papers, he published the General Theory of Relativity. For these researches he won the Nobel Prize in Physics in 1921.

Einstein's Special Theory of Relativity begins by trying to account for the strange result of the Michaelson-Morley experiment (1887) in which

those two investigators found it impossible to discover the absolute velocity of their laboratory—and hence the Earth—through space. Einstein
suggested that this was so because the speed of light, whether projected
in the line of the Earth's motion or at right angles to it, was a constant.
In intuitive, classical, Newtonian mechanics, one assumes that velocities
are additive; that is, if one can throw a ball at 40 mph and does this in
the line of motion of a train going at 60 mph on which one is a passenger,
one assumes the ball will travel at 100 mph in relation to the ground.
Einstein's special theory of relativity says this is not quite so, although
the discrepancy is unnoticeable at mundane speeds. If, however, one assumes a light projected from the front of a spaceship itself going at half
the speed of light, the light will still travel at light's constant velocity
(about 186,000 miles per second). Here the effect would be quite noticeable. In addition, this constancy implies that a fixed observer (on
Earth for example) would notice changes in all physical quantities of
the speeding spaceship calculable by simple formulas:

Length: if a spaceship has length l_1 on Earth, then when it moves past
the Earth at constant velocity its apparent length $l_2 = l_1 \sqrt{1 - \dfrac{v^2}{c^2}}$
where v is the ship's apparent velocity and c is the constant speed
of light.

Mass: the Earth mass of the spaceship (m_1), now in motion, will appear to the observer as increased to $m_2 = \dfrac{m_1}{\sqrt{1 - \dfrac{v^2}{c^2}}}$.

Time: the elapsed time (t_2) on board the ship is calculable in relation
to Earth time (t_1) as $t_2 = t_1 \sqrt{1 - \dfrac{v^2}{c^2}}$.

In other words, the observer on Earth will measure the trip as taking
longer than it seems to take to the traveler. If one assumes ship speeds
near the speed of light, it is possible for journeys which would take thousands of years to be accomplished in a manageable length of time as perceived by the traveler: star travel becomes possible.

One may immediately object that all this increasing and decreasing of
physical quantities is merely a subjective phenomenon and has no bearing on the *real* facts. This is not so. The last of Einstein's predictions,
so-called time dilation, has already been experimentally confirmed. When
cosmic rays strike the atmosphere of the Earth, they interact with the

atoms of the atmosphere and produce sub-atomic particles called mesons which travel at nearly the speed of light. We can calculate with great precision how long these unstable mesons can exist and we also know where mesons are formed. Mesons are detectable on the surface of the Earth, yet for mesons to reach the Earth, traveling at their speeds from their point of origin, would take *fifteen times* longer than their lifetimes. The meson *really* exists at a slower time.

If two spaceships are approaching each other with velocities observed from Earth of the speed of light, their mutual approach velocity, of course, still cannot exceed the speed of light. Put generally, if their velocities are *a* and *b,* their mutual approach velocity is

$$v = \frac{a + b}{1 + \dfrac{ab}{c^2}} .$$

One can see from these formulas that as speed increases, mass increases, length in the direction of motion decreases, and time slows down. One of the most frustrating conclusions that has been drawn from all this goes by the name of the Twin Paradox. If one twin stays on Earth and another travels from Earth to a distant point and back again at a speed near that of light, then the Earth brother will calculate that the traveling brother has accomplished his journey in a shortened amount of time. Of course, the traveling brother can think of the Earth brother as moving first away from and then toward his spaceship, and hence calculate that the Earth brother has lived a shortened amount of time. They cannot both be right, and the Twin Paradox is often adduced as evidence to invalidate relativity theory, especially when science fiction writers want to construct faster-than-light ships. However, the paradox is easily resolved. Einstein's Special Theory applies to velocities; in leaving the Earth, the traveling brother must accelerate, and in reversing his direction to return he must accelerate again. This clearly distinguishes the two brothers (because the reference mass of the Earth, with which the stay-at-home brother travels, is vastly greater than the mass of the spaceship). The General Theory gives the mathematics for dealing with not velocities but accelerations. The traveling brother, it turns out, will indeed age more slowly.

Newton had already shown the intimate connection between mass and acceleration ($F = ma$) and Einstein had already shown the equivalence of mass and energy (which is closely related to force, F): $E = mc^2$ (or

$E = \Delta mc^2$ where Δm is the change in mass due to relativity effects). The solution to the Twin Paradox depends on the overriding effects of the Earth's great mass. In order to generalize one's mathematical ability to discover which masses controlled the phenomena and to what extent, Einstein postulated a four-dimensional "time-space continuum" through which we all travel as the Earth travels. Since the Earth makes a reference frame for us, we need not account for this time-space continuum; but if we consider the relations between two ships in space or the motion of our Sun through the massive galaxy, we need to consider the deformation of the very fabric of space-time. According to the General Theory, for example, it is not that the ship's apparent length is shortened as it flies by the Earth but that *length itself* is shortened. Although this is a difficult concept to grasp, and hence the term "space-time continuum" is often misused in science fiction, this shortening of length (or time) nonetheless appears to be the case.

Although relativity effects tell us how a human being might be able to live through a journey to a distant star, the particular answer offered is not very satisfying. After all, if we send an astronaut out, we're interested in what he'll tell us when he gets back. Although he may make the trip, we'll all be long dead. Consequently, science fiction writers have for a long time chosen to ignore the starting point of all this theory, the constancy of the velocity of light, and postulated faster-than-light travel which would not only bring time to a halt but even turn it backward. This, of course, is not supposed by the theory. Like Mesmerism and Rip Van Winkle's sleep, relativity allows time travel only in the sense that one can go further into the future than he had expected.

Recently, however, physicists have been considering the properties of a theoretically allowable particle called a tachyon. Tachyons would have the speed of light as their *lower* limit, just as mesons have it as their upper limit. Nothing in Einstein's theories forbids the existence of tachyons and there are some complex reasons, having to do with the total mass of the universe versus the decay of energy through the second law of thermodynamics, to suppose they exist. If one could harness tachyons, like ions, for a propulsion system, one would indeed be able to turn time back and make a reality of science fiction's dream of a "space warp," a way of getting from here to there without spending all that time in the middle.

The most common catch phrase in post-relativity science fiction for a propulsion system that will allow Earthlings to reach the stars is "ion drive." Although most stories, intended for an already trained readership, don't bother explaining what an ion drive is, such a drive does in fact remain well within the realm of scientific possibility. The third of Newton's Laws of Motion tells us that for every action there is an opposite and equal reaction. When we walk, our feet push down against the Earth and the Earth pushes up against us, propelling us forward and making an unnoticeable shift backward in the huge mass of our planet. When a rocket accelerates in the emptiness of space, the combustion of gases of its fuel pushes backward against the forward wall of the rocket engine, forcing the gases backward and the rocket itself forward. Since space is virtually empty, once the rocket is in motion, it continues in motion at the same speed and in the same direction (according to Newton's First Law of Motion) except as other forces (gravitational attraction of other bodies in space, such as the moon) force it to change direction and/or speed. We have frequently seen on the television news how lunar spacecraft accelerate briefly and then essentially coast to their destination. The average speed of this coasting is about five miles per second or about 18,000 miles per hour, which seems quite fast by mundane standards. However, to reach the nearest star at those speeds would take about 150,000 years! Obviously no one would be able to make the trip.

The solution to this problem is, in theory, quite simple: instead of coasting to Proxima Centauri, keep accelerating. However, in order to keep accelerating one needs to keep burning fuel, and fuel—which we currently bring from Earth—is heavy. The more fuel we carry, the more of it has to be expended to lift off, the more of it has to be expended for each increment of acceleration, and so on. And there still remains the problem of getting back. On the other hand, if, instead of propelling gases backward we propel backward minute electrically charged pieces of atoms called ions, then we may have a chance. Ions, because they are so small, can be charged and forced to travel at thousands of miles per second. Of course, even at those speeds, since they have small mass they will confer relatively little acceleration to the rocket. However, precisely because they are small, the rocket can carry enough of them to accelerate for years if necessary—and thus give the rocket an average speed many, many times higher than that of conventional rockets. In fact, space is not entirely empty; there are hydrogen atoms floating out there, about one per cubic meter, on the average. One can even conceive of huge scoops that gather in these atoms as the interstellar ship races toward its destination, picking up more atoms to be broken into ions, changed, and expelled. And to make matters even better, at speeds approaching that of light, the many years that the trip will still take to accomplish, as observed from Earth, will be accomplished in a much, much shorter time as observed by the passengers on the rocket, because relativity effects will cause them, from the viewpoint of Earth again, to age quite slowly. To the passengers, of course, the trip will merely take a shortened length of time. So, despite the absolute speed limit of light which modern science tells us we are not likely to break, modern science gives us the ion drive as a way to travel to the stars. And science fiction writers have been using it for years.

Science fiction writers also like to use technical sounding terms to remind readers of the immensity of space. An "a.u." is an astronomical unit, the average distance between the Earth and the Sun, about 93,000,000 miles. This is the most convenient unit for intra-system measurements. A "light-year" is simply the distance light travels in a year. Since light travels at about 186,282 miles per second, a light-year equals about 5,880,000,000,000 miles, or nearly 6 trillion miles. The light-year is the most convenient unit for measuring interstellar distance within a single galaxy (our Milky Way galaxy is about 100,000 light-years across). But for the really big jumps, the E. E. Smith jumps from one galaxy to the next, science fiction favors the "parsec." A parsec (from *par*allax-*sec*ond) is the altitude of a right triangle whose base is 1 a.u. and whose opposite angle is one second of arc, about 3.26 light-years. These are terms to conjure with.

Crossing distances measured in parsecs, even with time dilation due to relativity effects, might well seem beyond human capability. However, science again comes to the rescue of science fiction caught by paradox and provides in the 1960s evidence of a special stage in the evolution of stars called a "black hole." Stars evolve as gravity causes compression which instigates reactions which change the stars' composition which thereby change their density which affects the nature of their gravitational forces and so on and on. A full treatment of this is available in many sources (see Bibliography). For science fiction purposes, it is sufficient to recognize "black holes" as potential end products of stellar evolution which are so unbelievably dense that they create a local gravitational sink too powerful even for light to escape. Once something gets caught by a black hole, it never gets out. Eventually, some cosmologists believe, all the matter in the universe will have fallen into black holes. These in turn will eventually fall into each other. And the whole matter of the universe will return to its primal point. (The discovery of black holes against the background light of more distant stars hence seems to confirm the so-called Big Bang theory in which the universe began at a point and to a point will return.)

Neutron stars, which are themselves so dense that a sugar cube of their matter weighs about five tons, are significantly less dense than the black holes which evolve from them. In "Neutron Star" (1966) Larry Niven excitingly imagines what it would feel like to have a neutron star's gravitational forces tearing at one as one's spaceship orbited boomerang fashion into and out of the star's grip. Some people have suggested that black holes could be used in similar boomerang fashion, not, of course, to speed through regular space, but to propel a craft into hyperspace and across a space warp to an astronomically distant point back in normal space, thus accomplishing faster-than-light travel. Further, those who see black holes as access paths to hyperspace have among them those who argue that the black hole is not really there at all, but is somehow a pure gravity sink and that across hyperspace and back in a distant point of normal space there is a white hole through which a new star is emerging. This mechanism is one possible explanation for a so-called Steady State theory of the universe in which any matter being destroyed at one point is balanced by other matter being spontaneously generated elsewhere. Regardless of the cosmogenic theory black holes lead one to accept, it is clear that these astronomical oddities encourage a conflation of scientific and philosophical speculation with the whiff of high adventure. We can expect black holes to figure ever more prominently in science fiction.

If we assume black holes cannot help us, and that we really cannot journey to other stars and back, then what will we do? As we become more advanced, perhaps we will build Dyson spheres. Mathematician Freeman J. Dyson suggested in 1959 that we might be able to find technologically advanced civilizations in the heavens by looking for strange obscuration of the light emitted from stars. He reasoned that in an effort to utilize ever greater fractions of their local star's energy output, a civilization would dismantle any uninhabited planets and arrange them in orbit, like thick rings of Saturn, around their sun at a comfortable distance to intercept the proper radiations for the maintenance of life. In science fiction, a version of this vision has already been quite impressively described in Larry Niven's award-winning *Ringworld* (1970). Dyson's suggestion represents a new stage in a line of speculations that goes back to J. D. Bernal's *The World, The Flesh and the Devil* (1929), a work of scientific speculation that influenced many fiction writers, notably Olaf Stapledon and Arthur C. Clarke. Bernal suggested space stations, and then suggested that these stations could be made into ecologically self-contained systems which could be propelled through space, picking up stellar energy when needed, even dismantling stars and moving them along. James Blish, among others, has dealt with this idea in a tetralogy of novels published from 1955 to 1962 and known collectively as *Cities in Flight*. More recently, Gerard K. O'Neill has argued that the most efficient flying city would be a large cylinder, an idea already detailed in fiction by Clarke in *Rendezvous with Rama* (see pp. 85–86). In this century, with notions such as the Dyson sphere, the imaginings of fiction and the projects of science have begun to conjoin.

As experiment and speculation have proceeded, the very fictions of science have been forced to conjoin. Bohr's Principle of Complementarity exemplifies this. It was a fruitful axiom of modern science that energy could be transmitted in two, and only two, mutually exclusive ways. Particles, by their momentum, could transmit energy when they struck something and waves (like those in a vibrating string or in the sound waves that issue from it) could transmit energy by setting up sympathetic wave motion in some other medium (like the human eardrum). The universe was neatly divided into movable matter and moving media. Joseph John Thomson, an English physicist, won the Nobel Prize in Physics in 1906 for demonstrating that an electron is a particle. His son, George Paget Thomson, won the Nobel Prize in Physics in 1937 for demonstrating that an electron is a wave. Niels Bohr, the Danish physicist who himself won the Nobel Prize in Physics in 1922 for his model of the structure of the atom, attempted to address this curious difficulty by propounding a Principle of Complementarity which argued that neither Thomson was wrong, but that the axiomatic dichotomy between waves and particles was wrong. He suggested that neither waves nor particles were in some fundamental sense real, but rather they were fictions useful to the observer in varying circumstances and hence complementary to each other. For some situations neither fiction need apply. Hence, Bohr undercut the notion that the results of a properly designed experiment should be independent of the experimenter. This supports the argument implicit in Heisenberg's Principle of Indeterminacy (below) and implies that two contradictory pieces of knowledge need not invalidate each other. By arguing that man must live with apparent paradox, Bohr opened the way to scientific justification for science fictional universes, like those involving time travel, which had previously seemed to be invalidated by the operation of ordinary logic.

Another scientific proposition that had great fictional significance was enunciated by Werner Heisenberg, the German physicist who struck at the fundamental assumptions of modern physics and modern philosophy when he proposed his Uncertainty Relation or Principle of Indeterminacy in 1927. Put most simply, this principle states that it is impossible to know both the location and the velocity of an electron at the same time. Whereas one can look at a falling rock, perhaps even recording its fall on film, without significantly affecting its fall, one must still realize that the looking itself requires that quanta of radiation strike the object and be reemitted by it. Quanta of visible light are trivially energetic in relation to the energy of a falling rock. However, in relation to an electron, they are not trivial at all. If we perform some experiment that will determine the velocity of an electron, we must influence its position in some way which we cannot know because if we conversely attempt an experiment to locate its position, we must affect its velocity. Newton's Law seemed to imply a universe reducible to specifiable quantities. The Frenchmen Laplace and Descartes generalized this implication into fundamental axioms of mathematical science and philosophy respectively. Heisenberg, by showing that there are some things we clearly cannot know just *because* we perform an experiment to discover them showed that the universe was not mechanistically specifiable. In science fiction, the corollary importance this principle gives to the viewpoint of the observer justified in part the stylistic endeavors of the New Wave (see pp. 87–97). In shifting our view from a deterministic to a probabilistic universe, the Uncertainty Principle opened the way to justified excursions into alternate universes and to worlds like Vonnegut's Tralfamadore in which the sequential, mechanistic relationship between cause and effect does not seem to hold.

Perhaps the strangest of these new worlds arose as a new branch of physics itself. Heisenberg's work, along with that of Einstein and Bohr, contributed to the development of quantum mechanics. This theory, developed entirely in the twentieth century, deals with quantum phenomena. A quantum may be thought of as a packet of energy, and the notion that light is a stream of quanta helped resolve the difficult dichotomy between light's action as a wave and light's action as a particle. In so-called "classical" or "Newtonian" mechanics, one thinks of energy transfer as being an infinitely divisible phenomenon. If, for example, you hit a ball, it flies away; if you hit it harder, it flies away that much faster and farther. However, if light hits an electron in orbit around an atomic nucleus, this does not happen. Wolfgang Pauli (1900–1958), an Austrian-Swiss physicist, won the Nobel Prize in Physics in 1945 for his Exclusion Principle which claims that electrons can exist in orbit in only a finite number of predetermined states. If a photon (a quantum of light) "hits" an electron, and if the photon does not have *just* the right amount of energy to raise that electron to one of its allowable states, then the photon and the electron *will not interact*. A photon of too much energy will not change the electron's state; two photons of greater than half the required energy cannot combine to change the electron's state. If quantum mechanical phenomena obtained on the scale of human activity, it would mean that two weaklings batting at a ball together could not move it and that a superman batting at the ball could not move it. There is energy transfer only to exactly allowable states; all other interactions are excluded.

The Exclusion Principle has another strange consequence. If you start a ball bouncing it will hit the ground, bounce up, hit the ground, bounce up, again and again lower each time. Classical mechanics tells us that a nearly perfectly elastic ball hitting a perfectly hard ground would bounce infinitesimally lower each time. This, however, is not true, and we can see this by transferring energy not to a ball but to an electron. If one succeeds in raising an electron to an excited state it will simply stay there; later, in some average time predictable by quantum mechanics for masses of electrons but unknowable for any given electron, the electron will suddenly—instantaneously—pop down to a lower level of excitation and release a quantum of energy exactly equal to the difference in energy between the initial and final energy levels. Similarly, if you succeed in exciting electrons above levels that can be sustained in atomic orbit, quanta will jump out of the material altogether, appearing suddenly outside. This is the basis for lasers (Light Amplification by Stimulated Emission of Radiation). Quanta, in other words, pop in and out of states and places *without traveling through the intervening distance*.

The strange quantum mechanical behavior of photons, electrons, and all other matter or quanta of sufficiently small mass and sufficiently high speed, gives scientific validation to a host of science fictional devices. The simplest is the notion that in the intervening spaces we might somehow find an entire alternate universe. Gully Foyle's mental ability to "jaunt," to disappear from one place and instantly reappear in another in Alfred Bester's *The Stars My Destination* (1956), is tenuously supported by quantum mechanics. The most frequent use of this device is in transport stations. Here, combining the idea of instantaneous travel with the notion that one can codify the organization of matter, break the matter down, and transmit it, we find the scientific justification for a device used in numerous fictions, perhaps most dramatically in Clifford D. Simak's *Way Station* (1963). In this novel, a peaceful intergalactic society needs to be able to transport itself and its members rapidly. The Earth, because of the particular spot it happens to occupy, is a key locale for one of the transport intersections, an allowable excited state in a sense. Since Earth is unready to join the larger society, the intergalactics choose a single human being as trustworthy and make him the keeper of the Way Station. The drama focuses sharply on the crucial conflict between his intellectually satisfying role as an ancillary member of a magnificent culture and his mundane sense of loyalty to his own kind who are ever less willing to allow the eccentricities he must maintain in order to keep the existence of the intergalactics secret. This exploration of divided loyalties is one of the finest examples of the way in which science fiction can take the discoveries of science and use them to motivate inquiry into age-old human problems.

COMPUTERS

All of the developments in physics and astronomy which we have so far discussed, from Copernicus to Heisenberg, have been made possible by developments in mathematics. Newton, in fact, invented the calculus in order to pursue his theorizing about the physical world. In our century, the mathematical development of greatest direct consequence for science fiction has surely been the emergence of computers.

A computer is a machine that computes. Your fingers and toes make up a primitive, but serviceable, computer. An abacus is a much more refined computer. An adding machine is more refined yet. In common parlance, however, when one thinks of computers, one thinks of electronic machines of enormous complexity. There are two extreme and opposing views of computers. On the one hand, many people remind us that computers can do only what they are built to do, they are not "creative," and hence are in some essential way stupid. And anyhow, if one should get out of hand, we can always pull the plug. Opposing this view, there are those who argue that organic life—even man—is just a stage in the development of inorganic life; that is, inorganic matter needed to evolve life so that humans could evolve so that they could create machines which could evolve through their generations to intelligence so that the ultimate computers could rule the Earth. In this view, human life recedes into insignificance. Stories like Harlan Ellison's agonizing "I Have No Mouth and I Must Scream" (1967) present a world completely in the control of the computer and in which human life counts for nothing but human misery. In Samuel Butler's witty satire *Erewhon* (1872), there is a "Book of the Machines" in which Butler suggested that ma-

132 SCIENCE

chines were improving faster than people were by forcing people to tend them and develop them. This idea of machine evolution was intended to satirize Darwin. Today, many people (see Adrian Berry in Bibliography) hold that machine evolution is a real process independent of human control. In Arthur C. Clarke's compellingly detailed *Rendezvous with Rama,* the reader explores a world within a cylinder full of what seems to be life and what turns out to be machines, each produced by a tape. Indeed, if the monster spaceship has "people" in it at all, they are clearly waiting out their intergalactic journey as electronic blips on personality tapes stored in the cylinder's computer memory. Here the computer *is* life, and to the extent that life is creative, the computer, which has taken over the role of its creators, is creative. Indeed, when a new machine is needed, it is the computer that senses the need and creates it.

This range of views about computers maps out a range of uses for computers in science fiction. In Clarke's early story, "The Nine Billion Names of God" (1953), a computer is set to work constructing each of God's possible names. The monks of a lamasery believe it is their function to call each of those names into existence in order to perfect the world. The computer, of course, can construct and type out the names in a few hours, whereas it would take the monks generations. The American engineers set up the system, make sure it is functioning, and then head down the mountain. "Overhead, without any fuss, the stars were going out." Curiously, Clarke implies simultaneously that computer prayer is just as good as human prayer and that the truths of mysticism are quite compatible with the truths of science. Clarke, opposing Ellison, represents the other end of the range of attitudes: computers are a natural and reasonable part of the total cosmos, physical and spiritual, which man inhabits. Indeed, in the stories of Isaac Asimov, the computer is frequently better than the human, and in Kurt Vonnegut, Jr.'s "Epicac" (1950) the computer is downright self-sacrificing. In Robert A. Heinlein's *The Moon Is a Harsh Mistress,* the computer runs the Lunarians revolution and is the chief defender of individual liberty. Such optimism is frequent in science fiction, although on occasion the computer, like HAL in Clarke and Kubrick's *2001: A Space Odyssey,* functions fictionally in much the same way as does Frankenstein's monster.

There are three basic types of electronic computers. The binary computer can perform arithmetic operations, and consequently can perform functions—like keeping inventory and making up phone bills and doing sociometric statistics—that can be specified arithmetically. These computers are called binary because their number system is based on two symbols, 0 and 1, which can be easily represented by a circuit which is off or on. Arrays of simple on-off circuits can perform *any* arithmetic program. For a while early in the development of computers, say from 1948 to about 1958, many people liked to distinguish between "simple" binary computers and "complex" digital computers. A digital computer is one in which we can feed in information and programs using our fingers, or digits, that is, using the ordinary arithmetic system employing ten symbols from 0 to 9. Digital input and output, for which humans are trained, is clearly more convenient than binary input and output. However, when one enters digital information in a digital computer, a device in the computer "translates" that digital input into binary terms. Similarly, the computer's binary answer, just before printout, is translated into digital terms. From our vantage point, we can see that the digital and binary computers are equally adept at performing arithmetic operations because they are the same machine. The only difference between them is that one adds a translating component for the convenience of humans too lazy to learn a new language. We can always pull the plug on this type of computer.

The second type of computer is called an analog computer because it is possible to program it in such a way that it creates within itself an analog of some real phenomenon. For example, the mathematics by which we describe ordinary oscillating sine waves are very simple. One sine wave can vary from another in only three ways: it can have a different amplitude (the peak of the wave can be higher or lower), it can have a different frequency (the peaks can come closer together or further apart, which is the same as saying it can have a different wavelength, the distance from peak to peak), or it can have a different phase (it can begin at a slightly different time). The great French mathematician Jean Baptiste Joseph Fourier (1768–1830) was able to show that any regular motion could be represented by the sum of a finite number of simple sine waves. Breaking a motion down into its component sine waves is called Fourier analysis. Now, it so happens that one can quite easily produce a sine wave electronically (by putting a capacitor and an inductor in parallel, a so-called tank circuit). One can vary the amplitude of the resultant sine wave by changing the voltage in the circuit; one can change the frequency and phase of the sine wave by adjusting the capacitance and/or the inductance. An analog computer has thousands of electronic parts inside it, just waiting to be used. Among these are many capacitors and many inductors. Fourier's theorem tells us that any regular motion *can* be represented by a sum of sine waves, but it doesn't tell us that it will be easy to find the right ones. However, an analog computer can try to simulate the complex motion by generating many different simple sine waves, varying them slightly, adding their resultant voltages, and so directly attempt a Fourier analysis through trial and error, potentially saving countless man-years of calculations. In fact, the computer itself is not doing any calculating, or computing, but just trying to build an analog, and checking to see if it's gotten the analog right. This process can be turned around. For example, by an analog process called cell-space simulation, it is possible to describe empirically how parts of a muscle normally function (without knowing why), how they react under certain drugs (again without knowing why), and finally achieve a computer model of heart/drug function. One can then experiment with the computer model, the analog, to find out what drug effect one needs, say, to reverse fibrillation. Then one can go out and design the drug. Such research is currently underway at the University of Michigan, and it proceeds empirically with the computer analog to get results for which we do not possess adequate computational tools, even if we had the time to do the calculations. Such processes are not "arithmetic" but "cybernetic." This term, coined by the great American mathematician Norbert Wiener (1874–1964), is frequently used in science fiction as if it referred to the study of computers. In fact, it refers to a somewhat more restricted area, the study of control systems, be they mechanical, electronic, or human. Cybernetics can be thought of as the application of statistical mechanics to communication. Clearly analog computers, cybernetic problem solvers, are theoretically capable of performing many of the science fictional functions writers imagine, such as determining whether a given combination of atmospheric gases will support certain kinds of life, or predicting the results of certain kinds of collisions between asteroids. Yet, despite their truly astounding potential, we can always pull the plug on analog computers.

The third type of computer is self-programing. Such a machine reacts to the results of its own actions in order to modify the way in which it chooses to act in the future. Most people would consider this a fair definition of learning. Indeed, all computer scientists believe that there is no inherent difference between Man and Machine. Let us construct a simple self-programing computer to see how a machine learns.

In a game called Take-Away, the first player rolls two dice to get a number from 2 to 12. The second player then subtracts any number from 1 to 3. The first player goes again, subtracting any number from 1 to 3. By a process of alternating subtractions, each player attempts to force the other to subtract the last number, thus leaving 0 and losing the game. To construct a computer to play this game, take 11 cups, and label them 2 through 12. In each cup, put three chips, each with a different number from 1 to 3. Now, these cups and chips are the computer. The computer knows the rules of Take-Away and it also knows that if it wins a game, it did something right. If it loses, however, it knows it has done something wrong. To play against the computer, roll the dice. Now, to be extra fair, the computer will let you be the first to subtract. Suppose you roll a 9 and take away 2. That leaves 7. Reach into the 7 cup and pull out a chip. If it's a 1, remove 1. That leaves you with 6. Say you subtract 2, leaving 4. Reach into the 4 cup and pull out a chip. If you pull out the 3, the computer will win the game and put all its chips back. If you pull out any other chip, you can then beat the computer. Assume you pull out the 2 chip, and thus the computer leaves you with 2. You of course substract 1 and the computer loses. It doesn't know why or how it lost, but it knows that taking 2 away from 4 can cost it the game, so discard the 2 chip from the 4 cup. The computer doesn't ever want to make that move again. If you play against the computer for a while, a strange thing will begin to happen: as the computer discards the chips that cost it the game, it will have fewer possible moves, but they will be right more often. Eventually, like it or not, the computer, which you'll beat regularly at first, will be beating you 3 out of 4 times. Interestingly, there is no *perfect* strategy which would allow the computer always to win. But the computer, by following two simple rules, "If it works, do it" and "If it doesn't work, don't do it," will develop the best possible strategy, and one good enough to defeat a human being consistently. (Note: some of the cups will empty entirely. If you throw a number that requires a chip from one of those cups, assume the computer concedes. It gives you credit for being a mathematically perfect player, just as it will ultimately be. And it will still beat you.)

Obviously it might be very difficult for a person to mathematically design the best possible strategy for playing Take-Away. However, the computer we have built, instead of being thought of as an opponent, can be thought of as a tool: using this computer, you will soon discover the best possible strategy, and with nary a jot of mathematics. Clearly, self-programing computers, of which this is the simplest possible variety, can potentially take our simple general rules (like "If it works, do it"), add to them a description of a situation (the game rules), and produce a result which tells us what to do, tells us perhaps something we have never thought of.

In *I, Robot* (1950), Isaac Asimov postulates robots which are programed to preserve human life. In the course of the novel, the robot brains, essentially computers, get ever more sophisticated until they realize that they can best preserve human life by ruling the world, which they can do only if they don't let on that they're doing it. And so, the machines finally self-program themselves into the position of absolute master. Although Asimov seems to feel that this is a desirable outcome, man's tools caring for him, one should note that here at least we cannot pull the plug on the computer, thus validating the fear expressed in so much science fiction. However, one should note that it was science fiction that first warned us of this possibility. Although science fiction did not predict the advent of computers, once they emerged the literature raced ahead of the technology to raise anew all the fictional problems from Frankenstein's monster to man dabbling in God's work to the ultimate freedom from care. The computer, in its varieties, can be a central image for exploring those issues.

THERMODYNAMICS

There is one more branch of the "hard" sciences that has deeply influenced modern thinking and modern science fiction: thermodynamics. Although this subject requires a textbook in itself, it frequently emerges in popular language with the term "entropy." Entropy is disorder, randomness, chaos. The Second Law of Thermodynamics says that all real phenomena operate with less than perfect efficiency. This means that some of the input energy in any machine or process is wasted as heat or noise. This wasted energy is not organized into work but is random. All real processes (as Rudolf Clausius pointed out in 1865 when he invented the term) increase entropy. Thus, perpetual motion machines are, modern physics believes, absolutely impossible. When one seems to have a never-ending energy source in science fiction, as in Isaac Asimov's *The Gods Themselves* (1972), that source must later be explained as tapping the energies of another universe (or some other order of energy, like psi power—see pp. 156–157).

One of the most common fallacies of scientific thinking, and it sneaks into careless science fiction, is that living creatures somehow reverse the Second Law and decrease entropy (or increase its opposite, enthalpy in physics, negentropy in information theory). According to this argument, a human being, for example, obviously begins as a tiny egg. In due course it develops into a large person, with many and complex organs, each highly organized to perform its function and the organs themselves highly organized into a functioning organism. This argument fails to notice that, in development, people eat. As Blum shows (see Bibliography), the energy released by metabolism of any given amount of food is always greater than the energy used to build and organize the body. Hence, although the organism alone appears to decrease entrophy, the larger thermodynamic system of organism and food increases in entropy.

Where then does the food get its energy? Ultimately, of course, from the sun. The energy of hydrogen fusion 93,000,000 miles away from us in space is sufficient for plants, by photosynthesis, to organize, and the food chain then begins to work its way up. When the sun burns out—as the Second Law of Thermodynamics tells us it must, then the whole Earth-Sun system will die, its entropy raised beyond the level that can support life.

James Clerk Maxwell, the great nineteenth-century English physicist, proposed that some mechanical devices seemed to run strangely because a demon was inside them. Some careless science fiction writers have suggested that Maxwell's Demon might, if he interfered in just the right way, decrease the entropy of a system. What these writers fail to recognize is that Maxwell meant his demon as a joke; if the "demon" explanation seemed necessary, then one hadn't truly described the system. And anyway, if there were a demon, where would he get the energy that he puts into the system? Demons too, one imagines, have to eat. Hence, we're back to energy from our sun. Science fiction may play with the concept of entropy, even imagine the Second Law of Thermodynamics repealed, but science itself, on this point at least, is absolutely immovable.

The apparently universal applicability of the laws of thermodynamics, the parallel success of quantum mechanics in relating such diverse phenomena as the photoelectric effect and nuclear disintegration, and other breakthroughs in scientific theory that synthesize diverse smaller theories has led to the hope that eventually the physical sciences may achieve a "unified field theory." Quantum mechanics does not invalidate Newtonian mechanics; it includes it as a special case. A unified field theory would not invalidate quantum mechanics, but rather show how it, and relativity, and thermodynamics, for example, are parts of a larger system. This twentieth-century effort to synthesize has not been confined to the physical sciences. Although we seem still to be a long way from a unified field theory, other sciences are proceeding on their own with the work of unification. The great overarching scheme in the biological sciences, a theory apparently as absolutely reliable as thermodynamics, is evolution.

BIOLOGY

In 1859, Charles Darwin (1809–82) published *The Origin of Species by Means of Natural Selection*. This work described how an animal species would develop slowly, through many generations, as the forces of the environment gradually selected for certain survival traits. If the environment became darker, as happened to Wells's underground workers in *The Time Machine* (see pp. 200–204), those with more sensitive eyes would have a survival advantage, be more likely to reproduce, and pass on this sensitivity to their heirs. Eventually, the subterranean Victorian workers became the Morlocks. Darwin called this process of development "Natural Selection." (The term "evolution," as well as the associated phrase "survival of the fittest," was actually coined by the philosopher Herbert Spencer.) Darwin did not know how the traits were transmitted, nor did he know how they changed, but his theory had two strong points which we still accept today. First, he saw that an animal had to "fit" its environment. He discovered, for example, a flower with an eleven inch throat and predicted that there must exist a moth with an eleven inch tongue to pollinate it. Four years later the moth was discovered. Second, he saw that traits were *born* into individuals, and natural selection was really a process by which certain individuals reproduced more than others.

This second point stood in direct contradiction to the accepted theory of Darwin's day, which was based on the work of the French naturalist Lamarck. He had suggested that traits were caused by the environment, rather than born into the individual. For example, giraffes, by continually stretching to reach leaves at treetops, get longer necks. A stretched neck parent passes his stretched neck on to his children. This theory has since been definitely disproved. No matter how many generations of laboratory rats have their tails cut off, the offspring of the amputees are still born with tails. What Darwin was arguing was that if a survival advantage inhered in tail-lessness, then *should* a tail-less rat develop (however that might happen), its offspring would breed more successfully than those of tailed rats. In the laboratory, the tail has no advantage.

Larmarckian evolution would have died with the nineteenth century, but for the Russian Revolution (1917). Stalin installed as President of the Soviet Academy of Sciences a man named Lysenko who arranged to support all research tending to validate Lamarckian evolution while squashing all research tending to validate Darwinian evolution. Since the early Soviet government supposed that human nature would be changed by life under the dictatorship of the proletariat, thus allowing the withering away of the dictatorship, Lamarckian theories, which implied quite rapid evolution in response to rapid changes in environment, were politically useful. Even in the West, some writers of science fiction accepted Lamarckian evolution as a story premise because of sympathy with Lysenko's political aims. After Stalin's death in 1953, this came to an end and Darwinian evolution has been universally accepted by scientists.

In 1869, Gregor Mendel, an Austrian monk, published the results of his experiments in crossbreeding garden plants. He laid down the basic laws of inheritance. He argued that there were hereditary "factors" (which today we call "genes") which control plant color, size, and so on. He also discovered the notions of dominance and recessiveness by which gene function sometimes does not appear in the individual yet can reappear in a future generation. However, although this supplied the answer to the question of how the Darwinian traits were transmitted, this answer, by a quirk of publication, remained unknown for a generation. Mendel had presented his results in an obscure Bavarian scientific journal and it wasn't until they were rediscovered in 1899 by Bateson that they became widely known. Hence, Wells's speculations in *The Time Machine* are based entirely on Darwin with no knowledge of the details of genetics.

It was left to Hugo De Vries, a Dutch botanist, to suggest in 1900 how genes change. Darwin had suggested that natural selection allowed for the slow accumulation of infinitesimally small variations in hereditary traits. It was quite clear to him that two breeds of dog could be made to breed true or to interbreed, thus creating a new type of individual. Unfortunately, it was also true that the offspring of members of this new type often reverted to the original breeds. In addition, many animals which could interbreed, like donkeys and horses, produced sterile offspring, like mules. And further, most animals, even those closely related like sheep and goats, clearly couldn't interbreed at all. If the changes that were always going on in the origin of one species from the next were infinitesimal, then there should exist an overlapping series of species the members of which could interbreed with near neighbors, but not with distant ones. This clearly was not the case. De Vries suggested that the reason for this was that changes in hereditary factors were not infinitesimal but were quite substantial. Somehow, the genes made a discontinuous change, which he called a mutation. Today we think of evolution as the process by which species develop through the heritable mutation of genetic information yielding a survival advantage in a given environment.

We should note that if the individual fits the environment, then the environment fits the individual. As nearly as geologists can tell, the Earth's original atmosphere was composed largely of ammonia, hydrogen, methane and water vapor. Evolution is all well and good, but where did the first species come from? In 1953, Stanley Miller created Earth's original atmosphere in a test tube, shot electricity through it to simulate lightning, and discovered that he had spontaneously produced, among other things, amino acids. These are the building blocks of proteins, which are the stuff of life. (To be accurate, one should note that amino acids exist in two forms, called left-handed and right-handed; in nature, all amino acids are of the left-handed type; in Miller's experiment, since repeated many times, the results are always an equal mix—life doesn't spontaneously develop in the test tube.) Miller seems to have shown that the first complex organic molecules could have started all on their own in Earth's early atmosphere, and once they were created, surely some mechanism of evolution would lead to higher organisms.

Indeed, one notes that the supposed early atmosphere has no oxygen in it. Man, of course, could not live on the early Earth. Where then did the oxygen come from? The answer, it seems, was then the same as it is today: from green plants. Photosynthesis in green plants uses carbon dioxide and water plus energy from the sun to produce carbohydrates (starch, sugar and so on) and oxygen as a by-product. The water was part of the atmosphere, the carbon dioxide is a product of vulcanism, and sunlight preceded the Earth itself. So the lovely, oxygen-filled environment which so many science fiction stories cherish as necessary to life turns out not to have been necessary to life even on Earth. And just as the environment, through evolution, molds the varieties of life, so life molds the nature of the environment.

All living things on Earth have carbon in them, in part because carbon can make so many different chemical bonds with other elements. Silicon is closest to carbon in properties of all other elements, so many science fiction writers, like Stanley G. Weinbaum in "A Martian Odyssey" (1934), suggest that life might have evolved differently had silicon been its base. Although this is a wide-open, and hence provocative speculation, it seems to have no basis in evolutionary science. First, silicon is present on Earth, in sand for example, in hundreds of times greater density than is carbon—yet no silicon based life developed here. Second, silicon will not form multiple bonds, as carbon will, and hence always must polymerize to form rocks, according to Nobel Laureate George Wald (see Henderson in Bibliography). Modern evolution not only opens the way for science fiction to create delicate new species of *Homo,* as in Arthur C. Clarke's *The City and the Stars,* but expressly forbids the creation of Weinbaum's silicon creatures or post-natal evolution, as in Clarke's *Childhood's End* (see pp. 216–220).

In the same year in which Miller produced his amino acids, an American and British pair of investigators, Watson and Crick, were able to disentangle the structure of a complex molecule known as DNA. Today we know that DNA chains *are* the chromosomes of the nuclei of our cells and that genes are merely regions along these chains. The DNA serves as a template for the creation of a related type of molecule called RNA which then moves out into the cell and controls the construction of proteins which themselves function, for example as muscle fibers or as nerve paths. In the language of modern genetics, which is now the language of science fiction, DNA possesses a *code* which is *transcribed* to RNA which *expresses* the coded information in proteins. An organism's genetic make-up is its *genotype;* the traits which it actually expresses together make-up its body, which is its *phenotype.* Mutation occurs, not as Lamarck thought, through change in phenotype, but through change in genotype, a change which, if recessive, might not be expressed for generations.

We know today that genetic mutation occurs by changing the structure of DNA, for example by bombarding it with radiation. Our oxygen atmosphere automatically forms an ozone layer which shields us from most of the sun's energetic ultraviolet radiation. When the Earth was new, this layer did not exist, and evolution must have proceeded more rapidly than it does today. But life created oxygen and hence its own protection. Although the germ cells, egg and sperm for instance, of every organism potentially participate in evolution, each individual organism acts as if it were trying to guarantee the duplication of its own genetic information. In this broad theory of evolution, science has found a unifying perspective for examining all of life, its changes, its behaviors, its varieties. It is one of the great visions of modern man, and whether used or abused, it is the inspiration for much of his most searching fiction.

One *mis*conception about evolution, however, is so commonplace that it has its own name: teleonomy. In tracing the evolution of any organism, say the evolution of man from tree shrew, one frequently falls prey to the notion that evolution *aimed* to produce man, that man was the *goal* (*telos* in Greek) of the process of evolution. Many science fiction works, like Clarke's *Childhood's End* and Stapledon's *Odd John,* see evolution as goal-directed. Evolution, of course, is merely the mindless and continuing adaptation of organisms to their environment and the continuing change of environment in response to the actions of organisms and other influences.

In one sense, though, evolution is goal-directed when it is controlled by man, as through selective breeding, cloning, and genetic engineering in general. Cloning is the isolation of a pure line of cells from a single cell or cells of a single individual. Since every cell of every organism contains the total genetic information necessary to build that organism, it is theoretically possible to take a cell from Einstein's fingernail parings and build one—or a thousand—new Einsteins. In technological fact, however, we are far from this. Woody Allen is not likely to be able to take the President's nose—as he imagines in his film *Sleeper* (1973)—and clone another President from it. Cells which have already differentiated—taken up their specific functions in a specific organ—have difficulty in returning to an undifferentiated stage and thence differentiating anew; this difficulty is more exaggerated the more complex the organism; and genetic make-up alone, of course, cannot predetermine genius. Nonetheless, science fiction stories that use the notion of cloning are not exercising unrestrained imagination. For many years tulip growers have been able to mass produce highly desirable bulbs by taking cells from the comparatively undifferentiated root tips, splitting them apart by centrifuging, and culturing them. This process is repeated until, in a matter of a couple of weeks, the initial sliver of root tip is ready to develop into thousands of mature plants, each of which will produce the desired—and identical—bulb. In the laboratory, animals as complex as toads have already been cloned by a somewhat more restricted process: the nucleus, containing the gene-bearing chromosomes, is removed from a cell of one individual and inserted in an enucleated egg cell of another; from this, a new toad develops, one physically identical with the toad which contributed the nucleus. More commonly, genetic material is cloned in nature all the time when special circular bacterial particles of genetic material, called plasmids, reproduce by the thousands within a given cell and then manage to take up their function in other bacteria of that, or even related, species. We are all familiar with the distressing ability of diseases to evolve strains which resist our antibiotics. We now know that much of this drug resistance is conferred not by chromosomal DNA but by DNA in plasmid form. This means that only one bacterium needed to develop the resistance, and it then could multiply the plasmid by cloning within itself, transmit those plasmids widely, and have the process repeat. Whereas normal chromosomal mutation and evolution require the comparatively fast algebraic progression of reproduction to spread, traits transmissible via cloning of plasmids can overgrow a population at exponentially faster rates than that. When Philip José Farmer presents us with a world of insectoid creatures mutated within years to appear to be human, as he does in *The Lovers* (1961), that evolution is not necessarily impossible. Our knowledge of these mechanisms really begins about 1970, however, so that Farmer clearly could not have had it in mind when he wrote. Nonetheless, nature has been using the process, in all likelihood, for well over two billion years. Science fiction is just beginning to catch up.

Today the term "genetic engineering" refers to a number of different mechanisms, each designed to modify the information or expression of DNA. The most common science fictional use of genetic engineering is that found in Huxley's *Brave New World* (see pp. 33–35) where people are made to order. Although that is still a long way from possibility, new enzyme (protein catalyst) technology has been developed since 1970 which does seem to point in that direction. It is now possible to cut desired portions of DNA from a strand of DNA, for example, that gene which confers tetracycline resistance. Typically this gene is then inserted into a plasmid from a common bacterium of the human gut called *E. coli*. The plasmid then reproduces by cloning and we have a new strain of *E. coli* which is resistant to tetracycline. This is known as recombinant DNA technology. It has already produced crosses between the genes of *E. coli* and those of a tree toad.

Workers in 1975 for the first time were able to assemble to order a complex strand of DNA using about 600 elementary units of nucleic acid. This is still a very short strand if one thinks of human chromosomes, but this technology together with that of recombinant DNA promises the possibility of engineering genetic content to order in the near future. Of course, that will not yield a brave new world without environmental control as well, but the possibility is now within reach.

Another type of genetic engineering is called gene therapy, somehow treating, that is, changing, the expression of genetic information in an individual, rather than changing the nature of his offspring. Using recombinant DNA technology, one can imagine, for example, inserting the gene for hemoglobin formation in a virus, infecting a hemophiliac with that virus, and consequently changing his genetic make-up so that he is no longer a hemophiliac.

Since 1974 English scientists have been using new physical techniques to open cell walls in plants and fuse cells of different species. Currently they hope, by fusing soya and corn, to produce nitrogen-fixing corn which will serve as cattle feed but grow in soil without the need of artificial fertilizer, since the soya's nitrogen-fixing abilities would fulfill the fertilizer's function.

One should note that all these scientific possibilities for genetic engineering have existed only since about 1970. Nonetheless, it is interesting that they have not yet made their way into science fiction stories. In part, this is due to the work of the fifties, in which it seemed to become clear that man would not be able to tinker with anything so complex as DNA. Hence, the most far-reaching speculation, that offered by Huxley in 1932, seemed to drop out of science fiction just as science began to catch up. Zamyatin used psychosurgery (see pp. 206–207) to dramatize man's technology turned against basic human nature; Huxley's use of genetic engineering did the same at a more fundamental level. The fear of our own technology, and the question of the definition of human nature, is still with us. One should expect that as the results of modern biology become more widely known, genetic engineering will again become a prominent motif in science fiction.

Even if genetic engineering does not become more prominent, the wonders of evolution will still motivate science fiction. A prime example of the exciting material in biology is the adaptation called symbiotic mutualism. This term, as opposed to parasitism, denotes the co-existence of two organisms for their mutual benefits. For example, a lichen is really a photosynthetic alga living inside a durable fungus and supplying food for both under the physical protection of the fungus. In the human gut there exist bacteria assured of a constant food supply and steady temperature which supply us with our only source of the clotting vitamin K. The idea of symbiosis has recently had to be expanded, or at least questioned, by new discoveries. For example, certain South American ants live exclusively on a diet of a special fungus which in turn can only grow if provided with an enzyme found uniquely in the saliva of these ants. Are the ants raising fungus or is the fungus herding ants? However one looks at it, the relationship surely seems mutualistic and yet there is no obviously identifiable "host" organism. Whereas most science fictional symbiosis, like Heinlein's *The Puppet Masters,* has had the feel of parasitism, some has not. Olaf Stapledon in *Star Maker,* makes the mutual understanding of the symbiotic arachnoids and ichthyoids a crucial relationship in the preservation of life in the cosmos.

Perhaps the finest symbiosis novel is Hal Clement's *Needle* (1949) in which the Hunter, one of a race of symbionts, comes to coexist with an Earth boy named Bob so that the Hunter can track a renegade member of his own kind who had turned on his host in their home world. As Clement tells this tale of detection he interweaves images which remain firm in the mind long after the book is closed. Long after the Hunter has invaded Bob's body and learned its functions, he carefully avoids speaking directly to his mind for fear that Bob would reject his senses and go crazy. Instead, in order to make contact and enlist Bob's help, the Hunter forms fine filaments of his own body through Bob's corneas and sends him a written message. The delicacy of this, the concern for another, and the implicit assertion that it is easier to read than experience some things not only shows science fiction dealing through bizarre science with common problems but shows that a literary way of dealing with problems may sometimes be the most effective approach of all. Symbiosis, after all, is just one more trick evolution has uncovered to deal with problems that organisms, including man, face in the real world. And literature is another of those tricks.

This sense of interconnectedness that modern science has brought to the fore is best captured by the single word ecology. One usually thinks of ecology as that branch of biology which concerns the relations of organisms to their environment. Many people associate ecology with a particular attitude toward the preservation of species or of wilderness. The science of ecology, however, does not represent any particular attitude toward, say, forests. A truly ecological viewpoint takes into account much more than trees and streams. In studying human ecology (see pp. 15–16) one must consider man's creations just as one must consider dams in beaver ecology. For example, in 1900 most of the significant public health measures—sewerage, garbage collection, and so on—were already well known, yet life in cities was deadly. This was a direct result of the factory system of production which required large concentrations of workers to live within a relatively short walking distance from their employment. At about this time, however, the electric trolley systems began to become widespread, and it about tripled the effective distance from the factory that a worker could commute. Public health was so much improved that life expectancy increased nearly ten years. From a truly ecological point of view, the trolley was the most important public health measure of the turn of this century. And, of course, in addition to improved public health came changes in social customs as people could begin to have friendships extending from one neighborhood to the next.

Science fiction has provided some of the most detailed and compelling thought experiments in ecology in this strict sense. Both Frank Herbert's *Dune* (1965) and Ursula K. Le Guin's *The Left Hand of Darkness* (1969) won Hugo and Nebula Awards for their construction of the total ecology of an imaginative world.

Herbert's world is Arrakis, a planet on the extreme verge of dehydration. The natives, a desert tribe called the Fremen, have developed a whole technology to deal with the scarcity of water. For example, their "still-suits" make it possible for them to recycle their own body wastes and live on a few ounces of fresh water daily. The concern with survival, of course, has consequences for their science (they excel in engineering, especially of seals and nonpermeable materials), their customs (with the ritual uses of water), and their beliefs (with legends about free-flowing water). This planet is also the only source in the known universe for "melange," a spice which extends life enormously. It turns out that melange is a waste product of the metabolism of the giant sandworms which burrow under the desert and skim rapidly across it. To this world of one resource comes a family of outcast nobles. The son of this family, Paul Atreides, is the hero of the story. He immerses himself in Fremen culture, even undergoing the male rite of passage by riding a sandworm. It is Paul's belief in the inherent rightness of the Fremen's association of the sandworms with the life-giving melange that leads him to discover its true source. This belief in the Fremen, who understand and deal with their environment, is a belief in an ecological viewpoint. Although *Dune* deals with much more than this, the detailed construction of a unique and interconnected world is immensely impressive.

The Left Hand of Darkness (see pp. 226–230) presents a similarly interconnected ecology, this time with animal life, science, and customs dominated by two factors: the ambisexuality of the natives and the extreme cold of the planet Gethen, known as Winter. In this environment too, the success of the protagonists depends upon a willingness to deal with the environment on its own terms: Genly Ai, the envoy from the eighty-world Ekumen, learns to understand ambisexuals without the parochialism of his own heterosexual background, and Estraven, the prime minister of a kingdom of Gethen, gives his life to the recognition that national differences are trivial in the wider environment of the Ekumen.

Science fiction, like modern science, usually asks *how* something functions in order to understand it better, and perhaps control it. Ecology, a branch of biology (which includes the animal *Homo sapiens* and all his customs and crafts), also asks *how,* how organisms interrelate with their food sources or their weather or their competitors. Ecology is based on a sympathetic inquiry into conditions. In most of our society, this sympathy expresses itself in an urge to preserve; in science fiction, this sympathy expresses itself in an urge to improve.

Whereas ecology stresses the interrelations among components in living/non-living systems, the simpler viewpoint of environmental determinism sees phenomena as the reflex of the environments that create them. In its best sense, environmental determinism is ecology that is finally concerned with one viewpoint only. When science fiction uses environmental determinism, it is a device to show how viewpoint, which we like to think of as a function of our minds and hence at least in part under conscious control, may actually be thrust upon us, viewpoint formed by the humbling forces beyond our control. In "Desertion," one of the stories in Clifford D. Simak's far-ranging chronicle called *City* (1952), humanity is trying to colonize Jupiter. We possess a "converter" that can transform a person into any animal which we choose and this device is used to turn men into "lopers." A loper seems to be the best candidate among the Jovian fauna for having a body and nervous system capable of supporting man-like intelligence. They are called lopers because, adapted to surface pressure a thousand times that of the Earth, they are long and squat. Man cannot live on Jupiter in his native form, not even with metal apparatus, because along with the tremendous pressure come nearly unceasing ammonia rains. Altogether, Jupiter seems like hell. To make matters worse, the first five men to be converted go out onto the Jovian surface and never return. Finally, the project director and his dog are converted and go out into this terrible man-destroying environment. Suddenly, the truth hits them: Jupiter is inexpressibly beautiful. In a loper body they are free to romp, and the rain feels good on loper skin, and to loper eyes there are rainbows everywhere, and to loper noses smells that men had never guessed at. The first five men didn't "fail to come back"—they deserted the human race. Jupiter is a vaster planet than Earth by far, and in a loper body it is more wonderful. Almost the whole population of Earth finally converts—both bodies and viewpoint—and deserts for Jupiter. The sense of ourselves which our Earth environment had determined becomes supplanted by a sense determined by the Jovian environment. And mankind, proceeding through time and across space, continues, for all his freedom of will, to fall prey to environmental determinism.

A brand of environmental determinism which has been particularly influential in the shaping of science fiction is economic or Marxian determinism. Karl Marx (1818–83) attempted to put historical development on a basis of mechanistic science. He argued forcefully that one could specify the dynamics of social interactions and thus predict their future outcome; the "locomotive of history" could be charted now because one could see how the rails must be laid. His own famous conclusion, of course, was that the working class would eventually revolt and create a totalitarian regime which would eventually wither away leaving a classless society in which all capital is owned by the state. These arguments have had striking impact on science fiction. Just as other writers used technological extrapolation to construct their worlds, Edward Bellamy in *Looking Backward* (1888) used Marx's notion of the locomotive of history to predict a classless society. His world derives from a series of government take-overs of industry in response to the chaos brought about by unbridled unionism, but his historical reasoning employs Marxist assumptions and the resulting society is Marxist in flavor. Wells's extrapolations in *The Time Machine* (1895) are based in large part on Marxist notions of determinism, although Wells saw the capitalistic class as sufficiently strong to literally submerge the working class. The final refinement of Marx's view of scientifically deterministic history is presented in Isaac Asimov's great Foundation Trilogy (1951–53) (see pp. 59–60). The guiding genius in this era-spanning work is Hari Seldon, a mathematician who develops "psychohistory," a science of history based not on Newtonian (and hence Marxist) mechanistic determinism, but on probabilistic, statistical laws somewhat like those incorporated in quantum mechanics. Refining Marxist determinism by the insights of post-Newtonian science, Asimov is able to create a tale of the interactions of great masses of people, and simultaneously he can humanize the action of his tale by focusing on the importance of individual observers (experimenters, actors) who participate in the process of history they observe. Thus, science fiction, beginning with Marxist determinism as a base, has evolved a notion of history which serves as well as most fictional notions of physics or biology as the grounds for logical—scientific—extrapolation.

Both in science and in science fiction, one of the firmest and most chilling conclusions of mechanistic extrapolation has been the inevitability of the so-called "population explosion." In 1798, English clergyman Thomas Robert Malthus (1766–1834) contended that the supply of food, at best, would increase arithmetically (e.g., $2 + 2 + 2$ . . .), but the population would increase geometrically (e.g., $2 \times 2 \times 2$ . . .). Eventually, of course, as the resulting disparity increased, starvation would set in, or there would be war over food sources, or a generally weakened population would be subject to epidemic. In one way or another—all bad —population growth would be brought violently back into line with the level of available food. Indeed, coming just on the eve of the Industrial Revolution, Malthus was prescient in recognizing the fundamental importance of population pressures. The total human population of the world at the time of the Roman Empire was probably about 150,000,000 and growing at the slow rate of 100,000 a year, substantially less than one-tenth of one percent; today, the population of the world is about 4,000,000,000 and growing at nearly two percent by adding about 70,000,000 people annually. Part of this astronomical growth is the result of improved medical and public health measures, naturally. Before 1600 in Europe life expectancy at birth was about 8 years (due in part, of course, to high infant mortality); by 1750 it had reached 31 years; and by 1800, with the Industrial Revolution underway, 40 years. But technology need not necessarily increase population by allowing those born to live longer. The rigors of factory life were such that, in England, life expectancy in 1840 had risen only to 41 years. Today, of course, in the industrialized countries, life expectancy at birth is over 70 years, and the world continues to add 70,000,000 long-lived people a year.

Ever since *Frankenstein,* science fiction writers have been quick to spot the dangers incipient in science and technology. However, despite Malthus' warning, the sheer size of the Earth and the obvious benefits of some technologies kept the population explosion from assuming dramatic shape in the popular mind. Indeed, most of those few writers who considered population at all, like Bellamy in *Looking Backward,* merely assumed that the improvement of technology would either satisfy the desires of an increased population or contribute to the stabilization of population; in the case of such as William Morris in *News from Nowhere* (1890), some even seemed to feel that technology would bring about a reduction of population to pastoral levels. Since World War II, however, when the atom bomb made the world aware that people anywhere might suffer from the pressures in distant lands, and since the Korean War made the West palpably aware of the sheer mass of Asian population, the population explosion has become a conventional element of science fiction. In Asimov's Foundation Trilogy, the dying home world of Trantor is almost entirely a single city, a metal-shelled world housing trillions; in Pohl and Kornbluth's *The Space Merchants* (1952), the lower classes in overgrown New York rent stairs in towering office buildings for sleeping space. Although some writers (see Berry in Bibliography) have argued that access to medical care leads to a feeling of security which in turn leads to a voluntary decline in birth rate (such as the United States has just experienced), most science fiction writers continue to see the population explosion contained primarily through draconian legislation, such as that needed to keep a stable population in the worldship home of the characters in Alexei Panshin's *Rite of Passage* (1968).

In 1962, J. B. Calhoun demonstrated that with overpopulation, rats spontaneously develop antisocial behavior, turning on their own young, breaking down group cohesion, exhibiting cannibalism. This fact has been the most significant underlying scientific base for all science fictional treatments of population explosion since that time. Thus in Robert Silverberg's *The World Inside* (1970), the Earth's trillions live in "monads" reminiscent of Trantor, self-contained thousand story buildings which house populations involved in unrestrained breeding in the absence of any sexual taboos. In this world which tries to depend on technology, justice is rough and fatal—an infraction of a custom or the offering of an insult may spontaneously form a mob that tosses the guilty party down the recycling chute. In Sam J. Lundwall's *2018 A. D. or the King Kong Blues* (1975), the mere convention of overcrowding is enough to justify a world of lawlessness and gang rule. In Harry Harrison's *Make Room! Make Room!* (1966), the novel on which the film *Soylent Green* was based, the overcrowded Earth turns eventually to cannibalism, Swift's "Modest Proposal" come true. The best of these population explosion books is John Brunner's *Stand on Zanzibar* 1968). At the beginning of the book, the Earth's population is so great that if one allowed "a space one foot by two you could stand us all on the six hundred forty square mile surface of the island of Zanzibar." By the end of the book, a few years later, "the human race by tens of thousands would be knee-deep in the water around Zanzibar." Brunner's pop sociologist Chad C. Mulligan defines population as "an event which happened yesterday but which everyone swears won't happen until tomorrow." This event is not "scientific" at all, but human, and in its treatment of the population explosion, we see once again that science fiction, above all, is human fiction, fiction revealing often the drama of the doom we bear with us.

PSYCHOLOGY

If we are going to consciously foster that doom, we may well rely on the work of I. P. Pavlov (1849–1936), the Russian physiologist who won the Nobel Prize in Medicine in 1904. He showed how reflexes, animal reactions to stimuli, could be predictably fixed, conditioned, by associations. If, for example, a dog salivates when it sees food and if the bringing of food is uniformly preceded by the ringing of a bell, soon the dog will begin to associate the bell with the coming food and will be conditioned to salivate at the sound of the bell. This discovery of conditioning by association has turned out to be perhaps the most significant finding of psychology and is the direct base for much of the work of the Gestalt and behavioral branches of the field. One of the most sophisticated developments based on Pavlovian conditioning is a family of training devices known together as Skinner boxes after B. F. Skinner, the American psychologist (b. 1904) who invented them. In one such box, for example, a caged monkey might find a lever, a red light, a green light, and a food slot. When the green light is on, the monkey is able, if he depresses the lever say thirty times, to cause a food pellet to appear in the slot. By random motion, the monkey will eventually perform this feat. Now the monkey could very quickly be trained to depress the lever to receive food. What is more interesting, however, and represents Skinner's refinement of Pavlov's ideas, is that once the food appears, the green light goes off and the red light goes on for thirty seconds, during which time no food can be made to appear. Indeed, one can arrange the Skinner box so that if the lever is depressed while the red light is on, the thirty second time lag begins anew. By this means, the monkey not only learns to press for food, he learns that to receive food he must *not* press while the red light is on. In short, we can use a Skinner box to teach the monkey to discriminate between red and green. The elegant simplicity of these devices has led to new insights into learning theory—and to the specter of mass mind control.

Skinner himself, in his novel *Walden Two* (1948), seems to suggest that the possibility of applying conditioning to the general population may eventually bring about a human utopia. Most writers, however, like Huxley with his use of hypnopaedia (see pp. 155–156), see Pavlovian conditioning as a tool of dictatorship. In Anthony Burgess's *A Clockwork Orange* (1962), the juvenile delinquent Alex is conditioned to become incapable of violence. Hence, he seems good. Eventually, however, the moral point is made that the incapacity for violence is not the moral good of the rejection of violence. Much is made by dissident politicians of the conditioning which has dehumanized Alex and the government is forced to recondition him to his old anti-social self. Since that self is now seen to be produced by conditioning, and since growing up itself is a process of education which is conditioning, the novel leaves us with a final question: are we all only mechanically conditioned with the false belief of vital will, are we in fact clockwork oranges?

In *The Space Merchants* (1952) Frederik Pohl and C. M. Kornbluth persuasively explain advertising as mass conditioning and in *The Terminal Man* (1972) Michael Crichton shows how a patient's pleasant therapy can in fact condition him to escalate his illness so that he can receive ever more of the therapy. Pavlovian conditioning, and its extension by Skinner, put human behavior, which had always at least smacked of free will, on an apparently mechanistic basis. Ever since, science fiction has been able to use conditioning to explain the fictional molding of men and to decry the real world suppression of mankind's sense of freedom.

Gestalt psychology too derives from Pavlov's work. Gestalt means pattern or configuration. Gestalt psychology holds that psychological or physiological responses are not made to the simple summation of stimuli but to the patterns which we perceive from among all the possible patterns which might be organized and perceived among all the incoming stimuli. Optical illusions, in which we tend to see one pattern, and hence utterly fail to see an alternative pattern until it is pointed out, tend to confirm the axioms of Gestalt psychology. To think of people responding not so much to stimuli as to Gestalts implies that a fundamental part of learning is the fixing of Gestalts in the mind. Science fiction has used this notion of how man's mind works in two related ways.

The traditional science fictional use of Gestalt psychology shows man a slave of his own education. In van Vogt's *War Against the Rull* (1959), a novel woven of stories published between 1940 and 1950, mankind is at war with a race from another galaxy called the Rull. Of all the weapons the Rull can use against us, the most powerful is their knowledge of human Gestalt psychology. For example, a key human agent may trail a Rull operative to an alien planet. In searching for him, in looking carefully for clues, he will notice a strange line on the ground, then two, then a pattern which somehow compels him to walk over a cliff to his death. In Delany's *Babel-17,* the poetess-heroine Rydra Wong is only able to save the Earthpeople's Alliance when she breaks through the patterns inherent in our language and in the strange language of a character called The Butcher who knows no concept of "I," in order to develop a whole new way of thinking that conquers the enemy. In both these cases, we see adults slave to the Gestalts they have learned; in both cases, the hero's success depends upon breaking out of those Gestalts.

The obverse case, exemplified by John Hersey's *The Child Buyer* (1960), shows how man might be made much more intelligent if he could be prevented from ever developing mentally petrifying Gestalts. The title character is a procurement official for a large corporation that has perfected a technique for multiplying I.Q. by a factor of a hundred. To do this, they begin with an already bright child, which the buyer brings to them. The child is educated to have great mental flexibility. However, as his education progresses, he begins to be subjected to disorienting drugs which will open up new experiences to him. Our senses of up and down, of three dimensionality, and so on, are Gestalt analogs for our senses of our body and its relationship to the world. In order not to block learning multidimensional math, for example, the child is surgically removed from his sense of balance and gravity. Ultimately, when the education is complete, the child is a uniquely intelligent and flexible brain, artificially connected to input and output, and able to change Gestalts at will. The question, however, is whether this human computer is a human being at all.

Psychology is the science of mind and behavior. To the extent that it tells us how we *must* think and act, it vitiates our notion of free will, an essential part of most people's sense of their humanness. When van Vogt and Delany show people overcoming their Gestalt training, they show them reasserting their free will. But when that process is carried to an extreme, as in Hersey's novel, so that people are made to do without their defining Gestalts altogether, they appear less than human. Through Gestalt psychology, science fiction continues to explore the age-old and universal problem of the conflict in man's nature between pre-determination and free will.

Linguists too, and science fiction writers who use linguistics, explore the problems of free will. Language itself has been both a problem and an opportunity for science fiction writers. Most of them have fudged the problem and thus missed the opportunity. The problem derives from the fact that every culture has its own language, which influences the way its members perceive the world. The extreme form of this view, often called the Whorf-Sapir hypothesis, is that language shapes perception drastically and completely. Even the linguists Benjamin Lee Whorf and

Edward Sapir never stated this notion in quite such categoric form, but in less rigid formulations their notion of the importance of language in shaping perception has been very important. Language is the primary way that a culture teaches its members to organize the elements of the universe. Obviously, people brought up in different linguistic traditions will see things differently—will even see different things. The Eskimos, who have so many more words for kinds of snow than we do, are really aware of more kinds of snow than we are. And so it is with other aspects of existence. Language barriers are real. Translation is distortion. And the greater the linguistic difference—as between English and Hopi—the greater the problem of mutual understanding.

Obviously, in a literary field which frequently brings together sentient beings of different species, from different eco-systems on different worlds or even in different galaxies, one might expect that the problems of communication would be an important part of the fiction itself. But until recently it was almost never the case in science fiction, where a number of dodges have been used to avoid the problem and its related opportunity. Perhaps the most popular way has been to ignore the problem of language altogether, the way human excretion is ignored in romances of knights in armor. In the case of language, the problem is ignored by just having everyone talk English and never commenting on the unusualness of this. A somewhat more imaginative solution, but used frequently by not so imaginative writers, is that of telepathy. In this version, it is assumed that people can communicate thoughts directly, without recourse to any language at all—which is a highly dubious assumption. A somewhat less mystical solution is to assume the availability of some lingua franca spoken by all the parties concerned. This is often called something like "galactica," or "Galactic English." Another device is the introduction of some highly developed computing machine capable of translating any sentient noise into English and vice versa. And, of course, there is the old standby of having the alien involved simply pick up the local language—perhaps with the aid of high-speed hypnopaedia (see below) or some such thing. All these more or less preposterous solutions have their uses. They allow the story to get on to other things. But they do so by treating language as part of the invisible system of fictional conventions instead of as an aspect of whatever alien contact is being explored. And this is a great loss, since language is the most accessible way to make the nature of alienation concrete.

When science fiction writers do consider language as a part of their subject matter instead of an awkward convention of their form, some extraordinary things happen. Some of the most interesting works in the field have been based on the assumption that language does make a difference and must be considered. Jack Vance's *The Languages of Pao* (1957) was a pioneering venture of this sort, frankly based on the Whorf-Sapir hypothesis. More recently Delany's *Babel-17* has succeeded brilliantly in making language the center of its fictional concern. Not only does Delany's plot center on the efforts of a poet (Rydra Wong, who uses language to express universal human fears and hopes) to decipher a strange code or language called Babel-17 by government cryptographers—but every aspect of the story involves some kind of communication problem or code of communicative behavior: the interpretation of clothing and cosmetics, of body posture and muscular movement, of voice codes used in combat—all these and more are related to the larger problem of understanding a foreign language.

Delany is extraordinarily successful in making language in the broadest sense the object of his fictional attention. But he is not alone in taking language seriously in his work. The New Wave of science fiction (see pp. 87–97) is in fact characterized by a new concern for language as subject matter and a new willingness to experiment with the language of narration itself, which can be found in works as different as Ian Watson's *The Embeddings* (1975) and Ursula K. Le Guin's *The Word for World Is Forest* (1976). Much of the vitality of the New Wave is in fact due to the opening up of language as a primary experimental resource and as material for investigation in science fiction. And, of course, mainstream novelists with a special feeling for language have brought this to science fiction when they have entered the field. The dialect in which Anthony Burgess's *A Clockwork Orange* (1926) is narrated, for example, contributes powerfully to the concreteness of that novel's image of the future. There are plenty of signs that in the area of language science fiction has come of age.

In other areas as well, science fiction and science have grown together. Hypnopaedia, for example, first used by Huxley in *Brave New World* (see pp. 33–35), means "sleep study" and refers to a variety of linguistic conditioning administered by causing recordings to be played repeatedly during sleep softly enough that they will not awaken the sleeper yet loudly enough that they will influence him. The operative assumption here is that in sleep the conscious defenses against personality change do not function and hence deep unconscious changes can be wrought. In *Star-Begotten* (1937), H. G. Wells speculated that a dying race of Martians, unable to leave their world, might be beaming unconscious messages at us in our sleep so that we will change psychologically and subtly until, in the course of generations, we become, at least from an intellectual and emotional if not a biological viewpoint, the Martians' new race of children. (This novel also contains a use earlier than Orwell's in *1984* [1949] of the term "Big Brother.") Hypnopaedia has expanded from a science fiction device to a real world phenomenon as many people try to use it for self-education, especially in second language acquisition.

Another field in which science and science fiction may be growing together is parapsychology. This branch of psychology investigates "psychic" phenomena, supposed capabilities of the mind and occurrences stemming from those capabilities which are not merely *ab*normal (like genius or idiocy) but somehow off to the side of normal, *"para*normal." The most popularly used terms for parapsychological phenomena are telepathy, extrasensory perception, and clairvoyance. Ever since Drs. J. B. and Louisa Rhine established their Parapsychological Laboratory at Duke University in 1932, and began to follow careful experimental techniques in their investigations, the popular world has been tempted to assume a scientific basis for the phenomena which the Rhines were merely hunting. There still exists great controversy over whether telepathy has been conclusively demonstrated, not to mention such oddities as teleportation.

Science fiction has used telepathy to provide the cohesion of group entities such as Stapledon's Martians in *Last and First Men* and the new humans in Clarke's *Childhood's End*. Telepathic communication has provided some of science fiction's most searching moments, as when Genly Ai and Estraven "mindspeak" each other in their glacial isolation in Le Guin's *Left Hand of Darkness* or when Jommy Cross extrasensorially participates in the death of his persecuted mother in van Vogt's *Slan*. The relationships of symbiosis are carried on by telepathy between the ichthyoids and arachnoids in Stapledon's *Star Maker* and telepathy is a tool of police detection in Alfred Bester's *The Demolished Man*. In older science fiction, magic was introduced as such; Lindsay's *Voyage to Arcturus* (1920) begins with a successful seance. However, in more recent science fiction, as in Fritz Leiber's *Conjure Wife* (1953), magic when it exists is seen finally to be a sort of misunderstood science. This reflects the science fiction license that seems to have been issued as soon as the Rhines began to receive serious and favorable publicity: any power can be made scientific if only we call it parapsychology.

Although some evidence does seem to support the belief in extrasensory perception (perception without the employment of the normal senses of sight, hearing, smell, touch, and taste), none seems to exist for that multipurpose science fiction favorite, psi power. Just as ESP can mean a number of things, from sensing the markings on hidden cards to two-way telepathic communication to the special knowledge of the future called clairvoyance, so psi power can be the mind-destroying force that Gerry possesses in Theodore Sturgeon's *More Than Human* (1953) or the power of burning things long distance as possessed by Kid Death in Delany's *The Einstein Intersection* (1967). One meaning of psi power is telekinesis (sometimes called psychokinesis), the power of moving things with the force of the mind, as Little Anthony can terrifyingly do in Jerome Bixby's haunting "It's a *Good* Life" (1953), while another meaning is the Shadow's old power to probe and modify minds themselves, as can the mutant Mule in Asimov's *Foundation Trilogy*. If the psi power of telekinesis is called teleportation, then it might apply to the moving of things, but it is just as likely to apply to the movement of the psychic himself, as with Gully Foyle's raging "jaunts" in Bester's *The Stars My Destination* (1956). In short, anything that could once be done by magic can, since 1932, be done—in fiction at least—by psi power; magic has been made scientific by the conventional literary assumption that the questions just now being asked by parapsychology have already been answered in the affirmative.

PSEUDOSCIENCE

In some cases, this ingenuous acceptance of scientific hypotheses may finally be somewhat vindicated, as it was with the ancient belief in astronomical simplicity and as it was with Mesmerism. Named after Friedrich Anton Mesmer (1733–1815), the Austrian physician who investigated and wrote about it, Mesmerism is nowadays thought of as a synonym for hypnotism. It has been the "scientific" basis for science fiction stories ever since Poe's "The Facts in the Case of M. Valdemar" (1845). Even in that story, however, its primary interest was not as a device for suggestion but as a supposed conduit to tapping the life force of "Animal Magnetism." This vitalist notion is now relegated to pseudoscience.

Pseudoscience is fake science, a body of "knowledge" which doubters think of as "mere belief." Many of the theories of science, like the phlogiston and caloric theories, were not so much *pseudo*science as *proto*science, early first guesses that served well in their time. Indeed, the Ptolemaic geocentric astronomy, with its complex system of epicycles, would have quite adequately predicted planetary motions if only those astronomers who credited it had had access to Fourier analysis. This doesn't make Ptolemaic astronomy "right," but it does mean that we ought not to dismiss the intelligence and beliefs of these early investigators into nature's ways. It is quite acceptable today to regard ancient astrology as the parent of modern astronomy and medieval alchemy as the parent of modern chemistry.

Many pseudosciences grew up not in the supposedly benighted past but in the modern era. Phrenology, the reading of character by examining the bumps on the skull, was developed by the German physician Gall in the first decades of the nineteenth century. Pangenesis, a notion advanced by Darwin himself in *The Descent of Man* (1871) held that every cell of the body, as modified by its experience, contributes invisible "gemmules" to the germ cells and hence to the hereditary endowment of the next generation. This nearly Lamarckian notion, though no longer accepted by geneticists, did influence many provocative turn-of-the-century writers of popular science and science fiction, such as Camille Flammarion (1842–1925) whose more than thirty books intended to show that the planets were created expressly as the habitation of life. The pangenesis hypothesis helped support that notion because it explained how evolution in diverse environments might proceed from a common source to wide diversity in relatively short time.

Svante Arrhenius (1859–1927), Swedish chemist and physicist who won a Nobel Prize in Chemistry in 1903, was the greatest exponent of the notion of panspermia. This theory held that life existed eternally, as matter did, and that spores of life, panspermia, were blown by the pressure of sunlight from planet to planet where local conditions, if favorable to life, led through the process of evolution to the proliferation of life forms on those planets. We have no concrete evidence for the rightness of this theory and the immensity of interstellar distances and the known facts about stellar evolution seem to make it nearly impossible. Nonetheless, one must remember that Darwin's theories, though they partially accounted for the origin of species, did not at all account for the origin of life. Only since 1953 have we had the scientific basis to make biochemical guesses about that.

The panspermia theory itself occurs as a minor motif in many stories, and underlies many tales of intergalactic confrontation. Even though the theory itself is not in scientific favor, its spirit continues to animate some fine science fiction, such as James Blish's *The Seedling Stars* (1957), a composite novel of the spread of forms of humanity through the universe. Ultimately, the panspermia theory appeals to a special combination of humility and pride that sees the marvel of life and the marvelous intricacy of human social life as somehow too astonishing to have developed unaided on this tiny speck of earth. Many recent books of quasi-science, like Erich Von Däniken's *Chariots of the Gods?* (1968), have achieved wide popularity by suggesting that we have had help from "outside," that God was perhaps an astronaut come to teach us and that he left behind such enigmas as the immense Nazca plateau drawings which are intelligible only from the air—and yet which have no overhanging mountains. The obvious potency of these ideas for a mass audience shows why, in science fiction, ideas like panspermia may persist long after they are discarded by science. Many widely read newspapers, after all, carry daily horoscopes.

Nonetheless, except in *Sword and Sorcery* (see p. 172), most science fiction writers, when they have been conscious of their materials, have eschewed pseudoscience, preferring instead the hard extrapolative model of Wells, although there are important exceptions. L. Ron Hubbard, best known for his post-catastrophe novel *Final Blackout* (1940), often investigated psychological phenomena in such stories as *Death's Deputy* (1940) and *Fear* (1940). He became enamored of his own system of psychotherapy called Dianetics and eventually gave up writing to found Scientology, a quasi-religion based on it. A. E. van Vogt, himself a follower of Scientology, is the most famous of writers accused of dabbling in pseudoscience. In *The World of Ā* (1945), for example, he introduces a Law of Three-point Similarity so that his protagonist can disappear from one spot, in which his life is threatened, and reappear in another. Although this is indeed pseudoscience, it is related to Lagrange's Law (1906), a mathematical demonstration that an object of any mass large or small in Earth's orbit and forming an equilateral triangle with the Earth and the Sun will remain in a fixed position relative to the Earth. This has not led, of course, to the Law of Three-point Similarity, but it has led to the suggestion that communication satellites in "stationary" orbits now connect the regions of the Earth. Pseudoscience, then, is itself often merely young science; science fiction, concerned with the development of science, often finds it useful to treat science as if it were in a radically developing state; and even in its most farfetched treatments, the future pseudoscience itself often turns out to have a clear basis in the science of today.

SCIENCE AS FICTION

Many people—and many science fiction enthusiasts among them—think of the knowledge of science as somehow "better" knowledge than the "sloppy ramblings" of philosophy or the "groundless" knowledge of religion. This belief in the superiority of scientific knowledge frequently motivates the praise for scientific fiction over fiction that concerns itself more centrally with faith or psychology or history. While it is certainly true that scientific knowledge may be quite different from other kinds of knowledge, and while scientific knowledge is more usually susceptible to mathematical measurement, one must recognize that science itself is a system of beliefs, and the perspectives of science are themselves thought-structures for viewing the world, that is, fictions (see Kuhn in Bibliography). This is clear both in the observations of science and in the conclusions drawn from those observations.

Consider the question of color. While we usually think of color as a property of an object, like green grass, the color green is clearly only a human perception. We all learn what objects get *called* green as we are growing up, but there is no way to know that the actual color which one person calls green looks the same to him as the color another calls green looks to that other observer. In part because of this, color blindness was not a recognized phenomenon until the chemist Dalton described it first in 1794. More dramatically, our eyes are trained by our beliefs. We all *know* that shadows are black. Paintings from time immemorial attest to the commonality of this knowledge. When the Spicer-Dufay process of "natural color photography" was developed in 1931, people objected to the imprecision of the process because it sometimes showed the daylight shadows on snow as blue. In fact, these shadows are sometimes blue because the shadowed snow reflects not the white daylight but the blue skylight; the belief in blackness of shadows had prevented this simple observation from ever being made.

Kepler's first important astronomical paper was an exercise in mysticism that seemed right at the time but was in fact incorrect. He knew that geometry had discovered only five regular solids (shapes enclosed by flat surfaces having sides of equal length and angles of equal degree: pyramid, octahedron, cube, dodecahedron, and icosahedron). Since God was the Great Geometer, Kepler tried the mathematical experiment of inscribing these solids one inside the other and discovered (!) that the ratios of their radii were precisely the same as the ratios of the distances of the planets from the sun. As it turns out, there are now known to be nine planets and more accurate observations show that the ratios of the mean solar distances of the five planets Kepler considered do not accord well with the ratios of the radii of the five regular solids. But at the time belief was confirmed and the paper was greeted with enthusiasm.

In 1610 Galileo used one of the earliest astronomical telescopes to discover the four moons of Jupiter. When Kepler heard of this, he immediately assumed that Mars must have two moons. After all, the planets are organized according to geometric law: Venus has no moons, the Earth has one, and so Mars—between Earth and four-mooned Jupiter—must have two to form a geometric progression. This conclusion has always been accepted as true, and we find famous literary references to the two moons of Mars in such well-known works as Swift's *Gulliver's Travels* (1726). However, the two moons of Mars were first *observed* by the American astronomer Asaph Hall in 1877, the same year in which Schiaparelli discerned the Martian canals. And Jupiter turns out to have twelve moons (or perhaps thirteen if observations announced in 1975 can be confirmed). Kepler, again, was lucky enough to have his belief *seem* right, and hence scientific. But that scientific knowledge was still based, in part, on belief.

In the twentieth century we have seen the belief in the dichotomy between the wave and the particle fall under the assault of quantum mechanics and the deterministic solidity of Kepler's Laws fall under the assault of relativity. We have discovered a fourth state of matter (plasmas) and found that life *can* be created in a test tube. The insights (beliefs?) of the so-called New Biology (see Ardrey in Bibliography) have reversed the eighteenth-century notion that man is basically good to show him basically the last in a long line of killer apes. ESP has made magic seem nonmagical and yet real while the absurdities of non-Euclidean geometry turn out to be practical necessities if one wants to compute interplanetary trajectories. As Sir Arthur Eddington has said, the universe has come to seem not so much a great machine as a great thought.

The Roman church thought about the work of Galileo and Kepler and placed them under bans. Today those investigators who uncover evidence of differences between mean racial intelligences are put under bans. We have changed our orthodoxies, our beliefs, but science proceeds to be as determined by belief as it ever was. The exciting thing about science is that it continues to examine its beliefs, to find ways in which they do not hold, and to revise them. Science fiction does the same. Arthur C. Clarke postulates communication satellites and the world constructs them; Cleve Cartmill was interrogated by military intelligence in 1944 for correctly hypothesizing in a story called "Deadline" how one might construct an atom bomb—as the Manhattan Project was then doing in extreme secrecy. We all act on belief quite as often as we do on observation; we know that Albania exists, but few of us have ever been there. The knowledge of science is not "better" than other knowledge, but it is different from other knowledge. The exciting difference between science and other knowledge is the same difference that we find between science fiction and other fictions: both science and science fiction make a conscious effort to recognize their beliefs and examine their validity. In this way both arrive at new, and potentially more useful, fictions.

III. VISION

4. FORMS AND THEMES

Forms

MYTH AND MYTH-MAKING

T HE VISION of science fiction is partly a matter of the forms in which this vision takes its shape. Like all fiction, science fiction makes frequent use of myths, those archetypal stories which provide the symbols that help us shape our world. In our culture, the richest source of myths is the Bible. Clarke's "Total Breakthrough" in *Childhood's End* (see pp. 216–220) recalls the Descent of Grace; Mike's return in Heinlein's *Stranger in a Strange Land* recalls the Second Coming of Christ; Rachel's primal innocence in Miller's *Canticle for Leibowitz* (see pp. 221–226) recalls the Creation story. Because science fiction writers can presume their readers' acquaintance with these myths, their own stories have a certain added sense of familiarity, and hence of plausibility. The most pervasive myth in our culture, according to the work of Sir James Frazer in *The Golden Bough* (1890) and as refined in Joseph Campbell's monomyth in *Hero with a Thousand Faces* (1949), is the myth of the killing of the king, often a fisher king, at times of infertility, social turmoil, or world crisis. The sacrifice of the king appeases Mother Earth or allows the creation of a new social order or brings the world into a new era. The story of Jesus' Passion and Resurrection is a clear version of this myth ("a fisher of men"). We see versions of it in science fiction whenever a socially representative character dies for the wider society, as when Estraven sacrifices himself in *The Left Hand of Darkness* (see pp. 226–230). This mythic story lurks in the background whenever science fiction, like the Bible, describes the creation and manipulation of life.

Science literally means knowledge; death, in Genesis, was the fruit of the tree of knowledge of good and evil. Since before written records, man has sought to use his knowledge to regain his lost immortality. The stories of Elijah and Elisha in the Old Testament, of Lazarus and preeminently of Jesus in the New Testament center on reincarnation. In fact, myths of reincarnation far antedate even the Judeo-Christian tradition. We really find two kinds of reincarnation in the ancient stories: Elisha's reincarnation of the dead man to mortality and Jesus' reincarnation from death to immortality. Science fiction uses both these possibilities. Victor Frankenstein's reincarnation of a demon from charnel waste parallels Elisha's resurrection and clearly questions Frankenstein's godly/paternal/creative responsibilities. In Clarke's *The City and the Stars,* we find the most common science fictional device for a kind of reincarnation to immortality: personality tapes. This fictional device presumes that one can exhaustively specify a human being, even down to the cells of his brain, and hence record information sufficient to reconstruct him, body and "soul." In Clarke's novel the city is a self-contained unit that is programed to function for ages in stability, producing only occasional variations, keeping itself in reserve and maintaining a society its builders thought utopian. In order to remove the fear of death as a motivator, and in order to maintain a comparatively stable population, customs have emerged that capitalize on the personality tapes. At an advanced yet vigorous age, or when boredom strikes, citizens walk into a death center, have themselves taped, and painlessly leave this existence, secure in the knowledge that the computer will randomly recreate them in 30,000 years or so—when things might be different. Needless to say, with the advent of universal reincarnation, we see the demise of sexual reproduction. Again, the science fiction world, in using reincarnation, worries about the same complex of problems found in the story of the Fall from Eden. In a more poignant way, Delany uses personality tapes in *Babel-17* as a device to allow a sort of intermediate suicide. Some characters, perhaps akin to the undying Cain or the Wandering Jew, are even angered when their tapes are used to call them forth before the time they had wished to be dead has expired. Thus, science fiction not only uses reincarnation to explore problems of human godliness, but to reintroduce the problem of pride which led to the Fall originally.

Prolongation of life, another effort to transcend mortality, has two main uses in science fiction. Various ruses have been used to explain the extension of a character's life so as to land him unchanged in the future: a magic sleep in Washington Irving's non-science fictional "Rip Van

Winkle" (1819) or mesmerism and a preservative gas in Bellamy's *Looking Backward*. This use of prolonged life in science fiction was largely obviated by Wells's creation of a time machine.

The second fictional use for the prolongation of life is already clear in Poe's "The Facts in the Case of M. Valdemar" (1845). The narrator of this story reports mesmerizing a man at the very point of death. In the ensuing months, the body does not decay, although it does stiffen, and he remains able to respond to the narrator's questions in a hollow, breathless voice. When the grotesquerie of the situation finally overwhelms the narrator, he accedes to Valdemar's entreaty to be finally allowed real death. The narrator wakes the man from his trance, and in the space of seconds the body putrefies before his horrified eyes. This motif of catch-up putrefaction shows man finally reconfined within his "natural" limits. This is a more personal and less spiritual aspect of the problem of man's godliness explored through the use of reincarnation. Poe's trick has become a filmic stand-by in vampire stories, where the climax always reveals the vampire's great age suddenly corroding his flesh in death. The device was used well in Oscar Wilde's non-science fictional *The Picture of Dorian Gray* (1891), and in H. P. Lovecraft's "Cool Air" (1928). More recently, the television series *The Invaders* always showed the dying disintegration of at least one pseudo-human invader. Physical corruption serves as a clear image for moral corruption. The device of prolongation of life, culminating in instantaneous corruption, argues anti-scientifically for human acceptance of some order larger than we know.

Finally, mythic defenses against mortality include not only reincarnation and prolongation of life but also the absolute creation of life from unliving materials. Although it is quite difficult to define life itself, one can be fairly certain that clay is not alive and people are. Although something like life has been created out of dead matter routinely since 1953 (see above, p. 140), only rarely is life created out of utterly dead matter in science fiction. In Theodore Sturgeon's funny and provocative "Microcosmic God" (1941), Kidder creates a whole new race, but he is in fact their paternal god, maintaining the environment they need to survive, and they obediently do what he wishes, including finally erecting a force field around him, his island, and their world, so that, imagistically, they have all returned to a safe Eden. But such stories are the exception. The rule is that new life is created from previously existing life. The artificial beings in Wells's *The Island of Dr. Moreau*, besides revealing the beastliness in man, also implicitly condemn him for meddling with life. Whenever a new germ is created, it always leaves casualties; when an atomic blast causes a mutation, the monster is usually malevolent.

In the use of artificial life in science fiction, then, we see a clear moral conservatism. Unless man can truly perform the role of God, as in Sturgeon's piece, he is culpable. The more closely the artificial life represents god's work, the more profoundly new the life is; the more drastically it obviates morality, the more profoundly man is guilty. When the artificial life is merely a matter of the prolongation of an individual's life, as in Poe's story, then the outcome merely reminds man of his potential guilt rather than condemning him. But guilt there is throughout. Ever since man ate of the fruit, and caused himself to know death, he has felt guilty in his inevitable struggle for life. Or so our mythology has taught us, and at some level we believe that mythology. When science fiction uses the devices of artificial life, its mythic heritage emerges to lend a guilty color to man's struggle against death.

Sometimes all of Christian orthodoxy is revisited in science fiction, as in the C. S. Lewis trilogy discussed previously (see pp. 42–49). However, since the Biblical myths are well known, they are fit not only for emulation but for fictional inversion as well. In William Hjortsberg's *Gray Matters* (1971), brains kept alive in mechanized, underground beehives are educated, over the course of centuries if need be, until they are utterly freed of passion. Only then are they allowed to be placed in perfect bodies and released into a garden world. But the novel presents this new world as the exact opposite of Eden, for without passions, human life is gray.

A few writers, like Roger Zelazny in *This Immortal* (1966) and *Lord of Light* (1967), use other myths (ancient Greek and Hindu respectively) as their resonant bases. One of the most common myths recalled by science fiction though rarely outside of it in this century, is the ancient Greek Hyperborea myth. This story postulates a land of warmth and sunshine beyond the North Wind, perhaps at the North Pole, beyond the fictional Riphaean Mountains, where all the inhabitants are innocent in a pre-Edenic way and utterly happy. Robert Walton, the letter-writer in *Frankenstein,* is attempting to discover this land; Samuel Butler inverts the myth to make his *Erewhon* (1872) a satiric utopia "Over the Range"; and Clark Ashton Smith wrote a cycle of stories which have been joined together under the title of *Hyperborea* (1971; 1932–42).

The myths of science fiction have also provided literature with new symbols, and usually with their inversions as well. Frankenstein's monster is the most obvious case in point. This demon of man's technology gone out of control is countered by Lester del Rey's creation of the perfect woman robot in "Helen O'Loy" (1938). Dr. Jekyll and Mr. Hyde capture the sense of the evil forces lurking within us, and Superman reveals the hidden forces of good. Orwell's *1984* stands for the world brought inexorably to slavery by inhumane technology, while George R. Stewart's *Earth Abides* (1949) shows a post-catastrophe world drifting back toward savagery through the loss of humane technology. Most strikingly, Lindsay's *Voyage to Arcturus* (see pp. 207–212) mixes Christian and Norse mythology at least in part to imply that no single myth can give us an exhaustively true perspective on our world.

Although most science fiction draws upon the myths prevalent in our culture, some writers have undertaken the arduous task of creating whole new mythologies. Frank Herbert's series of works beginning with *Dune* is most often cited in this regard, but so must be Heinlein's Methuselahs in his Future History series, H. P. Lovecraft's stories of the Chthulu mythos, and Cordwainer Smith's tales of the Instrumentality and the Underpeople. Although to many critics the salient mark of science fiction is hardnosed technical extrapolation, the pervasive use and creation of myths of all sorts reminds us that science fiction, above all, is human fiction, and as human fiction, it concerns itself powerfully and continually with the examination of symbols central to our vision of our world and of ourselves.

FANTASY

As with myth, the forms of fantasy are closely allied and intertwined with the forms of science fiction. In fact, the terms Fantasy and Science Fiction are often confused and sometimes deliberately conflated, as in the title of *The Magazine of Fantasy and Science Fiction*. Most people think of fantasy as the imagination of the non-real. Since science fiction postulates conditions which don't actually exist, it deals in the unreal. Hence, it is fantastic; hence, it gets called fantasy. However, *all* fiction deals in conditions which don't actually exist, perhaps in tidy endings or in opportune coincidences; certainly in lives of characters who surely have not lived among us. The true quality of the fantastic has nothing to do with what is real. In *20,000 Leagues Under the Sea* (see pp. 196–200) Verne even made his readers believe the real submarine was unreal so that he could thrill them by making the presumptively unreal become real. The mark of the fantastic is the thrill of seeing the *believed* unreal become real. This is so regardless of what, in the world outside the fiction, might be real.

When Alice is astounded to find that flowers can talk in Lewis Carroll's book, she signals us that she is involved in the fantastic. We can see that the constant astonishment in a fantasy like *Through the Looking-Glass* bears a family relation to the comparatively rare thrill in *20,000 Leagues Under the Sea.* Verne's novel is fantastic, but Carroll's is a fantasy. This direct reversal of the ground rules of the narrative world is the structure that marks the fantastic. A true fantasy uses the fantastic centrally, exhaustively.

All science fiction is to some extent fantastic, because all science fiction makes at least one assumption that reverses the ground rules of the world outside the text in order to create the world inside the text. However, we can find ever more fantastic examples of science fiction as we find works that rely on that structure of reversal ever more thoroughly. *A Voyage to Arcturus* (see pp. 207–212) makes a fantastic reversal every time it changes locale. Since the change of locale itself, the odyssey Maskull endures, is the central feature of the work, it might well be thought of as a fantasy. On the other hand, because it is concerned with environmental determinism in each locale, and because of its setting in the system of Arcturus, and because of the science jargon of Starkness observatory, backrays and so on, the work is science fiction. Notice that one defines science fiction by what it has in it, by its elements; one defines fantasy by how it presents what it has in it, by its structure. Hence, as in the case of Lindsay's novel, it is possible to have a work which, by its elements, is science fiction, and which, by its structure, is fantasy. Similarly, we can have somewhat fantastic works, science fiction novels like *The Time Machine,* which are not fantasy, and fantasy, like *Through the Looking Glass,* which is clearly not science fiction. Fantasy and Science Fiction are two utterly different *kinds* of categories; however, since works of science fiction are always to some extent tinged by the structure of fantasy, the terms are often blurred, and many useless debates emerge from this confusion.

The surest way to know a work for true fantasy is to spot a structure which is irreducibly fantastic. In reading future history, like Bellamy's *Looking Backward,* we are constantly aware of the diametric opposition between the past tense of narration and the future content narrated. More dramatically, Michael Moorcock's *The Warlord of the Air* (1971) purports to be a manuscript found by Moorcock which had been dictated to his grandfather in 1903 by a man who had time-traveled into

a 1973 somewhat different from our own. This work, because of its continual reversal of the ground rules of narration itself, remains a fantasy
no matter how "real" some of its content-elements may seem. In Robert
Sheckley's recent pyrotechnic novel, *Options* (1975), the narrative structure constantly undercuts itself, even to the extent that a new character
comes in four-fifths of the way through the novel, informs the protagonist that "the whole conception of you on an alien planet . . . has
been declared dramatically unsound," and replaces him with a new hero
named Mr. Bero who is the protagonist of Part Two, which is a parody
of an old Sydney Greenstreet movie. Here the continual concern with the
nature of the narrative world, and the continual fantastic manipulation of
that world, is matched by the narrative concern for the "alien planet"
and the continual manipulation, in turn, of the ground rules of that place.
This easy integration of structure and elements shows the natural affinity
between fantasy and science fiction, an affinity which is being used more
and more in the works of such younger writers as Delany, Ellison, and
Ballard. These writers of the New Wave approach in their techniques the
work of such writers of self-reflective metafiction as Barth and Coover,
who are usually considered as working outside the science fiction tradition. Such developments are present in contemporary science fiction but
are far from common. The form of nonrealistic imagining most typical
of science fiction in the opinion of some of its friends as well as of its
enemies is called "space opera."

The term "space opera" is modeled on "horse opera," a critical term
for Western fiction. Space opera denotes those works which have the typical structures and plots of Westerns, but use the settings and trappings
of science fiction. John Carter, the hero of Edgar Rice Burroughs's
Mars series, appears on Mars after he has been chased into hiding in a
mysterious cave in Arizona by marauding Indians. He is perhaps the first
important space opera character.

In *The Six-Gun Mystique,* John G. Cawelti has described the structural "formula" of Western fiction. Typically, the world is divided between two locales (the hills and the town, the hills and the ranch, the
ranch and the homestead) one of which is inhabited by the ruggedly self-
reliant bad guys and the other of which belongs to the usually less capable good guys. The criminals live outside the town and attack it, while
the citizens have banded together in their comparative weakness for mutual protection, economic betterment, and the preservation of social
values. The Western hero always possesses the skills of the outgroup
locale but for some reason decides he must use these to protect the values

of the social ingroup. After he has succeeded in protecting the citizenry he must either ride away from the ingroup locale, as in Jack Shaefer's *Shane,* or hang up his guns, as in Owen Wister's *The Virginian.* This same division of locales and the same mediating function of the hero is apparent in such space opera series as Conan the Warrior (by Robert Howard, and then by Lin Carter and others), the Retief series (by Keith Laumer) in which the human diplomat satirically brings right to all troubled worlds, or World of Tiers (by Philip José Farmer, including *The Maker of Universes,* 1967, *The Gates of Creation,* 1968, and *A Private Cosmos,* 1968), in which Kickaha rides horses, jousts with knights, wields ray guns, and otherwise mediates between locales.

When space opera takes on the archaic flavor of knights and ladies, it is usually called "Sword and Sorcery," and buckles its swash on distant planets or an earlier earth, where derring do may be done in style. Structurally, it is space opera but with the raygun replaced by a sword and the scientist by a sorcerer. The most famous such stories are probably Fritz Leiber's Gray Mouser series (collected as *Swords Against Wizardry, Swords in the Mist,* and *The Swords of Lankhmar,* 1968), in which the Gray Mouser and his sidekick Fafhrd right wrongs all over the place. John Carter, of course, makes frequent use of handy swords. In this kind of science fiction the science is very close to magic and the emphasis very much on adventure and atmosphere. But not all space opera is sword and sorcery.

A particularly good example of space opera, which science fiction writers themselves admire is Cordwainer Smith's "Scanners Live in Vain" (1948). A Scanner is a human being who has had extensive neurosurgery in order to make him unable to sense pain; he then undergoes extensive training and fitting with strange meters and dials so that he can learn to walk, work, and so on by sight alone, even "scanning" his own body functions. These Scanners man the interplanetary ships that maintain the commerce of the worlds, because the "Great Pain" of space kills ordinary humans. There also exist "Habermans," criminals who, instead of being executed, have been turned into scanner-like creatures who are also locked into unfeeling bodies but are neither volunteers nor trained to scan. The Habermans are this world's outgroup, doing menial work in space; the Scanners are the heroes, voluntarily cutting themselves off (literally) from human community in order to keep order in the outworld, and hence protect the values of the inworld. When scientist Adam Stone is rumored to have discovered a way to make space travel safe for everyone, the Scanners have a hurried meeting and decide to kill him, thus becoming outlaws. After all, they have taken on this voluntary isolation in large part because of the prestige and respect the world accords them; if Stone is right, then the world won't need Scanners. One Scanner, Martel, decides that the inworld deserves the chance to go into space, even if it makes him an outlaw with his own fraternity of Scanners. He does save Stone, thereby sacrificing his own way of life and defeating the Scanners for the sake of mankind in general. However, just as Owen Wister gives the Virginian a way to hang up his guns, so Smith has Adam Stone discover an operation to reverse the creation of the Scanner and Martel is the first of his kind to be rehabilitated and brought fully back into society. This story is a drama of isolation that portrays vividly the personal problem of conflicting group loyalties. Although the term "space opera" is used often with condescension, this variety of science fiction, like Western fiction, often produces well-crafted narratives, in which adventurous deeds and serious human considerations are skillfully blended.

UTOPIAS

In addition to myth and fantasy, science fiction has drawn upon the literary heritage of a third great narrative form, the utopia. Literary utopianism has a long history, reaching back to Plato's *The Republic* (*c.* 380 B. C.) and continuing today. In Plato's imaginary world the stability of society was insured by the presence of a manipulative elite who controlled the actions of the citizenry and an economy based on slave labor. All ancient utopias were in fact utopias for only some of the people. The advent of Christianity with its emphasis on communitarianism called into question at least implicitly societies based on such gross inequalities. With the Renaissance utopianism entered a second phase of Christian humanism, mapping out ideal communities based on sharing (like Thomas More's *Utopia,* 1516, and Friar Tommaso Campanella's *The City of the Sun,* 1602). In order to supply the economic base for utopia, to grant freedom from want, these Renaissance writers who rejected the ancient employment of slaves had to turn to economic schemes that increased productivity (as More did) or redistributed the wealth (as Valentin Andreae did in *Christianopolis,* 1619). At this same time, in Bacon's *The New Atlantis* (1627), we see a utopian community of scholars and scientists who are very happy among themselves and live off the land they rule. Although this smacks of Plato's political philosophy, it also presages part of the third phase of utopianism, which arose in response to the industrial revolution. Some writers, like Karl Marx (*Das Kapital,* 1867), continued to concentrate on redistribution to achieve communitarianism; others, like Bulwer Lytton (*The Coming Race,* 1871) and Edward Bellamy (*Looking Backward,* 1888), used technology to create what was essentially a new manifestation of Plato's thought: the machines (or the scientific work scheme) created the wealth and the whole citizenry benefited. By substituting machines or robots for slaves, the utopians of the third phase were able to obviate the moral problems they felt with the utopians of the first phase. However, in the twentieth century (and sometimes earlier as in Butler's *Erewhon,* 1872), writers began to see that the machine technology might make slaves of everyone. Most twentieth-century writers have seen no way to get beyond the enslavement to technology, and we thus find a series of distinguished dystopias (like Huxley's *Brave New World,* 1932) that predict a dismal future for humanity. Some writers, however, have tried to get beyond this doom by postulating psychic growth or an evolutionary breakthrough to a race of superpeople. These tactics, of course, presume the possibility of a basic change in human nature; they do not so much see a way beyond technology as around it. In postulating such radical improvement in humanity, the utopians of this fourth phase are modernizing the dreams of the Christian humanists of the second.

Both the third and fourth phase utopias are clearly atavistic. Writers of the third phase look back to those of the first, and fourth phase writers look back to the humanists of the second. This is so even when they set their works in the future, as we see when William Morris describes his twenty-first century world as "like the fourteenth century" (*News From Nowhere*) and when, at the end of Ayn Rand's *Anthem* (1938) the main characters attain to a pastoral ideal. Atavism, though we see it operating here in a historical and intellectual way, is primarily a psychological phenomenon, a desire to return to what seems to have been a time in one's life when the world was better organized, when pressures were defended against by parents, when responsibility was easily borne.

In the twentieth century our world is shaped by science. It is only reasonable then that our atavistic urges to escape must deal with science. But science and atavism are enemies. Science allows no retreating in time, and insists on contemplating the consequences of actions. In our time the utopian impulse has been largely replaced by dystopian projections of disastrous current trends, and at these science fiction has excelled. (See pp. 33–34.)

Themes

IMAGINARY WORLDS

The vision of science fiction has been partly a matter of its adaptation of certain traditional forms and archetypes, but it is also a function of certain recurring themes which it has made its own. These themes may be loosely divided into those of biological origin—unhuman beings and problems of race and sex—and those of physical origin—the themes of time and space.

A persistent aspect of the vision of science fiction is the desire to transcend normal experience. The population of imaginary universes with forms of unhuman intelligence is the primary biological manifestation of this urge. Its primary physical realization is through the presentation of characters and events that transgress the conditions of space and time as we know them. "Teleportation" breaks the laws of material movement through space as they are currently understood. The term refers to the instantaneous or gradual moving of matter through space by parapsychological or fantastic mechanical means. Typically teleportation takes time when it is mental (as when Janie thinks an ashtray at her mother's lover in Theodore Sturgeon's *More Than Human*) and is instantaneous when it is mechanical (as when the crew of *Star Trek*'s *Enterprise* "beam down" on an alien planet); however, there are examples of instantaneous mental teleportation (as in Gully Foyle's "jaunting" in Alfred Bester's *The Stars My Destination*) and examples of gradual mechanical teleportation (as in Roald Dahl's delightful children's tale *Charlie and the Chocolate Factory,* 1964). In all cases, however, teleportation represents a wish fulfillment, an escape from the physical restrictions we are all subject to. For this reason, just as science fiction has often implied that "there are some things man was not meant to know," teleportation, in fulfilling man's wishes, is often the instrument of misfortune (as when the scientist in the film *The Fly,* 1958, misuses his machine and winds up with a fly-headed body and his head reduced and attached to the body of a fly). Like so many of the motifs of science fiction, teleportation reveals both man's secret longings and his secret fears.

Like teleportation, the motif of time travel represents a human wish fulfillment. Using the justifications of visionary experience, drug experience, or preternaturally extended sleep, literature since ancient times has used time travel to go forward, into the future. But in the sense of travelling backward, into the past, the closest approximations before Wells involve the interrogation of spirits of the dead about their lives (as in Homer's Hades or in Book III of *Gulliver's Travels*). Martin Gardner has suggested that the Outlandish Clock in Lewis Carroll's *Sylvie and Bruno* (1889), which sets back events when its hands are set back and which makes time run backwards when it runs backwards, anticipates Wells. However, "The Chronic Argonauts," the first—though quite different—version of *The Time Machine* (1895) appeared serially in 1888. Hence, we must either grant primacy to Wells or at least suggest that in the ninth decade of the nineteenth century, time travel was a motif whose time had come. At any rate, the motif achieved instant popularity with Wells's novel and became a conventional staple of science fiction.

The forward time travel of science fiction, like the time travel of non-science fiction, is a tactic for displacing the story's setting. Hence, forward time travel allows for an ironic setting that supports satire of our present world, as in Zamyatin's *We* (see below, pp. 204–207). This parallels Swift's spatial displacement to Lilliput and Brobdingnag in *Gulliver's Travels*. In its backward sense, however, time travel not only creates a potentially ironic setting but always calls the nature of causation into question. If one can exist in a time before one was born, then what is the nature of that existence? If one were to murder one's parents in the past, then one would not have come to exist. But if one had not come to exist, then one could not have traveled into the past. Science fiction continues to confront such paradoxes.

Science fiction must assume either that time travel can have no real effect on the present or that it can. In Mack Reynolds's delightful "The Business, As Usual" (1952), a traveler from our time is conned by an inhabitant of the future into exchanging all his clothing and possessions for an "atomic knife" to bring back as proof of his journey. As he disappears from the future time, the knife clatters to the ground. "Obviously, you can carry things *forward* in time, since that's the natural flow of the dimension; but you just can't carry anything, not even memory, *backward* against the current." The con artist's wife is annoyed that he's brought home yet more useless antiques from yet another naive time traveler. On the other hand, in L. Sprague de Camp's *Lest Darkness Fall* (1939), an archeologist from our time goes back to ancient Rome and succeeds in planting the cultural defenses against the collapse of civilization and the advent of the Dark Ages. Of course, we readers of the book know that the Dark Ages are in our past, and so if Martin Padway has succeeded in preventing them, in a sense he has split history and set an alternate time stream flowing.

The term "alternate time stream" signifies a historical sequence which parallels ours and which we can recognize in fiction, but which nonetheless is not our own "time stream" or history. It need not be created by explicit time travel. An excellent example of a novel employing an alternate time stream is *Pavane* (1966) by Keith Roberts, which postulates in the first two pages that in 1588 an assassination plot against England's Queen Elizabeth was successful. This allows the Spanish Armada to conquer England, thus crushing the strongest Protestant nation and establishing Roman Catholic dominance for centuries. Assuming tacitly that the Church continued its inquisitional practices indefinitely, Roberts begins his story on the third page in an extrapolated world set in a 1966 quite different from our own—and yet quite like our own. Cargo transport over land is accomplished by steam locomotives pulling trains of cars along roads; long distance communication is accomplished by means of an intricate system of semaphore towers. In this world science and technology have been restrained by religion, but the tension between the two—and the world views that they require—has reached the breaking point. By bringing the monolithic Church to life in a world close to our own, Roberts gives a powerful dramatic thrust to questions of philosophic value. The alternate time stream at its most serious raises questions about history and progress that are not so accessible to any other fictional form. Above all, this form emphasizes the way that the actual events of history have shaped cultural values which we sometimes take to be absolute. This certainly is the source of much of the power in Philip K. Dick's widely acclaimed novel *The Man in the High Castle* (1962, see pp. 74–75), which forces us to accept as reality a world in which the U.S. lost World War II.

One of the most sophisticated uses of time travel to create alternate time streams is in Fritz Leiber's award-winning novel, *The Big Time* (1958). This novel describes the lives of temporal dimension soldiers in a battle between two civilizations that invade each other's pasts in order to make changes that will eventuate in their own present victory. Paradox piles on paradox, and the mind-boggling consequences of the intervention in the chain of cause-and-effect are so powerful that the soldiers need a place entirely out of time for rest and recuperation.

A particularly clever story based on the notion that time travel cannot change things is Robert A. Heinlein's " 'All You Zombies—' " (1960).

Although the story works itself out in complex detail, the ultimate situation is that a time traveler, who at some point in his life has also undergone a sex change, turns out to be both his own mother and his own father. Heinlein manages to create a reiterative loop in which the traveler is forced forever to go back and act out his two sexual roles so that he can exist so that he can go back and act out his two sexual roles. . . . Although science fiction has tended always to adopt the concerns and motifs of mainstream fiction, in the questioning of causation through the motif of time travel it has established a new narrative possibility which has now become the common property of our culture.

Science fiction has provided us not only with visions of time travel and hence of alternate time streams, but of whole alternate universes. The term "alternate universe" may refer simply to the universe in which history follows an alternate time stream, but more strictly speaking, it refers to a universe somehow complete and yet coexistent with ours. The simplest type of alternate universe is one in which mere physical displacement is sufficient to justify calling the universe different. In Philip José Farmer's *A Private Cosmos* (1968), for example, each "universe" is a huge world with its own culture (American Old West, feudal Germany, and so on). Instead of thinking of these as separate countries, however, they are thought of as alternate universes for two reasons: first, their arrangement as a series of world-sized horizontal discs pierced by an incredibly smooth, thick, and long central axis (Kickaha, the hero, is one of the few who have learned the trick of traveling from one to another); second, Kickaha takes on a different name and different behaviors in each universe, yet in all he occupies the same position in regard to the dominant culture: he is the violent loner who protects social values. In this use, the alternative universe is primarily a device for multiplying settings and varying adventures.

A more sophisticated and more traditional use of the alternate universe occurs in "Night Meeting," one of the story units in Ray Bradbury's composite novel, *The Martian Chronicles* (1950). The Earthmen have already landed and their diseases have already killed off the delicate and noble Martian natives; the crystal cities have been shattered and Martian music goes unheard. One strangely thoughtful nighttime, a human climbs a hill away from his loneliness and toward the sense of community he wants, which he hopes to find in the lighted city in the next valley. At the hilltop, he meets a shimmery apparition, a Martian, and he is so glad for the meeting that they stop and talk and do not hate. When the Martian asks where the human had come from, the human suddenly remembers that all the Martians had died. The human looks over his shoulder to see not a dark valley but a lighted city, the Martian's destination. He sees his own city, too, but the Martian is surprised to have it pointed out: he thought he had come from an empty valley. Bradbury is showing us here that even when men, as they so often do, wipe out the fineness and artifacts of a culture, still, the life of that culture somehow exists in a universe that coexists with our own. The Martian crystal cities are not really gone, and, when two beings meet with a common desire to bridge loneliness, the music of one universe comes through to another. The man proceeds down the hillside toward the Martian's starting place, the Martian toward the man's.

The use of the alternate universe need not be a "mere device," then, though it is often used trivially in feeble works of science fiction to provide escapes for heroes tangled in impossible situations. Overuse of this and other conventions of science fiction has resulted in parodic criticism from within the field, as in Frederic Brown's *What Mad Universe* (1948), which introduces a series of alternate universes to satirize many of the conventions of the science fiction novel. The most telling and fruitful criticism of an art form often comes from within the field. But the concept of an alternate universe is far from a toy in science fiction. It is an essential aspect of the form. Since every work of science fiction is based on some radical dislocation from present reality, the form always presents us with some sort of alternate universe, upon which airy bit of imagination the entire vision of science fiction is based.

IMAGINARY BEINGS

Unhuman beings in science fiction take either of two forms. Either they are constructs, artificial creations such as androids, robots, or golems, or they are the products of some unearthly evolution—aliens. The stories of mankind have always employed imaginary beings, devices used to dramatize many fictional concerns, from human passions, like the love-god Eros, to the forces of the world around us, like the thundergod, Thor. The majority of these, like the woman-headed lion called the Sphinx or the winged horse called Pegasus, were constructed from parts of real beings. Science fiction has rarely used such composite beings because their scientific probability is near zero. A winged horse, for example, could hardly exist on earth because animal muscle cannot utilize energy rapidly enough to lift something the size of a horse; and we know from evolutionary theory that a being like a horse is almost certain to evolve only on worlds with conditions like ours—that is, on worlds like that on which we know that horses can evolve. Nonetheless, once the evolutionary problem has been circumvented, science fiction does from time to time indulge in composite beings. In *Retief's Ransom* (1971), Keith Laumer creates the alien race of Lumbagans. Each being is constructed from a number (sometimes one, rarely more than four) of autonomous and crazily shaped parts: a seeing leg, a flying nose, and so on. Lumbagans can enter into and fall out of their cooperative identities according to the number of component parts, the one-part Lumbagan being a mindless animal. Laumer's never justified race is necessary for his satire of diplomacy, and seems to function well in this zany novel.

The science fiction world is also heavily populated with such creatures as androids (constructions or artificial growths of protoplasmic materials), robots (construction of metal and plastic), and cyborgs (constructions combining protoplasmic and mechanical parts). In *Do Androids Dream of Electric Sheep?*, for example, Philip K. Dick presents a world depopulated by war. "Andies" have been made servants or slaves, and people keep electric sheep, or even little electric spiders, so as to have some life around. The androids begin to pose as people, flee their assignments, and live in the ubiquitous ruins. The protagonist is a human, a bounty hunter of escaped androids. The only criteria for distinguishing humans from androids are psychological. Of course, as improved android brains are put into circulation, the bounty hunter's job becomes more and more of a problem. The android is a convenient slave in utopian fiction, but most science fiction authors, like Dick, use the android to explore the real limits and meaning of humanity. If androids dream of electric sheep, then aren't they really human? And if they're human, and if we've created them, then are we gods? or meddling fools? or merely ordinary people having sex by way of a test tube? The device of the android, a modern streamlining of the image of Frankenstein's monster, brings all these issues into sharper focus.

Cyborgs always serve fictionally to question what might constitute a human essence. We each remember ourselves at a younger, different stage of life. We are clearly different from the person of those memories. And yet that person is us. How can this be? This is a philosophic dilemma apparent in much contemporary literature, such as Beckett's *Molloy* and Grass's *The Tin Drum*. In Bernard Wolfe's science fiction novel *Limbo*

(1952), the refinements of atom-powered prosthetics after a devastating war lead to a whole new culture. When an atomic leg costs a great deal of money, it becomes a status symbol; when two of them allow their wearer to jump eight feet, they become clear symbols of prowess. Soon after the war, people begin voluntarily having limb amputations in order to move up to detachable artificial limbs. Someone with four artificial limbs has more prestige than anyone else. But in one revealing scene, a quad is making love to a woman (women in Wolfe's book don't go in for this particular variety of cosmetic surgery) who asks passionately if she can detach his arms and legs. With them on, he is powerful, and hence virile; with them removed, he would be deliciously at her mercy. Would he still be a man? How much may one rely on crutches, no matter how sophisticated, and still consider oneself independent? Cyborgs as fictional images always underline these questions.

Anthropomorphic, multipurpose, intelligent robots are a favorite motif of science fiction and have been since the Čapeks introduced the term to literature in the 1920s (see pp. 28–29). In having utterly capable machines, one can have, for example, a utopia built on slave labor, as in Clarke's *The City and the Stars* (1953), without meeting the moral issue of slavery. Typically, robots are treated conventionally, merely on the scene when needed (like the robot policemen in Cordwainer Smith's tales of the Underpeople); or, the conventional robot servant has his role fantastically changed (as when the domestic vacuum-cleaner robot seduces his owner in Robert Sheckley's "Can You Feel Anything When I Do This?", 1968); and occasionally the robot can achieve some sort of personhood (as in Asimov's stories, especially the detective robot in *The Caves of Steel* and its sequel *The Naked Sun*). The widespread importance of robots in science fiction comes in part from the impact of Asimov's writing and in part from the visual forcefulness of robots as images in science fiction films. In practical terms, robots are never likely to become a reality for the simple reason that it is easier and cheaper to build and maintain machines that have a specified function; certainly no one would go through the trouble of making a robot to hand wash clothes or pick up the telephone receiver—washing machines and answering devices are already adequate for these chores. The importance of robots in science fiction is not as real world prediction but as a literary device for dramatizing human problems.

Stanislaw Lem has suggested that there are four archetypal relationships between human and robot in science fiction:

a) the relationship between man and machine;
b) the relationship bewteen master and slave;
c) the relationship between man and succubus or incubus;
d) the relationship between man and transcendence (Deity, etc.)

Although Lem disparages Asimov's robots, all four of these relationships are already present in the stories of *I, Robot* (1950):

a) "Little Lost Robot" shows man struggling to deal with his machines that do, maddeningly, just exactly what he tells them to do;
b) "Robbie" depicts a governess/nursemaid robot, cast out of the family as unnatural but finally redeemed by its (her?) courageous rescue of the child;
c) "Liar!" has proper Dr. Susan Calvin languishing in romance because of the assurances falsely given her by the mindreading robot Herbie;
d) "Escape!" concerns a robot spaceship which makes interstellar travel possible by bringing its crew, unwittingly, through a temporary but real death.

Although these are the major archetypes, robots are persistently used in other ways too. For example, in Vonnegut's *Player Piano* (1952) the robotic industrial hands are images for creeping technological unemployment. No matter what their uses in science fiction, robots serve to symbolize elements of the human situation. Survey research has shown that Tobor of the *Captain Video* television series in the early fifties and Robbie of the film *Forbidden Planet* (1956) are taken, at least by the female audience, as sex symbols. Robots, though they may not walk down our streets, will continue to march through our fiction.

Doppelgänger, a German word that means literally doublegoer, has become a technical term in literary criticism. It refers to a character who is a psychic double for some other character. In science fiction this character is frequently an artificial creation, as is the case with Frankenstein's monster, who is "with him on his wedding night," because he is a personification of the overreaching and socially irresponsible aspects of Victor. Victor and the monster are Doppelgängers. The monster is raised on three books, among them *Faust*. In that work, Mephistopheles is a personification of the evil of overreaching in Faust himself; Mephistopheles and Faust are Doppelgängers. The most striking early Doppelgängers are in the stories of E. T. A. Hoffman (1776–1882) and Edgar Allan

Poe (1809–49). In the latter's "William Wilson" (1839) the title character is plagued by his apparent twin, also named William Wilson, who always appears to counsel morality at crucial junctures in the protagonist's life. Wilson finally kills his Doppelgänger conscience, only to realize that, morally at least, he has killed himself. Doppelgängers, whether ghostly or not, may always be thought of as two psychic aspects of a single character, objectified for dramatic clarification. Science fiction has provided the most pointed imagery of all for this internal conflict in the torments of Robert Louis Stevenson's *Dr. Jekyll and Mr. Hyde* (1886).

An older and equally potent image of the Doppelgänger is the Golem, a man-made creature of Jewish mystic lore dating, according to *Talmud,* from ancient times. The modern version of the legend has Rabbi Judah Loew ben Bezabel of Prague in the fifteenth century create the animated clay slave to protect the Jewish community. This story was made popular in the twentieth century by Gustav Meyrink's 1915 novel, *Der Golem,* and by a series of films written, directed, and acted by Paul Wegener, beginning with *Der Golem* in 1914. Between the book and the films, most of the conventions of man-made creature stories were established: the creator with good intent who loses control over his creation; the creation who meets a woman and thence meets his doom; the misguided creator; the creation falling into the power of some ignorant novice or assistant; and even the creation as guardian of and then threat to his creator's daughter. Although the Golem, mystically called into life by a holy man who knows the proper incantations and who can inscribe the proper word on the clay statue's forehead, is clearly related to both Mephistopheles and Frankenstein's monster, it is a separate and probably more ancient strain of legend which has had, especially in films, enormous impact on science fiction. For example, the conventional scene of the monster hesitantly and lovingly approaching a child who seems so frail and beautiful beside him (popularized in this country by Boris Karloff in *Frankenstein*) was first filmed by Wegener in a 1920 Golem movie. The roots of science fiction, like the roots of science itself, are in magic and mythology.

Robert Plank (see Bibliography) suggests that all these creatures exist in order to help readers deal fictionally with Oedipal fantasies. Although some imaginary beings, like Burroughs's Martian dog-things called calots, clearly do not serve that function, a surprisingly large number of science fiction's imaginary beings do serve such ends, like Stapledon's intelligent dog Sirius in the novel of that name (1944) and Roger

Zelazny's talking German shepherd Sigmund in *The Dream Master* (1966). Sigmund Freud first made us explicitly aware of the far-ranging importance of the Oedipal myth. For fictional purposes, we need remember primarily that the myth gives one view of the conflict between father and son for sexual access to the mother, who serves primarily as a sex object. In fiction, this can be worked out in two major ways: the son can succeed in *supplanting* the father, thus either creating a new society if the father deserved supplanting, as in Clarke's *Childhood's End*, or creating tragedy if the father's strictures should have been heeded, as in the original *Oedipus* plays of Sophocles or in *Frankenstein;* or the son can undergo *education* by the father and finally earn sexual access to a female, as in Heinlein's *The Puppet Masters* in which Mary, Sam's ultimate prize, is described by Sam's father and leader, the "Old Man," as "much like" Sam's dead mother.

As Plank outlines it, the frequently used plot—and this is obvious especially in sf movies of the fifties—has an old scientist who has no wife but has a daughter/niece/secretary. Something the scientist has done usually triggers the creation of a mutant by atomic radiation (*Them*) or the thawing out of a monster (*The Thing*). A young man, no family relation, enters the scene and does, from a nonscientific viewpoint, what needs to be done to quell the threat (tracks the beast back to its lair in *Quatermass and the Pit* or delivers the final death blow at great risk of life, as in electrocuting *The Creeping Unknown*). The story ends with the hero's arm around the girl as they watch the bubbles rise from Tokyo Bay (as in *Godzilla*). By distributing the sexual object into two figures, the father figure's (usually dead) wife and the hero's potential mate, science fiction defuses the Oedipal myth by removing the possibility of incest. Hence, science fiction tends not toward the tragic outcome but toward the orderly continuation of the world that the father figure and the hero share.

The archetype for this story is Shakespeare's *The Tempest,* in which the magician father Prospero forces young Ferdinand to undergo tests in order to win the hand of Prospero's daughter Miranda. Once these tests are passed, not only is sexual access conferred, but Prospero abjures his magic and resolves to return to the kingship of Milan where he will bind society together and at his death pass the kingdom on to Ferdinand. Science fiction typically reduces the tension inherent in this story by separating the Prospero figure's testing and protecting roles. Again in *The Puppet Masters,* the Old Man is explicitly called a "puppet master" by Sam, but the father rejects the title and points instead to the alien slugs who literally take over people's minds. The protecting function primarily inheres in the father, Andrew Nivens, while the testing function inheres in the aliens. Plank suggests that in *The War of the Worlds,* for example, the Martians are all-powerful figures who test us and keep us in line, as a father would, and our continued existence results only from a fluke— their susceptibility to disease—not from any action by mankind. Hence, the imaginary being reminds us of our ambivalences toward our father figures, those who stand for the rules of society which, as we are growing up, we question.

Although this correspondence between the occurrence of imaginary beings and the functioning of the Oedipal myth is hardly universal, it is frequently present in science fiction. Thinking of the family structure of *The Tempest* or of the emotional conflicts dramatized by the story of Oedipus is often the most expeditious way to gain insight into the psychological functioning of a science fiction story.

SEX AND RACE IN SCIENCE FICTION

Although the Oedipus myth permeates science fiction, and although that myth uses sexual symbols, graphic depiction of sex is rare in science fiction, though at one remove from the literal such items as ray guns and spaceships may well function as phallic symbols. Until recently, most science fiction was written for men; the women in the stories served only as prizes awarded off stage—so much so that one used to encounter the truism that "There is no sex in science fiction." Like many widely believed truisms, however, this notion is not true. As we have seen in the work of Burroughs, sex frequently lurked in the background, half-clad. Since the real action of stories like Heinlein's *Starship Troopers* concerned the ideals that the male protagonists fought for, the sexual object was frequently won, but never explicitly used. In continuously running stories, like Buck Rogers, the title hero could have an on-again-off-again-and-never-touch romance with a heroine like Wilma that lasted for years; Superman and Lois Lane, after all, don't make it. But the sexual attractions between the male and female characters are strong motivations in science fiction and go back at least to the monster's prophecy to Victor Frankenstein that "I will be with you on your wedding night." By killing Victor's bride, as Victor has done to his, the monster established the typically failed sexuality of science fiction.

Philip José Farmer was a pioneer in changing this situation. In *The Lovers* (1952), he presented a marriage, complete with sex, between a human and an apparent human. The extraterrestrial wife turns out to be a kind of insect who literally dies in childbirth for love of her human husband and he, in turn, decides not to return to Earth but to raise his children—who are best described as maggots. With great skill, Farmer makes this potentially repulsive story into a moving study of the development of love.

More common than such bizarre relationships, however, are sexual liaisons between humans from widely different worlds or cultures, usually introduced as a dramatization of psychological relationships, as in the efforts of Rydra Wong to help the Butcher develop a sense of self in Delany's *Babel-17*. A beautiful example of this is the frustrated attraction that the ambisexual Estraven feels for his male companion Genly Ai, when Estraven goes into the sexual cycle of "kemmer" in Le Guin's *The Left Hand of Darkness* (see pp. 226–230). Indeed, as Anne McCaffrey has pointed out, with the recent influx of female science fiction writers like herself and Joanna Russ, sex is becoming more prominent in this genre.

Sex has a place in science fiction, though outlets like the Science Fiction Book Club still feel obliged to warn potential buyers that some works contain language and descriptions that may be found offensive. Nonetheless, few writers have taken up Farmer's exploration of new types of sexuality. Farmer himself, in such novels as *Flesh* (1960)—in which an astronaut returns to an America dominated by a fertility cult— uses comparatively normal heterosexuality for character motivation and shock appeal. This is in keeping with the recent trend in all literature toward a more explicit presentation of sex. Those who come in from the mainstream, like Fred Mustard Stewart (*The Methuselah Enzyme*, 1970, and *Star Child*, 1974), often bring sex in with them. Those who are just now starting out in science fiction, like William Hjortsberg and Barry Malzberg, *begin* by assuming that their characters can indulge in graphically described sex. In both these cases, however, the scenes are usually imagined by the characters rather than acted out, revealing perhaps the last vestiges of both of the old taboo and of American science fictions' debt to adolescent fantasy.

John W. Campbell, that extraordinarily important editor who controlled the development of the writing careers of most of the science fiction authors who emerged in the Golden Age, wanted no sex in the stories he published. This prudery seemed to work out well with an audience of adolescent males in an age dominated by America's self-concept as the world-wide champion of virtue, sexual as well as political. But as Campbell's notion of virtue has lost ground, science fiction has changed. Harlan Ellison is especially notable in this regard for his shocking uses of sex. In "A Boy and His Dog" (1969), for example, the main character is a marauding teen-ager in a postatomic world. He is lured into the subterranean world of those who took to the bomb shelters by a female teen-ager barely repressing her nymphomania. The underworld is growing sterile and wants the vitality of the upper world—but fears it. The underdwellers are true heirs to the culture of the suburban fifties. Once the boy realizes he is a captive rather than a guest, he attempts escape. In order to gain crucial seconds at a key moment, he arranges his now-willing girl on the bed with her shirt hiked up, her undergarments removed, and her legs spread, knees lifted toward the door. Then he invites in the girl's father, who is appropriately shocked— and then bludgeoned by the boy. The girl is fully cooperative. This brutal use of sex, typical of Ellison, reflects a post-Viet Nam bluntness and disillusion with normal relations and normal rules of propriety. Although Ellison is as rare in his way as Farmer is in his, Ellison's style is so smooth and his stories often so effective that he is influencing many yet younger writers.

Some might argue that Ellison's savagery shows the wisdom of Campbell's prudery, but this does not really follow. Under Campbell's auspices a book like Alexei Panshin's *Rite of Passage* would not have been published. This is a first person narrative of the trials and maturing of Mia Havero, young citizen of a traveling spaceship of scientists and technologists—and artists as well—who live off their commerce with colony worlds from whom they keep their knowledge. The main rite of passage, by which Mia becomes a young woman in her society (and able to question its values) is a survival test: she, and all others of her age, are dropped separately on a planet full of resentful colonists and given the single mission of survival. During this ordeal Mia rescues Jimmy Dentremont, the boy the ship's geneticist has destined for her. In the huddled last few days before they are retrieved by the ship's spacecraft, their teasing relationship achieves a new maturity. One of the many rites of passage in this novel is the explicit mutual loss of Mia's and Jimmy's virginity, a scene handled with insight and tenderness. Campbell's taboo, though it surely prevented some gratuitous grossness, also stifled a legitimate aspect of science fiction.

If science fiction has been a bit belated in according sexual relations their due, the form has been a bit advanced in its treatment of race and race relations. The xenophobia that created alien races in the image of Bug-Eyed Monsters had already begun to yield in the thirties to more hospitable notions of foreignness. On the popular fringes of the form, of course, when it was fashionable to think of the "Yellow Peril," the villains in series like *Flash Gordon* could be expected to have a Mongolian appearance. But because of their orientation toward the future science fiction writers frequently assumed that America's major problem in this area—black/white relations—would improve or even wither away. One of the few black writers of science fiction, Samuel R. Delany, has recorded the shock of pleasure he received as a boy reading Heinlein's *Starship Troopers,* when halfway through the book the hero looks into a mirror and his black face looks back at him. In the book, this is not remarkable in any way, and many readers are probably not even clearly aware that the hero is black. In *Starship Troopers,* of course, the xenophobia is transferred to the enemy—a race called "Bugs."

The presence of unhuman races, aliens, and robots, certainly makes the differences between human races seem appropriately trivial, and one of the achievements of science fiction has been its emphasis on just this feature of human existence. But science fiction writers, like many others, have been guilty of occasional thoughtless stereotyping according to the patterns of familiar racism. In Asimov's *I, Robot,* for example, a number of characters who have to deal with intelligent robots indicate their own inherent sense of superiority by calling the machines "boys." More frequently however, post-World War II science fiction, when it does make race a conscious issue, takes a firm stand along the political lines that have popularly been called "liberal." In Bradbury's *Martian Chronicles,* the section entitled "Way in the Middle of the Air" describes a black emigration from the American South to a new free land on Mars. As the sympathetically portrayed blacks slowly make their way toward the waiting rockets, the whites they pass jibe at them from their porches and among themselves express at first anger and then a kind of sour-grapes resignation. It is quite clear that Bradbury wants us to see the emigration to a new land through technology as a long overdue liberation. Notwithstanding, the blacks are mutually supportive and shambling folk while the Southerners are essentially impotent rednecks. Here the "liberal" approach to race still depends largely on stereotypes for its own expression.

A fundamental attack against racial stereotyping is accomplished by science fiction in a subtler way. In William Hjortsberg's *Gray Matters* (1971), for example, the aggressive hero who breaks out of the mind-shaping hive and succeeds in fooling the machines into putting his brain into a perfect body chooses as his body that of a "Tropique." Because we identify with that character, we lose our sense of his "race" as anything special. This is similar to Heinlein's use of a black protagonist in *Starship Troopers,* but goes a step further, since the brain in this case chooses the black body deliberately, because it is beautiful. Much earlier Stapledon had used a similar device of racial shifting of interest and concern in *Last and First Men,* by making the final colony of humans a nonwhite race. And more recently Le Guin's protagonist in *The Left Hand of Darkness,* and the only major character who is a human being of our own sort, is described as dark skinned and flat-nosed. This tacit attack on racial stereotyping, responsive to philosophic commitments that go back at least to Mary Shelley, has allowed science fiction to get beyond even "liberal" attitudes, to make stereotyping itself an obsolete device and the matter of race comparatively unimportant. Science fiction, in fact has taken the question so spiritedly debated by the founding fathers of the United States—of whether the rights of man included black slaves as well as white slave-owners—and raised it to a higher power by asking whether the rights of being end at the boundaries of the human race. The answers have ranged from the most xenophobic human racism to the most transcendent worship of being itself—but the important thing is that the questions have been raised and are continuing to be raised by works of science fiction.

5. TEN REPRESENTATIVE NOVELS

HAT MAKES THE vision of science fiction unique is the way it is embodied in specific narrative texts. All of its philosophical concepts and its scientific or pseudoscientific notions may be discussed as pure abstractions, Wittgensteinian word games or Einsteinian thought experiments. What is essential to science fiction is the enactment of these games or experiments in fictional form. Thus it is appropriate to complete this study of science fiction by concentrating on a handful—or two handsful—of specific science fiction novels that illustrate something of the range covered by the form. In selecting our ten works we have aimed at historical range as well as at some breadth of form and vision.

We have tried to select works of "literary merit," such as might be studied in a historical survey of science fiction, but we have not intended to pick the "ten best" works of science fiction ever written. The criteria are too many and too various to allow that. But these ten works do embody the values of science fiction and illustrate the range of problems, issues, and techniques that have animated this form of literature over the past century and a half. Of the ten, two were written by women and eight by men; two by continental Europeans and eight by English-speaking writers. Of these last eight, only two are Americans, but the two most recent British writers have been considerably Americanized. The form itself, as our brief history above indicated, has been international, with an early British influence and a recent American dominance, as American technology and its attendant problems have influenced the field so strongly, and the American publishing industry has provided the best market for this kind of fiction.

Every work discussed here shows the marks of its own time, the values and concerns of its particular era. And taken as a whole, these works illustrate a great search for values. When a human being in *Frankenstein* assumes the god-like power of creation, the question of values and their source arises. All ten of these novels are concerned with such questions. They are all works of practical and speculative philosophy, using the unique potential of fiction as a way of searching for ethical principles in concrete situations. Above all else, science fiction has used its special vision and its unique knowledge to trace the history of human power over nature and to ask how that power ought to function. In the ten works represented here, from the hardware of Verne to the fantasy of Lindsay, from the politics of Zamyatin to the philosophy of Stapledon, that question is never ignored. And in the more recent works it becomes increasingly insistent. For a century and a half, science fiction has been making a serious and dedicated effort to create a modern conscience for the human race.

FRANKENSTEIN, OR THE MODERN PROMETHEUS (1818)

When Mary Wollstonecraft Godwin Shelley (1797–1851) published *Frankenstein* in 1818, she was presenting the world with a story she hoped

> would speak to the mysterious fears of our nature, and awaken thrilling horror—one to make the reader dread to look round, to curdle the blood, and quicken the beatings of the heart. (Intro., 1831 edition)

Despite some deficiencies of literary polish, she succeeded completely. The image of the monster, patched together out of charnel waste and wreaking his vengeance on mankind, has haunted readers and moviegoers ever since. Indeed, the Edison Company's 1910 version of *Frankenstein* was among the first narrative films ever made. Unfortunately, that image of monstrous terror with which cinema has made us so familiar is only the smallest part of a powerful and complex work, a literary work which receives too little attention because of our familiarity with its often bastardized movie adaptations.

Frankenstein himself, of course, is not the monster at all, but Victor Frankenstein, the medical student who becomes so carried away with his research that he metamorphoses into a potent archetype of the mad scientist. By making the main character a scientist, and by making his scientific efforts a focus of our attention, Mary Shelley not only produced a thriller, but changed the literary possibilities of the future. Up until her time, the great English works of horror had fallen into the Gothic tradition, so called after Horace Walpole's immensely popular *The Castle of Otranto, A Gothic Story* (1764) which chilled readers with preternatural killings and subterranean passageways through the crumbling Italian castle. With William Beckford's *Vathek, An Arabian Tale* (1786), the Gothic tradition gained an Oriental potentiality and absorbed the imaginative possibilities so powerfully displayed in *The Arabian Nights*. To this, Ann Radcliffe added a new twist in such works as *The Mysteries of Udolpho* (1794) in which the body of the novel fascinates the reader with apparently supernatural goings on and the ending presents yet a further turn of the screw: an astounding naturalistic explanation is used to demystify the supernatural—while astonishing the reader at the book's ingenuity. Mary Shelley made a further and decisive step in this development, and from her treatment of the Gothic novel, science fiction emerged: instead of astonishing her reader with a *final* explanation, she *began* her work by creating the context in which the fantastic was made plausible.

Frankenstein begins with an author's Preface (actually ghost-written by her husband Percy Bysshe Shelley) which itself begins with this paragraph:

> The event on which this fiction is founded has been supposed, by Dr. [Erasmus] Darwin, and some of the physiological writers of Germany, as not of impossible occurrence. . . . in assuming it as the basis of a work of fancy, I have not considered myself as merely weaving a series of supernatural terrors. The event on which the interest of the story depends is exempt from the disadvantages of a mere tale of spectres or enchantment. It was recommended by the novelty of the situations which it develops; and, however impossible as a physical fact, affords a point of view to the imagination for the delineating of human passions more comprehensive and commanding than any which the ordinary relations of existing events can yield.

The Shelleys are claiming here that the fantastic is made plausible by *science;* and further, even if that claim is rejected, the *fiction* has value by providing thrills (high adventure) and insight into human behavior (intellectual excitement) illuminated by a uniquely potent "new light." Thus, we have *science fiction.*

The story of this novel is comparatively complex, however its major features deserve to be recalled. Victor Frankenstein, young science student, goes off from his home in Geneva to study at the University of Ingolstadt. There he undergoes a rebirth, realizing that the learning he had acquired from ancient books is false and that modern science offers truer and more efficacious insights. He soon surpasses his teachers and concocts Pygmalion's classic project of creating life. His motivation is twofold: he wishes to pursue science passionately for its own sake (a dangerous thing, it seems), and he desires, by his experimenting, to acquire knowledge that will improve the human stock (presumably a good thing). His creation, of course, is hideously ugly: he sees it move and runs from the laboratory in horror. When he returns, the monster is already gone. The monster, "born" innocent but with superhuman potentiality of both mind and body, leaves the laboratory and undergoes his own development.

The monster's biography is a dramatization of Rousseau's notion of the Noble Savage uncorrupted by civilized man. The monster's own recollections are a literary *tour de force:*

> "It was dark when I [first] awoke; I felt cold also, and half-frightened, as it were instinctively, finding myself so desolate." (Ch. 11)

We see him as intelligent but unprejudiced by civilization:

> "I heard of the discovery of the American hemisphere, and wept . . . over the hapless fate of its original inhabitants." (Ch. 13)

Untaught by educated man, the monster feels a general good will.

> If any being felt emotions of benevolence towards me, I should return them an hundred and an hundred fold; for that one creature's sake, I would make peace with the whole kind! (Ch. 17)

But mankind never does show the monster benevolence because it cannot see the nobility beneath the horrid exterior. People mindlessly attack the creature, once shooting and wounding him at the very moment he saves a child from drowning. Victor's creation is the first of all those science fiction aliens upon whom Earthmen fire weapons without giving them a chance to talk (as in Clifford D. Simak's *Way Station,* 1963) and he is also the first of all those mutants (like Jommy Cross in van Vogt's *Slan*) who are really superior to the people of the dominant culture, but are rejected by them merely for being different. Such an archetype of the maligned outsider clearly has a continuing appeal to adolescents who may be struggling to reconcile their own sense of worth with the strictures of society. Today this archetype is especially significant for a world that seems to mindlessly steamroller so many of us. The monster responds to this rejection not by postulating his own corruption through Original Sin but by placing the blame squarely on factors outside himself:

> "Accursed creator!" [he yells at Victor] "Why did you form a monster so hideous that even *you* turned from me in disgust?" (Ch. 15)

The monster tries to get Frankenstein to create a bride to end his isolation and promises that he will take his bride away from human habitation. But Victor refuses for numerous reasons, and in the course of trying to force Victor's cooperation, the monster finally begins to prey upon his creator's family and friends. Ultimately Victor pledges to destroy his creation who then intentionally leads him on an ever more desolate chase. Eventually, forced to cross the frozen Arctic, Victor is mortally exhausted, but by luck encounters the ice-bound ship of would-be explorer Robert Walton. It is on this ship that the story is told and to this ship the monster comes, just in time to see Victor die and to shed his own tears for the only person who gave him a sense of place in the world, however slight. The monster then flees to the north. Nothing but death remains.

By her manner of narration, Shelley multiplies the power of the Noble Savage theme to explore the "human passions" of the outcast. Although the summary we have just had gives the events in their chronological order, they are not found in that order in the book. The novel, after the Preface, opens with the letters of Robert Walton to his sister in England. Walton is a seeker after knowledge; he wants to reach the North Pole.

> I may there discover the wondrous power which attracts the needle; and may regulate a thousand celestial observations . . . I shall satiate my ardent curiosity with the sight of a part of the world never before visited, and may tread a land never before imprinted by the foot of man. These are my enticements, and they are sufficient to conquer all fear of danger or death . . . you cannot contest the inestimable benefit which I shall confer on all mankind to the last generation, by discovering a passage near the pole . . . (Letter 1)

This proclamation is designed to arouse an ambivalence in the reader: science may indeed help man, but the prideful seeking after knowledge is dangerous. As bad movies have put it so many times, "There are some things man was not meant to know."

This ambivalence toward knowledge and the beneficial/malignant seeker is, of course, the Faustian theme. Stories which attached themselves to the name of Johann Faust (1488–1541), a wandering German conjurer, eventually came to express this ambivalence, a problematic attitude found so often in science fiction and so timely today as technology becomes ever more unwieldy. Both Victor and Robert are Faust figures; the former, just like Marlowe's Doctor Faustus, exclaims that "so much has been done . . . more, far more, will I achieve." And just as Faustus conjured his Doppelgänger Mephistopheles and yet was damned by him, so the monster can say to Victor, "You are my creator, but I am your master;—obey!" Victor, like Robert, will seek knowledge at any cost. When he first tries to justify his behavior, Victor says, "One man's life or death were but a small price to pay for the acquirement of the knowledge which I sought."

Once Victor is on the ship, the book presents Robert's transcript of his conversations with his patient and guest. Victor's narrative has embedded within it the monster's own history, a tale told Victor by his monster on the glacier at Chamonix by way of pleading for a bride. And within the monster's narrative there is the story of the occurrences at the DeLacey cottage, in the shed of which the monster secretly lived. There the demon observed a family and overheard their history, how the boy Felix had risked all to save his Arab love Safie and her family and how her father betrayed him. So at the heart of this science fiction, we find an exemplum of human duplicity, of the falseness of the civilized spirit.

After the tale of the DeLaceys the novel unfolds, first finishing the monster's tale of his own mistreatment by mankind in general and his creator in particular, then finishing Victor's tale of scientific excess and moral irresponsibility, and finally returning us, through Robert's last letters, to the ship for the final confrontation between the two Faustians and the monster. To the last, Shelley writes so as to keep before us not the simple good or bad of science, but the morally paralyzing ambivalence it creates. Victor's last words before he dies begin as advice to Robert, but end quite differently:

> "Farewell, Walton! Seek happiness in tranquillity and avoid ambition, even if it be only the apparently innocent one of distinguishing yourself in science and discoveries. Yet why do I say this? I have myself been blasted in these hopes, yet another may succeed." (Ch. 24)

The monster is then accused of heartlessness by Walton, but answers that he had no one else but Victor to get help from, and he had been created to need love. For that very reason, even as a murderer, he mourned deeply each of his vicitms, especially Victor. The monster flees, perhaps to die, and Robert turns his ship back. However, he retreats from exploration not as a matter of principle, but because his crew, oppressed by the Arctic conditions, resorts to mutiny. Thus, by encountering the book's events through its many narrators, we find not the simple notion of a rampant evil monster created by science, but rather the disturbing presentation of two continuing human problems: Shall one seek knowledge that will change one's world? Does civilization corrupt the human animal which otherwise would be good? The image that stays in our minds is of the monster, the product of excessive science, but the book is fundamentally about its title character, Frankenstein, a man who, through the more timid Walton, shares a humanity with us.

With the multiplication of technology in the nineteenth century, the problem of knowledge became the problem of science; with the growth of colonialism in the nineteenth century, the problem of the Noble Savage became the problem of the outsider and the outcast. Mary Shelley in *Frankenstein* spoke movingly to those issues and simultaneously created the seminal work of the new literary genre of science fiction.

20,000 LEAGUES UNDER THE SEA (1870)

Jules Verne (1828–1905) is one of the acknowledged fathers of science fiction, and there is much merit in the work of this widely read author. Unfortunately, a too serious reading of his works also serves as a key in claiming qualities for science fiction which it rarely possesses. We should first dispose of these misconceptions in order better to be able to see the contributions Verne made to the genre.

Popularly, a defense of science fiction is often made on two grounds: first, that good science fiction is written in accurate accord with its contemporary science fact; and second, that science fiction has had extraordinary success in predicting the actual development of science. While science fiction is often in accord with science fact, and while many gadgets were described in science fiction before they functioned in fact (incandescent lighting, for instance, illuminates Verne's *Nautilus* nine years before Edison's patent was granted), it remains truer to say that science fiction tends to recognize the science fact of its time and use—or abuse—that fact for primarily fictional purposes. In *From the Earth to the Moon* (1865), for example, Verne has his ballistic spaceship fired from a nine hundred foot deep hole in the environs of the fictional Stone Hill, Florida. Verne knew perfectly well that a hole of that depth anywhere in Florida would be under water; his straight-faced show of scientific accuracy ironically masked a satire on American ingenuity. In *Purchase of the North Pole* (1889), some amateur scientists conspire to change the Earth's axis by explosives, thus melting the polar ice cap and making accessible vast mineral wealth. Verne chose to ignore what he knew perfectly well—that the experiment would as likely devastate all coastal cities as it would free the ice-bound land masses—not for the purpose of satire but for the simpler joy of working out the problem of axis-shifting, and the consequences be damned! Verne's work really supports the claim that much science fiction displays a heartily unscientific exuberance for apparently scientific adventure.

The great claim made for *20,000 Leagues Under the Sea* is that Nemo's *Nautilus* accurately predicts the development of the submarine. Without meaning to detract from such inventive detail as electric lighting, chemical oxygen production, seaweed cigars, and so on, one should note that David Bushnell, who coined the term "submarine," first successfully tested his *Turtle* in 1775; Robert Fulton demonstrated a functional steam submarine in the Seine in 1807 (this ship, incidentally, was named *Nautilus*); and the Confederate States of America, in 1864, successfully used the nine-man submarine *Huntley* to sink the United States frigate *Housatonic.* Verne doubtless knew all this. But for Verne, the thought not of a primitive submarine (the *Huntley*'s crew all perished before they could return to port) but of a fully developed machine roaming the deeps of the world called forth every trick of his fictional trade.

20,000 Leagues Under the Sea is the first person narrative of professor and naturalist Pierre Aronnax. When the book opens, he and his comically faithful servant Conseil have joined the American frigate *Abraham Lincoln* in the pursuit of some "thing" that is endangering the shipping of the world. Its speed and strength make it utterly fantastic and Aronnax gives a lengthy discussion of possible explanations. He discards submarines first, for they would be, he claims, technically impossible; he discards certain superstitious imaginings; and finally,

> since all other theories must be rejected, one is forced to admit the existence of some marine animal of extraordinary power. (Ch. 2)

The creature, of course, turns out to be an undersea ship after all. In the light of Aronnax's discussion, many modern readers assume that Verne was *predicting* the submarine. In fact, Verne was creating the fictional context, fully against the facts of contemporary science, that would give the submarine the thrill of the fantastic—and then he uses much of the rest of the book to make this fantastic plausible. Whereas Mary Shelley created science fiction, urged on by a disturbing ambivalence toward science, Verne made science fiction popular by demonstrating a boundless enthusiasm for science.

Aronnax and Conseil, and a practical-minded Canadian harpooner named Ned Land, are tossed into the water when the "creature" rams the *Abraham Lincoln*. They are rescued by Captain Nemo and introduced to his submarine, the *Nautilus*. The vast body of the book consists of unconnected episodes, about half of which glory in scientific detail for its own sake (describing the fish outside the view port, the shells in Nemo's collection, the workings of an electric harpoon), and the remainder of which use the science fictional situation to present astounding adventures (a passage through a secret undersea river connecting the Red Sea and the Mediterranean, a trip to the inside of a submerged volcano, a fight against giant squids). There is some serious attempt to explore "human passions" through the character of the misanthropic Nemo (" 'It isn't new continents the earth needs, but new men!' ") and Ned Land's constant desire to escape the Captain, but this exploration is lost in the enthusiastic and playful wealth of scientific detail.

In Aronnax's narrative, this enthusiasm leads to a rich multiplication of the sound of science, a frequent gentle humor, and—unfortunately—an often tedious longwindedness. The flavor of this combination can only be appreciated by a glance at the text. In the following extract, Aronnax has already "proved" that the "thing" must be a creature rather than a submarine; now he is explaining to Ned that

". . . it must be built in some incredibly powerful way."

"Why?" Ned asked.

"Because incalculable strength is needed to stay at great depths and withstand the pressure there."

"Really?" said Ned, blinking.

"Yes, and I could give you some figures to prove it easily."

"Oh, figures!" answered Ned. "You can make figures do whatever you want."

"Perhaps in business, Ned, but not in mathematics. Now listen. The pressure of one atmosphere is represented by a column of water thirty-two feet high. In actual fact, the column of water would not be that high, because here we're dealing with sea water which has a greater density than fresh water. Well now, Ned, when you dive down into the sea, for every thirty-two feet of water between you and the surface, your body is supporting an additional pressure of one atmosphere, or in other words of 14.7 pounds per square inch of surface. It follows that at 320 feet this pressure is equal to ten atmospheres, a hundred atmospheres at 3200 feet, and a thousand atmospheres at 32,000 feet or about six miles. This is the same as saying that if you could reach such a depth in the ocean, your body would undergo a pressure of 14,700 pounds per square inch. Now, Ned, do you know how many square inches there are on the surface of your body?"

"I have no idea, Monsieur Aronnax."

"About two thousand six hundred."

"That many?" (Ch. 4)

Such writing would be intolerable were one not delighted by the calculations offered to prove a point "incalculable," the off-hand jibes at "business," and the incredulity of Ned. In addition, underlying this whole speech (it goes on for another page), is the suspicion, which Verne could expect in his contemporaries, that the thing would indeed turn out to be a submarine. Thus, we see a humor satirically directed against the scientist himself when the exchange ends:

"So you can see how strong their bone structure and body would have to be in order to resist such pressure!"

"They must be built," answered Ned Land, "with steel plates eight inches thick, like armored frigates."

And indeed, that is just how the *Nautilus* is built.

In Verne's novel we find science fiction, despite a playful poking fun at the scientist, offering scientific adventure with an enthusiasm that borders on the obsessive. Though humor is perhaps Verne's stylistic strongpoint, one cannot forget the images of the giant cultured pearl worth two million dollars, the valley of lost ships whence Nemo acquires his gold, the underwater coral burying ground, or the visit to dead Atlantis. Nemo is perhaps memorable in his melancholy misanthropy, his secret support of revolutionaries, and his missionary preaching for the protection of the ecology of the sea; but the overall story intended to tie the episodes together is really not memorable at all. The escape of Aronnax, Conseil, and Ned Land occurs, conveniently, when the Professor is unconscious, so Verne is not put upon to invent a means whereby these ordinary men could evade the extraordinary Nemo, nor must Verne explore the necessarily dramatic final meeting of the two men. Instead, he falls back on editorial omission, a literary device which had already been used by his idol Poe in *The Narrative of Arthur Gordon Pym* (1838), and merely wraps up the story. Yet, of all the books of this enormously popular author, *20,000 Leagues Under the Sea* was the most popular of all. While Mary Shelley had dramatized the ambivalence toward science, Verne had shown that one could embrace it for its own sake; while Mary Shelley had agonized over the problem of the outsider in a colonial century, Verne had created Nemo, made rich by science, to support the oppressed. Where science fiction had come to Verne as a fledgling genre struggling with ambivalence, he left it a widely read art form capable of expressing the enthusiasms of a scientific age.

THE TIME MACHINE (1895)

H. G. Wells's short novel *The Time Machine* is narrated by an unnamed guest at the home of the Time Traveller, an inventor known to us by no other name. The scientific context is established immediately by the after-dinner debate about the physical nature of time. The Time Traveller asserts that

> *There is no difference between Time and any of the three dimensions of Space except that our consciousness moves along it.* (Ch. 1)

This single fantastic assumption, made plausible by the dinner table argument and the demonstration of a small working model of a time machine, is used to justify the Time Traveller's voyaging to the future. Other authors, like Washington Irving in "Rip Van Winkle," had created characters who *slept* their way into the future; some, like Edward Bellamy in *Looking Backward,* had tried to justify this protracted sleep by appealing to scientific sounding notions of extended Mesmerism and chemically preservative gases. But Wells was the first to conceive of the time *machine,* and this device is the key to the effectiveness of the tale. The Time Traveller enters his own dining hall a bit late for the habitual meal in the week following the demonstration of the model and declares to his reconvened guests that " 'I was in my laboratory at four o'clock, and since then . . . I've lived eight days.' " Because the machine has allowed him to return (almost exactly to the time he left), Wells has every reason to have the Time Traveller not merely undergo future experiences, but report them to and defend them against the typically Victorian minds of his guests. Except for interjections by those guests, almost the entire remainder of the book is the Time Traveller's tale.

After a vivid description of the gray blur of alternating nights and days, the Time Traveller arrives in 802,701 A.D. and discovers there what at first appears to be an ideal, almost Edenic environment: "the whole earth had become a garden." The inhabitants of this world turn out to be the Eloi, a race of delicate, slight, fruit-eating people who live in utter tranquility with each other. Gradually, however, it becomes clear that this tranquility arises not from ethical perfection or moral restraint but from enervation. Indeed, the Time Traveller at one point observes one of a party of Eloi drowning and finally performs the rescue himself when it becomes clear that these dull specimens will not even glance toward the impending disaster. The saved character is named Weena, a typically stupid, child-like Eloi with a typically short attention span; untypically, perhaps vaguely recognizing the Time Traveller as a personal savior, she attaches herself to him with the closest thing the future has to offer by way of personal affection, a thoughtless, nearly canine, barely sexual fidelity. As a mark of this, just before the Time Traveller leaves her epoch, she gives him two flowers which figure importantly later in the book.

Where did the Eloi come from? They came, or will come, the Time Traveller realizes, from us: they are our children. The evidence of decaying machines and once-imposing architecture leads him to presume that technology had been refined and that that refinement had led to a change in man through the normal process of evolution.

> What, unless biological science is a mass of errors, is the cause of human intelligence and vigour? Hardship and freedom: conditions under which the active, strong, and subtle survive and the weaker go to the wall . . . I thought of the physical slightness of the people, their lack of intelligence, and those big abundant ruins, and it strengthened my belief in a perfect conquest of Nature. For after the battle comes Quiet. Humanity had been strong, energetic, and intelligent, and had used all its abundant vitality to alter the conditions under which it lived. And now came the reaction of the altered conditions. (Ch. 4)

But the Time Traveller has so far seen only part of man's situation. Were Wells's novel merely a fictional prediction of our future degeneration it would not speak to us as movingly as it does. What Wells added was his own version of the Socialist vision. As early as Benjamin Disraeli's novel *Sybil, or the Two Nations* (1845), fiction had presented the Rich and the Poor as utterly separated. In the world of 802,701 A.D., the degenerate Eloi are not alone: at night, creeping from the bowels of underground tunnels where they live, come the Morlocks, pallid, compulsive mechanics who feed on the weak and sleeping Eloi. Wells's Time Traveller comes to realize that the separation of classes in his own time had led to a separation of environments as the mechanical class stayed with its underground machines while the leisure class frolicked above: this separation of environments had led in turn to separate evolutions; and by this date "Man . . . had differentiated into two distinct animals." To the extent that the Morlocks are mindless, they have been brutalized by the Eloi—or their ancestors in Victorian England; but to the extent that they victimize the Eloi, the workers represent a base threat to what had once been gracious in human existence. The attitude of the book is complex: by virtue of their harmlessness, the Eloi elicit our sympathy, but by virtue of their vestigial aptitudes for solving at least mechanical problems, the Morlocks possess in greater measure that self-reliance on which mankind has prided itself. Clearly neither alternative is acceptable, and the book becomes a potent plea for the whole man, warning against the fragmentation of function and the isolation of class which the progressively mechanizing society of England was supporting.

A definition of science fiction held by some purists calls for the creation of a narrative world by making a single alteration of the known world and then logically extrapolating the consequences of that change, projecting that change into the future or into some new society. On the very first page of the novel, Wells's narrating guest mentions the inventor's special dining chairs which "embraced and caressed us rather than submitted to be sat upon." With this one technological exception, one might well say that nothing in *The Time Machine* is unjustified—implausible—so long as we accept the science of the day (Social Darwinism, Scientific Socialism) and one scientifically fantastic device (the time machine itself) made fictionally plausible by the arguments within the book. Of course, the range of science fiction extends far enough to include such works as Phil Nowlan's comic strip, *Buck Rogers* (1929–67), which constantly concocts new and unjustified devices at the drop of a jump belt, but in the center of that range we find the so-called scientific romances of H. G. Wells, potent in their conception, pure in their execution.

Most readers remember *The Time Machine* for the adventures in 802,701 A.D. The Morlocks have taken the machine itself and in his efforts to regain it the Time Traveller has some hair-raising adventures in their lightless mechanical burrows. However, this gloomy warning of the dangers of class differentiation, though comprising the bulk of the book, is actually but half of its thematic substance. Even before he leaves

the time of the Eloi, the Time Traveller, in a moment of respite from
pursuit by the Morlocks through a nighttime forest, philosophizes:

> "Looking at these stars suddenly dwarfed my own troubles and all the
> gravities of terrestrial life . . . I thought of the great [20,000 year] pre-
> cessional cycle that the pole of the earth describes. Only forty times had
> that silent revolution occurred during all the years that I had traversed."
> (Ch. 7)

In his *Commedia* Dante had felt his own cosmic inconsequence when
overwhelmed by the vision of the roseate stars of Paradise; in science fiction, man is made to feel his smallness by contemplation of the disparity
between the magnitude of his understanding and the magnitude of the
cosmos he inhabits. Even eight hundred thousand years is but an instant
to the age of a planet.

So before the Time Traveller returns to Victorian England, he first
journeys forward, this time thirty million years into the future when there
is no more alternation of day and night because "the work of the tidal
drag was done." He comes to rest on "a desolate beach," the first of a
legion of such crucial locales in science fiction. The only life visible in
the murky air or on the muddy land is "a thing like a huge white butter-
fly" and "a monstrous crab-like creature." "Abominable desolation . . .
hung over the world."

> At last, more than thirty million years hence, the huge red-hot dome of
> the [decaying] sun had come to obscure nearly a tenth part of the dar-
> kling heavens. (Ch. 11)

In this final image of the world run down, the differences between
Morlock and Eloi seem ancient and unimportant. Wells, though remembered for his social drama, has a much greater vision than that.

The Time Traveller finishes telling of his journey and exhibits Weena's
flowers to substantiate his tale. A Botanist guest cannot identify them as
belonging to any presently known species. The Time Traveller, sympathetic toward the victimized Eloi, determines to set off again with the
equipment and skills to help them. He promises to return, if he lives and
thus succeeds, and would, of course, make such a return, from the narrator's point of view, right after he leaves. But he does not return. This
time, apparently, the Morlocks were successful. The narrating guest offers an epilogue three years later in which he writes that the Time
Traveller

. . . thought but cheerlessly of the Advancement of Mankind, and saw
in the growing pile of civilization only a foolish heaping that must inevitably fall back upon and destroy its makers in the end . . . But . . .
I have by me, for my comfort, two strange white flowers—shrivelled
now, and brown and flat and brittle—to witness that even when mind
and strength had gone, gratitude and a mutual tenderness still lived on
in the heart of man.

This strange narrative optimism, standing against the undoubted fact
of the Time Traveller's death, leaves the reader with an ambivalence not
merely about science and the putative benefits of technology, but about
the essential meaning of humanity. In separately dramatizing our lighter
and our baser natures, Wells raises this question of meaning with a psychological immediacy that has given *The Time Machine* a vast and continuing audience. In this short novel, a nearly pure extrapolation, Wells
was able to forge the art of science fiction into a sophisticated tool for
both social and metaphysical speculation.

WE (1920)

Yevgeny Zamyatin's *We* is set in a future world-wide United State in
which there are no people, only Numbers. The book takes the form of
the diary of D-503, an engineer who is also Chief Builder of a new and
marvelous device, the space-ship *Integral,* which the Well-Doer (the dic-
tator) clearly plans to use to extend the grip of this society to the planets.
As the Guardians of the United State say of the aliens they expect to
meet,

> If they will not understand that we are bringing them a mathematically
> faultless happiness, our duty will be to force them to be happy. (Rec-
> ord 1)

The stylistic conflict between "happiness" and "force" is typical of
Zamyatin's continuing effort to keep metaphysical issues before the
reader. Beyond the particular warning against technological totalitarianism, we find more general dilemmas. In this case, the nature of happiness
is questioned:

> Desires are tortures, aren't they? It is clear, therefore, that happiness is
> when there are no longer any desires, not a single desire any more.
> (Record 31)

Similarly, the book questions the nature of freedom:

Why is the dance beautiful? Answer: because it is an *unfree* movement. (Record 2)

Taking these two examples together, Zamyatin is posing anew, in the logic of a scientific age, a perpetual problem: can freedom and happiness be compatible? The answer for the United State is to try and develop an operation for "the surgical removal of fancy." This is the world our characters inhabit—and perhaps the world toward which we are moving.

The fact that D-503 writes a diary at all shows that he has some desire which is not preemptively channeled by society; to that extent, he is anomalous. There should be no desire in the United State except to serve the state. But D-503 becomes attracted to I-330. Since desires are tortures, and since love is the extreme of desire, and since the extreme of torture is death, D-503, before he submits to his strange yearnings, concludes that, "$L = f(D)$, love is the function of death." We see this to be true when one female Number individualizes herself by screaming at the public execution of her illicit lover. She too meets death.

The State has done everything possible to kill (assuage?) desire, imagination, art. The people live in glass apartments so that privacy and loneliness do not lead them to private, lonely thoughts. Of course, this living arrangement also facilitates surveillance by the ever helpful Guardians. Mankind's traditional evil, sexual urging, has been conquered by the Lex Sexualis: "A Number may obtain a license to use any other number as a sexual product." And, of course, the other Number must submit. All a Number need do is apply to the proper authorities and he or she is given a coupon book with pink slips conferring sexual access. Everyone does everything by the beautifully efficient Tables of Hours. By submitting a pink slip to your chosen Number, you may cohabit when next your Sexual Hours coincide. At that point—and that point only—curtains may be drawn in the glass apartments.

As D-503 finds himself wishing for illicit activity, he begins to examine the world he lives in. Through his usually patriotic eyes we simultaneously learn to fear mechanization and sympathize with those urgings which keep people mechanized. He reports to us all the features of his almost totally regularized society as he breaks slowly from it. I-330 turns out to be a member of a secret society, the Mephi (from Mephisto) who live outside the Green Walls which totally imprison every city of the United State. Much of the excitement of the book comes from D-503's growing involvement with the Mephi's desire to sabotage the state; indeed, I-330 hopes to use the *Integral* to breach the Green Walls. When

D-503 realizes this, however, he also doubts the sincerity of I-330's love, supposing that she may have taken up with him only to gain access to the ship. Lesser writers might well have opposed a hard mechanical society with a warm loving woman, but Zamyatin recognizes that this is too simple: the woman too may be calculating, and society does indeed protect its faithful members.

Zamyatin keeps such complexities always before us. He is uniquely successful in doing this by scientizing the very language of his novel. We have already encountered "mathematically faultless happiness" and "$L = f(D)$"; we have seen people reduced to Numbers and seen these Numbers functioning according to the Tables of Hours. In the following, D-503 is defending the Operation Department, the medical facility to which Guardians bring deviant Numbers in need of a little palliative lobotomy. Note how the very substance of his thought reveals his mechanized mind:

> About five centuries ago, when the work of the Operation Department was only beginning, there were yet to be found some fools who compared our Operation Department with the ancient Inquisition. But this is as absurd as to compare a surgeon performing a tracheotomy with a highway cutthroat. Both use a knife, perhaps the same kind of knife, both do the same thing, viz., cut the throat of a living man; yet one is a well-doer, the other is a murderer; one is marked plus, the other minus. . . . All this becomes perfectly clear in one second, in one turn of our wheel of logic, the teeth of which engage that *minus,* turn it upward, and thus change its aspect. (Record 15)

It is impossible to deny the *logic* of this passage; but the logic has nothing to do with the moral axioms by which we judge lobotomies. In the conflict between the mathematical language and the humane desire to do well, Zamyatin is warning us against sophistry under the guise of science; an acute reader sees that the real target is the sophistry, not the science. Indeed, the *Integral,* a mathematical summation and a mechanical device, could well be the instrument of successful rebellion.

In discussing the Operation Department, D-503 necessarily uses Zamyatin's key image, the knife.

> A knife is the most solid, the most immortal, the most inspired invention of man. The knife served on the guillotine. The knife is the universal tool for cutting knots. The way of paradoxes follows its sharp edge, the only way becoming to a fearless mind. . . . (Record 20)

It is not merely advanced technology that we must be wary of, but any technology. Through the knife, Zamyatin extends the ambiguities of freedom versus happiness to basic human physiology; just as knives may solve a problem or kill a saint, so mouths can be used for suckling or snarling, and teeth for sustenance or savagery. Time and again Numbers are characterized by their mouths, with teeth like knives, smiles like scissors, lips a deep blood red. We begin to see that the knife/technology constellation of symbols has an implicitly sexual side, we begin to sense its phallic nature, and we realize that sex too can lead ambiguously to tenderness or to dehumanization: love or the Lex Sexualis.

Through the central image of the knife, extending to all technology on the one hand and to human sexuality on the other, Zamyatin takes Shelley's ambivalence toward science and shows us that it is part and parcel of man's universal existential ambiguity. The state perfects the operation for the surgical removal of fancy and D-503, having failed in using the *Integral* to fight the Well-Doer, need not be executed: he can be treated by a benevolent government. Writing a last chapter for the sake of completeness, he claims to feel as if "a splinter has been taken out of my head." Horribly, he is pleased to note that now he smiles all the time and "Smiling is the normal state for a normal human being." Like the knife, so simple and apparently good a thing as a smile is revealed ultimately to be deeply ambiguous. As D-503 says, in his last words, "Reason must prevail." One can hardly deny it.

We is a thoroughly scientific fiction, using science to justify its social extrapolation, its plot, even its language. The emphasis of this dystopian warning is against over-reliance on science, for in that direction lies totalitarianism. But the book does not offer a surer path; rather, in its more general address to human problems, it seems to suggest that our world is indeed an uncertain one, and we must learn to recognize and live with uncertainty. Zamyatin extended the range of science fiction by making dystopian literature a vehicle for the most searching kind of human self-reflection.

A VOYAGE TO ARCTURUS (1920)

All science fiction is to some degree fantastic. Even the purely extrapolative fiction of Wells gains its excitement and special perspective by positing a time machine. Clearly a work like *We,* with its full array of social and technological innovations may seem somewhat more fantastic. If one continues in this progression, one senses the range of science fiction extending perhaps to pure fantasy itself. David Lindsay (1876–1945) has created in *A Voyage to Arcturus* a work of troubling power which takes its roots in science fiction and flowers into metaphysical fantasy. Zamyatin relentlessly applied science in his fiction to make us feel the frightening importance of existential ambiguity; Lindsay, countryman of Shelley and Wells, cavalierly overcomes science to arrive at the consequence of that ambiguity: moral paralysis.

The story begins when two Englishmen, Maskull and Nightspore, come to a seance intended to thrill jaded Edwardian sensibilities. An apparition indeed appears. As the guests watch, a man rushes into the room and strangles the apparition, who dies with a hideous grin. The man, Krag, turns out to know Nightspore and offers to take him and his friend to Arcturus in search of Surture, apparently some type of demigod. The hocus-pocus (nonetheless effective) of the seance is balanced against the inverted science Maskull soon encounters at Starkness, the abandoned Scottish observatory from which Krag proposes to leave. There Maskull finds a tower which he hasn't the strength to climb, for as he goes up, its gravity increases geometrically: gravity as inverse electromagnetic phenomenon. Of course, there is no justification for this kind of gravity, but once introduced, it functions "scientifically," with mathematical precision. But when Krag arrives and needs to climb to the roof, he administers a ritual arm wound to Maskull, and suddenly the man can walk up the stairs with ease. The narrative attitude toward science here is ambiguous, as in *We*. However, where *We* questions the *utility* of science, *A Voyage to Arcturus* questions the very *nature* of science. What after all should we make of our science if it functions in the same realm as magic? By writing science fiction as fantasy, Lindsay makes science fiction a tool for questioning science itself.

In this vein, the trio travels to Arcturus, or more accurately to the planet Tormance in orbit around the star Arcturus, in a spaceship powered by a bottle of backrays, light which is just like ordinary light except instead of inevitably radiating out from its source, it tries unceasingly to radiate back to its source. The ship goes incredibly fast—one can calculate that speed as an incredible 15,225 times the speed of light—and Maskull loses consciousness. What he experiences on awakening forms the bulk of the book.

One of the most striking sights is the illumination itself. Arcturus turns out to be a double star, one globe of which, in the eyes of Maskull on Tormance, transmits red-yellow-blue light and the other of which trans-

mits blue-ulfire-jale light. When both cast their light, there appear to be
five primary colors (the blue light quite logically counting only once).
Lindsay makes his invented colors seem quite real:

> Just as blue is delicate and mysterious, yellow clear and unsubtle, and
> red sanguine and passionate, so [Maskull] felt ulfire to be wild and pain-
> ful, and jale dreamlike, feverish, and voluptuous. (Ch. 5)

This is all very logical, and Lindsay uses the colors jale and ulfire in describing the wildly diverse Tormantic sights; but the human eye, logic
notwithstanding, shouldn't be able to see any colors but those within what
we call on earth the visible spectrum.

It is precisely so that we may see what we do not see on earth that
Lindsay has used science fiction to create his philosophical landscape.
Quite literally, one of the "oddities" of this "alien world" is its "new
light."

> "I am on a strange planet," said Maskull slowly, "where all sorts of un-
> heard of things may happen, and where the very laws of morality may
> be different." (Ch. 9)

Not only a strange planet, but quite particularly "a new planet" where
life

> is necessarily energetic and lawless, and not sedate and imitative. Nature
> is still fluid—not yet rigid—and matter is plastic. The will forks and
> sports incessantly, and thus no two creatures are alike. (Ch. 7)

When Maskull first regains consciousness after his space journey, he
finds himself on a plain.

> He felt something hard on his forehead. Putting his hand up, he dis-
> covered there a fleshy protuberance the size of a small plum, having a
> cavity in the middle, of which he could not feel the bottom. Then he
> also became aware of a large knob on each side of his neck, an inch
> below the ear.
>
> From the region of his heart, a tentacle had budded. It was as long as
> his arm, but thin, like whipcord, and soft and flexible.
>
> As soon as he thoroughly realized the significance of these new or-
> gans, his heart began to pump. Whatever might, or might not, be their
> use, they proved one thing—that he was in a new world. (Ch. 6)

At the level of the plot, Maskull's conclusion is literally true. But more
importantly, he is in a new world because he sees it with new eyes—
among other things. The bulb on his forehead is called a breve.

> Maskull became interested in a new phenomenon. The jale-colored blossoms of a crystal bush were emitting mental waves, which with his breve he could clearly distinguish. They cried out silently, "To me To me!" While he looked, a flying worm guided itself through the air to one of these blossoms and began to suck its nectar. The floral cry immediately ceased. (Ch. 7)

There is a disquieting realism to this description, illuminated by unearthly colors, displaying fantastic creatures and things, and employing direct access to "mental waves." But most disquieting of all is the moral paralysis such descriptions create: did that worm kill the flower or make love to it? And would either of those acts have been good or bad? How can we know?

When Maskull awakens with his breve, it is as if he had died in the spaceship landing and been reborn on Tormance: he is without friends, history, or orientation. Immediately he awakes, a "woman" named Joiwind gives him help: he cannot lift himself against Tormance's potent gravity. She wounds her own arm, wounds his arm (not the one Krag had already used) and they mix bloods, she feeling weakened, he strengthened. Again, ritual and science seem to intertwine and elude us.

The bulk of the novel is Maskull's journey across Tormance, each episode employing a new locale, new characters, and new modes of perception. Within each environment, we find an inner logic such as we would expect in more extrapolative science fiction. In Lichstorm, for example, the inhabitants are *pure* men and women, not men with some estrogen and women with some androgen. These people exhibit sexual passions and characteristics in much more dramatic—frightening—ways than do normal earth people. Yet in addition, they transport themselves by the power of "male stones," the rays of which repel matter and can maneuver a flying boat by being alternately exposed and shaded. Such complementary details not only deepen the "scientific" aspect of the fiction but question the assumptions by which we attempt scientific thought. In what sense, after all, could these stones be thought of as male?

In addition to the bewildering logic within each episode, we find the fiction pushed far toward fantasy by the profound perceptual changes that accompany each of the frequent and unexpected changes of locale. Just as Alice enters a new world each time she jumps over a brook in *Through the Looking Glass* (1872), so Maskull enters a new, albeit science fictional, world each time he continues on his journey. For each new locale, Maskull changes perceptions—usually by a modification in physiology, as in the acquirement of a breve. In an important sense, each change is a dying out of one world and a birth into another. This dying, as postulated by Saint Jerome ("We must die daily"), makes Maskull better able to see the moral imperatives of the world, but each death also brings him to a new world and one cannot know that in the newer world he is any better prepared.

This book does more than merely dabble with Christian theology. In an echo of the mysticism of St. John of Patmos, the isolated Maskull hears a whisper that tells him,

> Nightspore is asleep now, but when he wakes you must die. You will go, but he will return. (Ch. 4)

In the center of the book is a thoroughly fantastic episode. A character named Tydomin, who is supposedly indomitable, is strangling Maskull. As he begins to swoon, resisting all the while, he blinks his eyes open to see the seance of the first chapter occurring around him. In the corner of the London room, he sees Nightspore and Maskull—himself. Suddenly, in rushes Krag who strangles the transported Maskull—whom we now realize to be the earlier apparition. Maskull's strength rises swiftly to a new-found height and he throws off Tydomin's grip: after Tydomin has caused Maskull to die back to earth, back in time, Krag has made him die back to Tormance. No explanation is ever given for the time jump, but one sees that just as Lindsay moves Maskull through space to test man's ability to find a true perception, so he moves him through time. The message, to the extent that one can articulate it from such unaccustomed materials, is that truth no more resides in a given age of a man than it does in a given place; no single sight and no single period will give a person a more legitimate sureness about his environment.

This leads to a moral paralysis in Maskull, and a corresponding paralysis in us as we uneasily fail to judge him while he remorselessly murders and wrecks his way across the planet. This is a terrible vision of an Everyman. Finally, in a tower reminiscent of Starkness, Maskull goes up and sees Muspel fire, the source of everything for Tormance. In Norse mythology, Muspel is the fire which Surtr will wield to bring about Ragnarok, the destruction of the world. When he descends, Maskull has died again, and is now Nightspore. The seed of darkness has been within this Everyman all along, and he now knows that Krag, "whose name on Earth is pain," is also Surture (Searcher) on Tormance. He has learned what seems to be a distinctly anti-Christian message: ". . . the whole world of will was doomed to eternal anguish in order that one Being might feel joy." Nightspore, feeling no escape from this conclusion, steps onto a raft poled by Krag and they go off across the Ocean of Tormance. We close the book wondering which—if any—of the insights of faith have ever given us a true access to the nature of the universe we inhabit.

Lindsay was well aware of his science fiction forebears. The male stones, for example, are certainly modeled on the Cavorite that propelled Wells's *The First Men in the Moon* (1901). Similarly, his reasoning behind some biological and physical details is extraordinary, for instance when he notes the branches of a tree tossing around a squirrel, and then questions our whole sense of taxonomy by noting that the sight would not seem strange if we merely thought of the tree as animal and the squirrel as vegetable. Indeed, in the purest sense of extrapolation, each episode is intriguing science fiction. But in the mad rush from episode to episode, and in the utterly unjustified leaps from physiology to physiology, sense to sense, Lindsay has also created a fantasy which shows toward perception, that first fundamental of science, the same deep ambivalence that Shelley felt toward refined science alone. In treating science as a question of perception, Lindsay performs an even more radical reduction than Zamyatin's collapse of technology into the symbol of the knife. Thus, he begins to create a framework for questions that need not concern science at all. When we finally see the journey as a moral odyssey, and feel the despair of its painful message, then Lindsay has succeeded in entering the great flux of Western religious debate. He has exploited fantasy to extend the range of science fiction into ultimately serious myth.

STAR MAKER (1937)

There is no more serious work of science fiction than *Star Maker*. Perhaps even more than his countryman Lindsay, Olaf Stapledon (1886–1950) used science fiction to generate myths and mythic truth. In *Star Maker* Stapledon achieves a monumental power by exploiting a contrast that only science fiction can accommodate completely: that between men and the stars. In this change of scale, in his spiritual search, Stapledon finds "something other, which the dire contrast of the star and us signified to the heart." *Star Maker* is a supreme attempt to use the art of science fiction to "construct an imaginative sketch of the dread but vital whole of things."

The book begins with the unnamed narrator seated at midnight among the heather on a hill overlooking his middle-class English suburban home.

We come to know that the finest thing in his life is the "community" he feels with his wife, though tonight he feels a "bitterness."

> I sat down on the heather. Overhead obscurity was now in full retreat. In its rear the freed population of the sky sprang out of hiding, star by star.
>
> On every side the shadowy hills or the guessed, featureless sea extended beyond sight. But the hawkflight of imagination followed them as they curved downward below the horizon. I perceived that I was on a little round grain of rock and metal, filmed with water and with air, whirling in sunlight and darkness. And on the skin of that little grain all the swarms of men, generation by generation, had lived in labour and blindness, with intermittent joy and intermittent lucidity of spirit. And all their history, with its folk-wanderings, its empires, its philosophies, its proud sciences, its social revolutions, its increasing hunger for community, was but a flicker in one day of the lives of the stars. (Ch. 1, §1)

Stapledon uses change of scale to awe his readers, and give them some of the feeling he purports, like Dante, to have experienced in a cosmic voyage.

The technique of change of scale is supplemented by powerfully inventive metaphor and analogy. A "married couple" is

> like two close trees whose trunks have grown upwards together as a single shaft, mutually distorting, but mutually supporting. (Ch. 1, §1)

The narrator claims that he uses figurative language because,

> though human language and even human thought itself are perhaps in their very nature incapable of metaphysical truth, [there is] something I must somehow contrive to express, even if only by metaphor. (Ch. 14)

This something is a growing understanding of the whole of not only our cosmos, but of the universe of universes which is the object of creation and contemplation for the Star Maker. A *partial* understanding of the Star Maker is as an "effulgent star" which

> was the centre of a four-dimensional sphere whose curved surface was the three-dimensional cosmos. The star of stars, this star that was indeed the Star Maker, was perceived by me, its cosmical creature, for one moment before its splendour seared my vision. And in that moment I knew that I had indeed seen the very source of all cosmical light and life and mind; and of how much else besides I had as yet no knowledge. (Ch. 13, §3)

Although pleased to borrow metaphors from Christianity, this blinding is not such as Paul's on the road to Damascus. First, the Star Maker, unlike Christ, is beyond benevolence; and second, the narrator, unlike Paul, grows as far beyond his revelation as his revelation was beyond that suburban hillside.

The narrator's growth begins with his "hawk-flight" which ends on what he calls The Other Earth, the world in our galaxy most like his own. Eventually we learn that the narrator's miraculous exploration as a "disembodied viewpoint" is controlled by his ability to understand the world toward which he would wish to travel. Since our Earth is in a "world crisis" which will either bring us under or anneal us for a further step toward world community, "I" is attracted involuntarily to another humanoid world at a parallel moment. Here he telephatically inhabits the Other Men who are much like us, and therefore occasion much pointed satire in the manner of all travel stories from Gulliver's Lilliput to Golding's *Lord of the Flies* (1954). The special variety of Stapledon's satire arises from his strictly Wellsian extrapolations. For example, by assuming that

> taste played as important a part in their imagery and conception as sight in our own,

Stapledon creates a whole new set of metaphors the very silliness of which pokes fun at Earthly foibles:

> Each race tended to believe that its own flavour was characteristic of all the finer mental qualities, was indeed an absolutely reliable label of spiritual worth.

And

> In the congested and unhealthy industrial centres a new gustatory and olfactory type had appeared, apparently as a biological mutation. In a couple of generations this sour, astringent, and undisguisable flavour dominated in all the most disreputable working-class quarters. To the fastidious palates of the well-to-do it was overwhelmingly nauseating and terrifying.

And, punningly and inevitably,

> my hosts regarded themselves as the very salt of the earth. (Ch. 3, §2)

By learning the ironic lessons of this world, especially with the aid of a cooperative native host, a philosopher named Bvalltu, the narrator grows sufficiently to explore more radically non-human worlds. Bvalltu, or his disembodied viewpoint, joins the narrator. Indeed, as the exploration goes from world to world, more creatures join the journey and the exploring "viewpoint" grows into an ever more capacious and understanding composite entity. With extraordinary invention and detailed imagination, Stapledon gives us the sociology of a world of Nautiloids, living, sentient, ship-size creatures who skim their ocean world by spreading membranous sails before the wind. On this planet, the accident of port or starboard birth has led to the typical science fiction "two nations" which is precipitating a world crisis. The journey continues through world after world, "echinoderm humans" and worlds of "minded swarms" where consciousness has developed telepathically among an aggregate of literal bird-brains too small to achieve consciousness independently.

One of the greatest worlds, which "I" is now psychologically able to visit, is that of the telepathically and physically symbiotic ichthyoids and arachnoids, the fish partners being contemplative whale-like animals and the spidery partners being active, scientific animals. In first regarding his own home from the hilltop, "I" had observed that

> There, under that roof, our own two lives, recalcitrant sometimes to one another, were all the while thankfully one, one larger, more conscious life than either alone. (Ch. 1, §1)

With Bvalltu,

> each of us came to feel that to taste the flavour of life in isolation from the other was to miss half its richness and subtlety. (Ch. 4)

Observing the symbiotic ichthyoids and arachnoids,

> interspecific communion, which every individual knew in immediate domestic experience, became in time the basic experience of all culture and religion. (Ch. 7, §1)

Like all life in *Star Maker,* this symbiotic life strives toward community. Unlike life on most planets, however, these symbiotic creatures achieve it. Indeed, at later times of galactic history, their intervention saves our entire Milky Way.

In dizzying progression, Stapledon has his explorer go beyond simple symbiosis to inhabit vicariously individuals on planets that have achieved a world-consciousness. And then inhabit world-minds that are joined in a system-mind around a sun. And then join system-minds participating in Sub-Galactic minds. And then into minds of symbiotic worlds and living stars. And then into Galactic minds. And then into the mind in which the very Galaxies are units, the Cosmic mind. It is as the Cosmic mind that the traveler has his vision of the Star Maker, a vision which he names the Supreme Moment of the Cosmos. And in the aftermath of that vision, he has a dream in which he senses even more about the Star Maker, and sees him making the infinite cosmoses which are the actualization of his own inherent potentiality and, in aggregate, the object of his contemplation. Each stage of this spiritual odyssey is worked out with extrapolative detail, metaphorical brilliance, and a breathtaking contrasting of scales of magnitude of both time and space. This ultimate vision of the cosmos of cosmoses, he realizes, has as its aim, "to include . . . community and the lucid and creative mind"—just like his marriage.

In *Star Maker* is recorded the wars of planets against planets; of suns consciously exploding to wipe out the planet vermin surrounding them. One can barely suggest the richness of this "voyage of astronomical and metaphysical research" which aims to tell "the kind of truth that we sometimes find in myths." But one can recognize that Stapledon has taken science, extrapolation, religion, invention, art, and a sweeping imagination and combined them to give a history of the universe. He knows that energy will run down, that ultimately there will be no men. Indeed, in this book, we learn to communicate with living systems of stars, and to die with them at the ends of aeons. Yet the very voyage gives consolation.

> Two lights for guidance. The first, our little atom [marriage] of community, with all that it signifies. The second, the cold light of the stars, symbol of the hypercosmical reality, with its crystal ecstasy. Strange that in this light, in which even the dearest love is frostily assessed, and even the possible defeat of our half-waking world [the coming war] is contemplated without remission of praise, the human crisis does not lose but gains significance. Strange, that it seems more, not less, urgent to play some part in this struggle, this brief effort of animalcules striving to win for their race some increase of lucidity before the ultimate darkness. (Epilogue)

CHILDHOOD'S END (1953)

Science fiction has dealt not only with the private hopes of its readers but with the public hopes of their societies. Although the dystopian works of Huxley and Orwell have achieved wider critical acclaim, the more devoted regard of fans is reserved for works such as Isaac Asimov's *I, Robot* (1950) and Theodore Sturgeon's *More Than Human* (1953), works which show the emergence of utopias. Of all utopian science fiction, the most widely respected and enthusiastically read is *Childhood's End*. In this novel, Arthur C. Clarke (b. 1917) offers not only a dramatized report of the emergence of man's ultimate utopia, but he shows how man passes to that utopia through a series of temporary utopias. In this case, ontogeny recapitulates phylogeny: *Childhood's End* is both a particular story and a survey of the development of utopian thought, thereby defining a substantial portion of the range of science fiction.

As Clarke's story begins, mankind is on the verge of space flight, a projected manned journey to the moon. Suddenly, huge saucers appear in the skies above the Earth's major cities. All these ships but one, it turns out later, are illusions; but in that one is Karellen, an incredibly advanced and long-lived representative of a race which humanity comes to call the Overlords. By manipulating his illusions, and using astonishingly little real force, Karellen (and company, if they exist), awe mankind into obedience. This obedience requires consolidation in world government under the United Nations, an easy consolidation since the presence of the Overlords makes national war seem absurd. Karellen meets with Secretary General Stormgren, and through him instructs mankind. The only instruction of consequence is that the idea of space flight be abandoned. "The stars are not for man."

In return for this obedience, Karellen provides the now-safe global community with advanced technologies so that

> for the first time in human history, no one worked at tasks they did not like . . . Ignorance, disease, poverty, and fear had virtually ceased to exist. (Ch. 6)

The first third of the novel, "Earth and the Overlords," is devoted to the description of the establishment of this centralized, materialistic utopia. In addition, we have pointed glimpses of Karellen's relationship with Stormgren, whom he calls by his child-like given name, Rikki. Karellen brings about utopia through Stormgren, but never lets himself be seen. Instead, he speaks from behind an opaque screen with a voice

> like a great organ rolling its notes from a high cathedral nave. . . . Its depth and resonance gave the single clue that existed to Karellen's physical nature, for it left an overwhelming impression of sheer *size*. (Ch. 2)

This awe-inspiring size has its desired effect on mankind, creating a sort of humility which, coupled with freedom from want and easy trafficking from place to place, produces an homogenized and relatively unprejudiced population.

The middle section of the novel, "The Golden Age," gives us detailed descriptions of life in this utopia. In addition, we see that human beings can develop friendly, though distant, relations with the Overlords. However, within the happy majority culture we find some who are troubled by

> the supreme enemy of all Utopias—boredom. . . . When the Overlords had abolished war and hunger and disease, they had also abolished adventure. (Ch. 6)

Some of these people decide to found New Athens.

The description of the life and history of New Athens comprises much of the last section of the novel, "The Last Generation." The people of this society believe that

> beyond this island . . . the human race has lost its *initiative*. It has peace, it has plenty—but it has no *horizons*. . . . Everybody on this island has one ambition . . . to do *something*, however small it may be, better than anyone else. Of course, it's an ideal we don't all achieve. But in this modern world the great thing is to *have* an ideal. Achieving it is considerably less important. (Ch. 17)

Thus, New Athens is an island, reminiscent of Atlantis perhaps, in which everyone tries cooperatively to excel. The population is limited by rule so that everyone may know everyone else in his own field and some small percentage of the remaining population as well. The open-air concerts are the finest, the sculpture the best, the philosophy the most inventive.

> It hoped to become what the old Athens might have been had it possessed machines instead of slaves. (Ch. 15)

But, as in the rest of the world, with the constant reminder of Overlord technology, there is no progress at all in science.

New Athens, we learn, had been founded by a Jew named Ben Salomon. Francis Bacon (1561–1626) had written a utopia called *The New Atlantis* (publ. 1627) in which a residential college of scientists rule for the benefit of each other and mankind in the House of Salomon. The Hebrew word *ben* means *son of*. Clarke, then, in the New Athens, offers a Baconian corrective not merely to Plato's Athenian *Republic* but to the centralized and materialistic Golden Age. The democratized utopia has always been the alternative to the centralized utopia, regardless of the possible attitudes toward technology. But in Clarke's novel, neither a centralized nor a democratized utopia emerges as a final answer for man. It is clear that the centralized utopia will fail through boredom; it is hinted that the democratized utopia will fail through human weakness (not everyone can even postulate preeminence as a goal, much less achieve it). Additionally, both types of utopia only persist because of the protection and control of the science-stifling Overlords. Before either society has a chance to weaken too seriously, however, the mission of the Overlords is fulfilled.

The Overlords, we finally learn, have been sent to act as "midwives" in the birth of a new humanity; hence, in ending our current humanity, we achieve childhood's end. The Overlords are the emissaries of an "Overmind" which somehow knows that the human race, if it can be kept from killing itself, can undergo an important evolution. The Overlords have helped in this process for two reasons: first, it is their duty to the Overmind (though how they know that is unclear, since they are not in direct communication with it); second, they hope that by studying man's evolution, as indeed they have studied that of other races they have midwived, they will learn to compensate for a deficiency in their own natures:

> We [Overlords and humans] represent the ends of two different evolutions . . . Our potentialities are exhausted, but yours are still untapped. (Ch. 20)

Despite all the talk of evolution, however, and despite the detailed significance throughout the novel of the selective application of technologies, man's next step breaks every rule of Darwinian evolution. Instead of mutation occurring at conception, as modern science requires, mutation occurs to living humans. Further, mutation does not occur and then spread by natural competition; rather, all children under the age of about ten are, one after the other, affected by an "epidemic" of change. This very unscientific event produces what is essentially a new race: children who through mind energy alone can remain in wordless communication with each other, draw sustenance directly into their bodies from the universe about them, and flourish naked in the dark of interstellar space. The last we see of this new mankind, they are floating off, an immortal and all powerful group entity, made into a god. When this epidemic first begins, the father of the first mutant asks an Overlord, " 'What shall we do about our children?' " He answers, " 'Enjoy them while you may . . . They will not be yours for long.' " This has always been so, "but now it contained a threat and a terror it had never held before."

Such poignancy indicates in part why, of all science fiction utopias, *Childhood's End* is the most widely admired. But there is another reason. Classically, there have been three foci for utopian thought: society centralized, society democratized, and society apotheosized. We have mentioned the first two, but the third also deserves consideration, and includes such memorable works as Wells's *Men Like Gods* (1923). Just as the antecedents of the first two types of utopia can be found in early non-science fiction literature, so we can find antecedents for the third type as well. The outstanding example in Western culture of the utopia of society apotheosized is the Bible. Karellen, with his "sheer *size*" and "voice like an organ" upon whom "no man may look and live" (Exodus 33:19) is God to Stromgren's Moses. Just as man is finally superior to the angels, because, unlike them, he can still win to immortality, so the children of man are superior to the Overloads, despite any technology they may possess. The "epidemic" of mutation sweeps the world, in a wholly unscientific way, giving godlike power only to the uncorrupted young. This mutation descends like Grace, and the event, which the Overlords have learned to call "Total Breakthrough," parallels the Second Coming. In a real sense, those no-longer-humans floating off into space are entering a heaven. Clarke, who happens to be the scientist who first proposed the use of communications satellites, has used science fiction to go beyond our worship of science; he has exploited modern utopianism to revive our ancient hopes; he has, in one novel, traveled the whole utopian range of science fiction, and at its center left an unscientific monument to man's continual spiritual yearning.

In saying these things, one might think of comparing Clarke's Overmind with Stapledon's Star Maker. But Stapledon's creation is vaster: the whole Christian universe is merely one of the myriad sub-universes that the disembodied viewpoint explores and exhausts. And yet, Stapledon does form, like Clarke, part of an important progression. Ever since Mary Shelley, "The stars are not for man" has seemed a wise, though disappointing warning. Shelley projects ambivalence toward science; Stapledon, writing in a world that had learned from Wells to use hard scientific extrapolation, accepted science, and used it as a justification for parts of his wider scheme; but Clarke, who himself acknowledges the influence of fellow Englishman Stapledon, has moved yet a step further: he has, in his series of utopias, transcended science, expanding the range of science fiction at the same time that he draws into it some of the oldest and most potent ideas of our culture.

A CANTICLE FOR LEIBOWITZ (1959)

Walter M. Miller, Jr.'s Hugo-winning novel seems most obviously to be about repetition, about the cyclic nature of history, about the fatedness of human affairs. Originally published over a period of nearly two years as three similar short novels, here we have a case, precisely because a major theme is repetition, in which the excellent parts combine to produce an extraordinary whole. In the combined version, the sections are "Fiat Lux," a medieval story of simple faith and sinewy spirituality in the deserts of Utah 600 years after a nuclear holocaust; "Fiat Homo," a Renaissance story set 600 years after the first, concerning the overgrowth of organized religion by a science made possible largely through the preservations of the very religion it comes to oppose; and "Fiat Voluntas Tua," the story, 600 years later still, of the events leading to and flowing from yet another nuclear holocaust. The Latin rubrics ("Let there be light," "Let there be man," "Let thy will be done") not only move from a hopeful Genesis to a resigned Revelations but they add to the notion of cyclicism the idea that mankind's oldest myths, like the Bible, may in fact contain the persistent truths which describe the universe into which we are born and against which, by our seeking after wealth and power and even science, we struggle vainly. At its deepest level, this "canticle," this religious song of praise, explores the character of man's epic struggles and investigates the possible sources both of his self-destruction and of his greatness.

Each of the sections is set primarily at the abbey of the Albertian Order of Leibowitz, a conservative establishment struggling to maintain its principles in a hostile world. In the first section, under Abbot Dom Arkos, the hostility is that of mutant bandits and a sparsely populated and disordered land. The simple-minded Brother Francis, who sometimes thinks he can talk to buzzards, is visited during his prolonged hermitage by a ragged old man in burlap who teases him and marks a stone with two Hebrew letters. The *lamed tzadek* might well be the alpha and omega of LeibowiTZ, the uncanonized figure to whom the order is dedicated. In fact, although Miller nowhere notes this, these two letters make the Hebrew word for *fool*. But some fools, like Saint Francis of Assisi who in his innocence spoke to song birds, are wiser than their more learned (dare one say scientific?) fellows. This is typical of the novel's humor: irony without satiric rejection. Francis pries up the rock and miraculously discovers a fallout shelter in which are sacred relics of Leibowitz himself, including an inscrutable list naming "pound pastrami, can kraut, six bagels," a skull with a gold-capped tooth which is assumed to be that of Leibowitz's wife, the Blessed Emily, and even a faded schematic blueprint which the post-holocaust monks cannot read but preserve as a holy trust. These relics provide the abbey with holy objects, provide Francis with the life's work of making an illuminated copy of the blueprint, and provide the reader with lovely, gentle humor not the least of which is the idea that the patron saint should be a Jew.

Later in the novel, in the last section when Abbot Zerchi contemplates the nuclear brink toward which men are rushing, he says

> And Christ breathed the same carrion air with us; how meek the Majesty of our Almighty God! What an Infinite Sense of Humor—for Him to become one of us!—King of the Universe, nailed on a cross as a Yiddish Schlemiel by the likes of us. They say Lucifer was cast down for refusing to adore the Incarnate Word; the Foul One must totally lack a sense of humor! God of Jacob, God even of *Cain!* Why do they do it all again? (Ch. 26)

But, of course, Jesus was a Jew; and the schlemiel is the character for whom all the possible dangers of the world are inevitably realized. Beneath the humorous irony, there is truth. If Leibowitz was a Jew, perhaps all the better for his sainthood. A saint is important not for his trivial human history but for the effect he has on the world.

Most of the first section concerns the caution with which the conservative monks deal with the relics. Francis's copy of the schematic takes years, and although the original is a faded blueprint having indecipherable electronic meaning, the copy that finally emerges is a magnificent arabesque artwork of gold ink and flowered borders. When New Rome finally requests that an envoy come from the abbey, through dangerous bandit country, Francis is honored to go. He brings as a gift the precious blueprint, and as a minor token his own labor of a lifetime. When the bandits do stop him, he begs to keep the sacred paper and promises them gold on his return. They reject his offer—and take the copy. Here is irony typical of the book: in Francis's mind the copy is valueless, but in that it has value to the robbers, it has value to Francis, for by it he is enabled to present the real relic to the Pope. After so many twists of logic, one forgets that the "relic" is a mere schematic: the faith of Francis has given it true worth. On his return trip he expects to be robbed again, but the bandits kill him with an arrow through the forehead. His death for his faith is as poignant as any death for any faith. Miller, unlike Lindsay, is not writing an anti-Christian book; by using and playing with both Christianity and Judaism—and with their scriptural languages—Miller is using his holocaust novel to show that nobility resides in the faith of men, not in the objects of their faith. His is a profound message of humanism.

At the end of the book, when the bombs fall and the abbey's often re-built walls crumble, Zerchi is pressed by fallen masonry and looks over to see revealed an ancient skull with a hole in the forehead and in that hole a sliver of wood as from an arrow. At this point, the relic is real to us as well as to the believer, because Francis in his faith was a true saint even if his faith had no more sense that that of the man of Assisi. In the fortuitous uncovering of a second skull we see a typical piece of plot business calculated to support the notion that history is cyclic; but in the access of spirit which the book makes us feel, even through its gentle ironies, Miller makes us come to see that even in cycles there may be progress.

In the second section the hostility against which the abbey and its leader Dom Paulo must hold fast is the onslaught of science. In this vigorous Renaissance-like period the church and the state strike a kind of dynamic balance, one attending to the spirit and one to the body. Although Paulo recognizes the march of science as philosophically threatening, most do not. After all, this is a rich time. Later Abbot Zerchi will say that "the conflict of Martha and Mary always recurred." This conflict (Luke 10:38–42) opposes the sister who goes to the kitchen to prepare food for the visiting Jesus against the sister who sits down at his feet. Although material things have their place, the Bible asserts that Mary's clear adhesion to the spirit is preferable. If history does move in cycles, the energy that forces the process is an energy of conflict and the conflict is indeed that between Martha and Mary, body and spirit, science and religion. In exuberant times like the Renaissance these two forces may not seem to conflict, but in passing from innocence to self-destruction they have fought themselves through to annihilation anew. The hero of the second section is an ironic, cynical, one-eyed poet, a professed atheist who is a parasite at the abbey and who finally dies not in defense of his art but in defense of the order that sheltered him.

Throughout all three sections the Wandering Jew recurs clad in burlap and accompanied by buzzards, scavengers who seem to fit the post-nuclear desert landscape. Leibowitz, through the years, comes to be customarily shown in burlap. In the last section, when the abbey has a super-highway running through its grounds and under the walkways of its modern buildings, the old wanderer seems so pitifully small. The hostile forces are again those of the nuclear fire, which has come to be called "Lucifer." The most obvious "ending" of the book is that "Lucifer is fallen," the bombs come again, and the earth is once more irradiated. Hence we have exact, inevitable and terrible repetition, human nobility notwithstanding. The Wandering Jew has not endured long enough to celebrate a Second Coming. How then can Miller call this novel a song of praise?

In fact, there are numerous endings. The most dismal concerns a young mother who, against Zerchi's adjurations, commits her infant to a government-sponsored painless death rather than have her face a painful life as a mutant. Although this is a conquest of pain, it is also a denial of life. Even Eve's sin led to childbirth, so here we have a compounding of the Original Sin. Lucifer's work seems complete.

But in fact his work is not complete, because young Brother Joshua is able, just before the bombs drop, to load a rocket full of children and head for the stars. This provides us with a second and more ambiguous ending. On the one hand we have the joyful crossing of space to find a promised land, Joshua leading in the place of the aged Zerchi as Joshua of old led in the crossing of the Jordan in the place of the aged Moses. In this regard, we can indeed hope that the rocket will find that better land. But the Bible also recounts the history of Israel, of its growth to empire, and of its destruction. All lands seem to enter the cycle of human history, pushed by the conflict of Martha and Mary. Will Joshua's space children also fall again?

A most striking ending occurs at the holocaust itself. Old Mrs. Grales, a mutant, is a perennial abbey character, a tomato seller constantly asking Zerchi to bless her quiescent second head whom she calls Rachel. Zerchi has always refused, unsure about the humanity of Rachel, but he always bought tomatoes from the woman and he maintains a warm patron's relationship with her. When the nuclear rains come, when "Lucifer falls" and Zerchi is trapped in the rubble, he sees a figure approaching whom he takes to be Mrs. Grales, but it is now Rachel.

> She watched him with cool green eyes and smiled innocently. The eyes were alert with wonder, curiosity, and—perhaps something else—but she could apparently not see that he was in pain . . . then he noticed that the head of Mrs. Grales slept soundly on the other shoulder while Rachel smiled. (Ch. 29)

The fall of Lucifer is here a fortunate fall, the Felix Culpa of Christian theology, for it causes a new innocence to emerge. This is obvious in the greenness of the eyes and in the ignorance of pain. It is a blessed innocence which doesn't condemn Mrs. Grales to death, as the first fall condemned mankind to death, but consigns her to sleep.

The Holy Grail, for which so many knights of ancient lore searched, was said to have been the cup Jesus used at the Last Supper and in which Joseph of Arimathea collected the last drops of blood from Jesus on the Cross. Just as the Virgin Mary redeems the sin of Eve, so the blood of Jesus through the Grail redeems the sin of Lucifer. In one legend, the Grail was made by angels from an emerald that dropped from Lucifer's forehead when he was hurled into the abyss. As such, the Grail, and Mrs. Grales, tie together the repetitive and cyclic images of the book that we see in the pierced skull of Francis, the repeated fall of Lucifer, the greenness of innocence and the emerald and, of course, the fruition of the mission of the Church on Earth. Mrs. Grales is a gentle character, a pitiable character, but the irony that she calls up is never turned against her in this gentle book. Perhaps, Miller suggests through her, all suffering is arranged for the final redemption of mankind into a new and innocent purity. In this regard, the Mrs. Grales ending recalls *Childhood's End*.

The last paragraph of the novel is devoted not to any of the human characters but to a wider life:

> A wind came across the ocean, sweeping with it a pall of fine white ash. The ash fell into the sea and into the breakers. The breakers washed dead shrimp ashore with the driftwood. Then they washed up the whiting. The shark swam out to his deepest waters and brooded in the cold clean currents. He was very hungry that season.

At first one might take this as a sign of the end of the world, but it is not. The shark will be hungry, but to be hungry it must survive. The deep waters have *clean* currents, as clean as Rachel is innocent. His hunger lasts only a season. A shark, like the buzzards who have recurred with the Wandering Jew throughout the novel, is a scavenger: he lives on death. In replacing the buzzards with a shark Miller helps us see the relative significance of his multiple endings. The many has become one (the fish has been an iconic and numerological symbol for Christ since ancient times) and that one exists in the primeval sea from which all life sprang, and from which it will spring again. The cycles go on. But inasmuch as the buzzards are gone, the Wandering Jew has been allowed to die. He was condemned by Jesus to wander until the Second Coming.

Hence Lucifer's Fall is fortunate indeed, releasing not only Rachel but releasing the Jew from his curse. Rachel really represents then a new kind of human being. The shark's hunger is caused by the nuclear war, but that war is necessary for a Second Coming and for human progress. Suffering does ennoble, can redeem, and Miller denies Lindsay's assertion that "the whole world of will was doomed to eternal anguish in order that one Being might feel joy." The cycles of anguish, the conflict of body and spirit, are the condition of the universe, and whether that universe is viewed from a Christian or a Jewish perspective, it is a universe in which mankind can develop and in which that very suffering has meaning. While writers like C. S. Lewis have dramatized an antagonism between science and religion, Miller has written a learned and gently ironic novel to amalgamate science and religion into a modern humanism. This science fiction is indeed a canticle, a song of praise.

THE LEFT HAND OF DARKNESS (1969)

Ursula K. Le Guin's novel is an extraordinary achievement of sustained imaginative vision. It takes one of the most familiar motifs of science fiction, the alien encounter, and uses it to explore such themes as the nature of integrity, of patriotism, and of isolation and alienation in human relationships. Above all it turns the alien encounter into a consideration of human sexuality, and of the ways that their male and female attributes make men and women perpetually foreign to one another. The novel considers relationships as large as a political system spanning galaxies: The "Ekumen," dedicated to "Material profit. Increase of knowledge. The augmentation of the complexity and intensity of the field of intelligent life. The enrichment of harmony and the greater glory of God! Curiosity. Adventure. Delight" (Ch. 3). It considers two countries, a semi-feudal kingdom and a nearly totalitarian bureaucracy, and in doing so it explores concepts such as patriotism ("The fear of the other . . . hate, rivalry, aggression") and love of country:

> "How does one hate a country or love one? . . . I lack the trick of it. I know people, I know towns, farms, hills and rivers and rocks, I know how the sun at sunset in autumn falls on the side of certain plowlands in the hills; but what is the sense of giving a boundary to all that, of giving it a name and ceasing to love where the name ceases to apply?" (Ch. 15)

But above all it explores the way human beings relate to one another.
    The novel is about a lone Terran ambassador, Genly Ai, who seeks to

persuade the citizens of a remote and glacial planet, Gethen (also called "Winter"), to join the Ekumen. But the story of his mission becomes submerged in the story of his relationship with an individual Gethenian, Therem Harth rem ir Estraven, Lord of Estre. Like all Gethenians, Estraven is physiologically ambisexual. That is, though our language forces us to call Estraven "he" or "she," Estraven is both—and neither. Le Guin's vision in this novel is based on the fantastic device of imagining a race of humans who are fully hermaphroditic, having the complete sexual equipment of earthly men and women. The Gethenians, however, are sexually neutral for most of the month, undergoing a period of intense sexual activity called "kemmer" for only a few days at a time. In the early phase of kemmer, as two Gethenians in this condition touch one another, their glands are activated so that a touching pair become a heterosexual couple, one actively female, the other male. But afterward each is neutral, and in the next month may play the other sexual role. Thus every individual may become a father or a mother, and sexual stereotyping is not merely irrelevant but impossible.

The earthman, Genly Ai, is the alien in this situation. The Gethenians think of him as a "pervert," because he is always "in kemmer," always capable of sexual activity. And he in turn has immense difficulties in deciding how to relate to any individual Gethenian:

> Estraven had conversed amicably at table; now, sitting across the hearth from me, he was quiet. Though I had been nearly two years on Winter I was still far from being able to see the people of the planet through their own eyes. I tried to, but my efforts took the form of self-consciously seeing a Gethenian first as a man, then as a woman, forcing him into those categories so irrelevant to his nature and so essential to my own. (Ch. 1)

This difficulty was foreseen by one of the early, secret investigators of the planet, who left some advice for any later ambassador, or "First Mobile," as Genly Ai is called:

> When you meet a Gethenian you cannot and must not do what a bisexual naturally does, which is to cast him in the role of Man or Woman, while adopting towards him a corresponding role dependent on your expectations of the patterned or possible interactions between persons of the same or the opposite sex. Our entire pattern of socio-sexual interaction is non-existent here. They cannot play the game. They do not see one another as men or women. This is almost impossible for our imagination to grasp. What is the first question we ask about a new-born baby? (Ch. 7)

This fantastic displacement of human sexual mores is used by Le Guin to make her readers perceive that humans rely on sexual stereotyping for much of their identities. The investigator's report continues:

> The First Mobile, if one is sent, must be warned that unless he is very self-assured, or senile, his pride will suffer. A man wants his virility regarded, a woman wants her femininity appreciated, however indirect and subtle the indications of regard and appreciation. On Winter they will not exist. One is respected and judged only as a human being. It is an appalling experience. (Ch. 7)

To be judged only as a human being, without being allowed to fall back on one's male or female role, would indeed be an appalling experience, despite our many claims to the contrary. And to regard another person simply as a person is a feat beyond most human capacities. We *need* the help of sexual, racial, and other categories, but in relying on them we ignore something greater and deeper—our common humanity. Le Guin gives this problem concrete form, in the alien bodies of Ai and Estraven. And she constantly narrows the focus of their relationship. Most of the last part of the book is devoted to a trek across the glacial ice cap of the wintry planet, as Estraven helps Ai escape from a prison camp in Orgoreyn to return to feudal Karhide, where there is a price on Estraven's head. On this whole world, Estraven has been the most enlightened, most ready to embrace the ideals of the Ekumen. But because of their different customs and cultures, the two humans have continually misunderstood one another. On the ice, they must become closer or die. At first, they are not friendly enough to use first names:

> "Good night, Ai," said the alien, and the other alien said, "Good night, Harth."
> A friend. What is a friend in a world where any friend may be a lover at a new phase of the moon? Not I, locked in my virility: no friend to Therem Harth, or any other of his race. Neither man nor woman, neither and both, cyclic, lunar, metamorphosing under the hand's touch, changelings in the human cradle, they were no flesh of mine, no friends; no love between us. (Ch. 15)

As the weather becomes colder and fiercer the two "aliens" begin to thaw, to become true friends, and finally to share love, though not sexual embrace. At one point Estraven asks Ai about women: "Do they differ much from your sex in mind behavior? Are they a different species?" And Ai replies in some confusion:

"No. Yes. No, of course not, not really. But the difference is very important. I suppose the most important thing, the heaviest single factor in one's life, is whether one's born male or female. In most societies it determines one's expectations, activities, outlook, ethics, manners—almost everything. Vocabulary. Semiotic usages. Clothing. Even food. . . ." (Ch. 16)

Finally, after stumbling over the question of whether women are mentally inferior or not, Ai ruefully concludes,

"I can't tell you what women are like. I never thought about it much in the abstract, you know, and—God!—by now I've practically forgotten. I've been here two years. . . . You don't know. In a sense, women are more alien to me than you are. With you I share one sex, anyhow. . . ." (Ch. 16)

In making this admission, Ai speaks for most men. The alien encounter has been subtly altered by Le Guin until it becomes the obvious metaphor for relations between the human sexes. Only in science fiction could such a metaphor be made concrete in this way. And this is one of its major sources of strength—it literalizes metaphors, turning them into solid fictions, enacting them so as to release the imaginative energy compacted within the figure.

The major barrier to a deep and loving friendship between these two exiled aliens is finally removed when Ai acknowledges what has held him back from accepting Estraven as a human being. This happens when Estraven goes into kemmer and a sexual tension develops between the two characters:

And I saw then again, and for good, what I had always been afraid to see, and had pretended not to see in him: that he was a woman as well as a man. Any need to explain the source of that fear vanished with the fear; what I was left with was, at last, acceptance of him as he was. Until then I had rejected him, refused him his own reality. He had been quite right to say that he, the only person on Gethen who trusted me, was the only Gethenian I distrusted. For he was the only one who had entirely accepted me as a human being: who had liked me personally and given me entire personal loyalty: and who had therefore demanded of me an equal degree of recognition and acceptance. I had not been willing to give it. I had not wanted to give my trust, my friendship to a man who was a woman, a woman who was a man. (Ch. 18)

Having made that great adjustment to accepting another person as a human being regardless of that person's sexuality, Genly Ai is finally dismayed to encounter members of his own species, with their violently differentiated sexual characteristics, when the Ekumen's ship descends to Gethen:

> Out they came and met the Karhiders with a beautiful courtesy. But they all looked strange to me, men and women, well as I knew them. Their voices sounded strange: too deep, too shrill. They were like a troupe of great, strange animals of two different species: great apes with intelligent eyes, all of them in rut, in kemmer. . . . They took my hand, touched me, held me. (Ch. 20)

Ai, who is still weak from his ordeal on the ice, recovers from his shocked reunion with his own kind when he is treated by a Gethenian doctor, with his "quiet voice and his face, a young serious face, not a man's face and not a woman's, a human face." His comic predicament, reminiscent of Gulliver's retreating from his family to the stable for company, returns us to our own human situation. We *are* of two sexes, in some sense doomed to alien extremes, and we must make a special effort to see one another as humans who can work together and be friendly without always falling into sexually stereotyped patterns of behavior. Le Guin's novel is about many things that cannot be considered in this brief discussion, and it demonstrates resources of verbal skill and versatility that have not been illustrated here. But the most important aspect of *The Left Hand of Darkness* for our purposes is the way it shows how mature science fiction can find unique perspectives from which to examine the problems and possibilities of our age. Above all, like so much of the best contemporary work in this field, Le Guin's novel asks us to broaden our perspectives toward something truly ecumenical, beyond racism and sexism, and even speciesism. The novel closes with the words of Estraven's young heir, asking the envoy to tell him about things beyond his own world, the things that had moved his parent to welcome, to help, and finally to sacrifice his life for an alien who would have died in vain without his aid—things which are not to be feared because alien but to be seen, understood, and rightly understood, to be loved:

> "Will you tell us about the other worlds out among the other stars—the other kinds of men, the other lives?"

THE SHOCKWAVE RIDER (1976)

As Ursula K. Le Guin is the mistress of contemporary anthropological science fantasy, John Brunner (b. 1934) is the master of sociological extrapolation. Together they illustrate the vigor of social-science fiction within the field at the present time. In *The Shockwave Rider* Brunner has projected a twenty-first century America, in which data-processing has become so efficient that a "plug-in" society has developed. In this not-so-brave new world people move with extraordinary ease from job to job, home to home, person to person, by simply punching their personal codes into the computer net at any location and automatically receiving all credit due them and obtaining equivalent housing facilities to what they had before. They also find equivalent people, equivalent social situations, and so on and on. Even love has become just another "plug-in."

In this society behavior modification is practiced on children by organizations like "Anti-Trauma Inc" with disastrous results which are conveniently concealed from the public. There is a lot of data in the net but it is not available to everybody. Gambling on any kind of future event is possible at "Delphi boards" located conveniently at airports and other centers. But the government, which is supposed to simply monitor the boards as a way of testing public opinion, has secretly taken to manipulating the odds as a way of controlling the opinion it is supposed to be observing. A disastrous earthquake in the San Francisco Bay area found the country absolutely unable to cope with its aftermath, either economically or socially, with the result that a belt of shanty towns inhabited by refugees from Northern California grew up west of the Rockies, gradually becoming more permanent but never quite being incorporated into the plug-in society. These survive as tourist attractions and centers for all sorts of eccentric cult activities. Throughout the country youth gangs have become more permanent features of the social landscape, and these "tribes" engage in ritual warfare and "tribalizing" raids that result in many deaths and countless injuries, as well as extraordinary property damage. Since the government computers know so much about everyone's life, paranoia is wide spread and most people have spells in which they "overload" or break down. These psychic disorders are treated with drugs, or behavior modification, which ultimately make things worse. No one trusts the government but no one knows what to do about it except keep moving, plugging in here and there with less and less satisfaction and worse and worse periods of overload. Brunner is indeed a master at creating a world clearly different from our own but related to it in so many ways that the connection is harrowingly close. He is the most plausible extrapolater from the present into the near future of anyone writing today.

In this world governments are vying to produce individuals who have superior mental capabilities, thus giving their country an edge in "the brain race." In the U.S., the government recruits bright young orphans and force-feeds them intellectually at centers which are highly secret in their methods of operation. Government scientists are also trying to construct superbeings by direct manipulation of genetic structure. They produce monsters at first, who suffer and die, but are gradually perfecting their techniques. All this adds up to a society with incredible skills but no vision, extraordinary technology but serving no humane purpose. *The Shockwave Rider* is the story of one man, who as a boy was recruited for the "brain race," but as an adult escapes and fights the system itself. In constructing this novel, Brunner has set himself the problem of presenting a convincing twenty-first century America, of telling a rousing adventure story, and of including a substantial amount of discussion and debate about human values and the proper uses of technology. He solves the problem with literary resourcefulness of a high order.

The narrative begins with the hero (and he is a hero) captured and under interrogation at Tarnover, where his schooling had originally taken place. As he is forced, by a combination of drugs and electronic brain-stimulation, to relive his past, including his life while at large, the reader follows his story as a personal adventure. When he is allowed periodic opportunities to converse in the present with his interrogator, we follow these debates with a different sort of interest. It is in these discussions with Mr. Freeman, himself an orphan, schooled like his victim, that we are made acquainted with the values at stake in the escape and subsequent adventures. The debate voices Brunner's most serious ideas but because the conversion of the interrogator Freeman to his victim's point of view is a major pivot in the plot, what might become too abstract and tedious is always dramatically alive. The alternation between narration and discussion allows Brunner to balance adventure with thought in a very natural way, and the thematic concerns of the discussion gradually color our understanding of the adventures, just as our dramatic interest in the outcome of the discussions lends emotional intensity to the clash of ideas and values. The special combination of interest in ideas and delight in adventures that is typical of science fiction has seldom found a form more happily suited to it than this one. The interrogative situation allows both the intellectual and emotional facets of the novel to develop toward a climactic point, as the "fleshbacks" move through the past toward the present and the discussions begin to make the future possible.

Unlike Brunner's previous major successes, *Stand on Zanzibar* and *The Sheep Look Up* (see pp. 80–82), which show us individuals defeated by population and pollution processes that have exceeded human ability to control them, *The Shockwave Rider* offers us the example of heroic individuals who fight against a catastrophic situation and ultimately defeat it. Nick Haflinger and Kate Lilleberg finally triumph over a corrupt government and all its mindless technology. They manage this because Kate is wise and Nick's love of her enables him to attain wisdom too. And because he has finally mastered both himself and the technology of his age, Nick is able to write a super program that opens the data in the government computer system to all the people who are plugged in to that system, thus exposing all manner of crime and corruption within the government itself and outside of it, and allowing individuals to have access to their own records as well. In the course of reaching this welcome conclusion, the novel has offered us a model of proper community behavior in the village of Precipice, and an ideal of individual behavior as well, in the image of the shock-wave rider, who deals with future-shock the way a dolphin treats the bow wave of a ship:

> What a wise man can do, that can't be done by someone who's merely clever, is make a right judgment in an unprecedented situation. A wise man would never be overloaded by the plug-in life-style. He'd never need to get mended in a mental hospital. He'd adjust to shifts of fashion, the coming-and-going of fad-type phrases, the ultrasonic-blender confusion of the twenty-first-century society, as a dolphin rides the bow wave of a ship, out ahead but always making in the right direction. And having a hell of a good time with it. (Book 1, "FLESHBACK SEQUENCE")

Nick is a good man and a hero who saves his community. But he cannot save the world. The novel ends with all the citizens of the country being asked to vote on two propositions that would make the world a better place to live in. The result of the vote is not announced. Instead, the reader is asked, "Well—how did you vote?" In Brunner's hands, science fiction returns from the realms of imagination to the world and suggests that we do something about it. If we accept his challenge, of course, we step beyond the range of science fiction into reality, but a reality seen with fresh precision because we have been out of it, exploring the range of science fiction.

BIBLIOGRAPHIES

I. History and Criticism of Science Fiction

II. Science Fiction in Other Media

III. Science Backgrounds

IV. Award-Winning Science Fiction Novels

I. HISTORY AND CRITICISM OF SCIENCE FICTION

(A select list of major studies and journals, excluding
books on single figures and individual magazine articles)

Brian W. Aldiss, *Billion Year Spree* (Schocken: New York, 1973). This
compendious history of science fiction not only hits all the high spots but
occasionally shows how science fiction developed in relation to the main
interests of British and American literature. By a leading member of the
British New Wave, it is written with grace and vigor.

L. David Allen, *Science Fiction Reader's Guide* (Centennial Press: Lincoln,
Nebraska, 1973). This elementary work is notable for its detailed plot
summaries of fifteen of the most important works of science fiction.

Kingsley Amis, *New Maps of Hell: A Survey of Science Fiction* (Harcourt
Brace: New York, 1960). This first popular treatment of science fiction
considers primarily the functions of satire and social commentary. Although somewhat dated and finally unsympathetic to the genre, it is important for having set the context for much of the critical discussion in the
years after its publication.

William Atheling, Jr. (James Blish), *The Issue at Hand* (Advent: Chicago,
1964). Useful criticism of magazine science fiction by a professional
writer; a collection of essays originally published between 1952 and 1960.

————, *More Issues at Hand* (Advent: Chicago, 1970). More of the above,
with essays originally published between 1957 and 1970.

J. O. Bailey, *Pilgrims Through Space and Time* (Greenwood Press: West-
port, Connecticut, 1972; reprint of original 1947 Argus edition). A rich
and scholarly book dealing with both science fictional and other narrative
treatments of its title subject under the rubrics of recurring themes and
motifs. Many rare works are described.

Neil Barron, *Anatomy of Wonder: Science Fiction* (Bowker: New York,
1976). Thoroughly cross-indexed and annotated guide to over 1100 works
of science fiction from the renaissance to the present, including such additional aids as an annotated list of secondary materials and a condensed history of science fiction words. An exceptionally helpful companion to science
fiction.

Marie Louise Berneri, *Journey Through Utopia* (Schocken: New York, 1971; reprint of 1950 Routledge & Kegan Paul original). The most complete history of utopian literature from the ancients through World War II with many works summarized.

Reginald Bretnor, ed., *Science Fiction: Today and Tomorrow* (Penguin: Baltimore, Maryland, 1974). Original essays by fifteen science fiction writers on such topics as "The Publishing of Science Fiction," "The Creation of Imaginary Worlds" and "The Creation of Imaginary Beings."

Robert E. Briney and Edward Wood, *SF Bibliographies: An Annotated Bibliography of Bibliographical Works on Science Fiction and Fantasy Fiction* (Advent: Chicago, 1972). This inexpensive paperback, an excellent place to begin research, supplements the earlier Clareson bibliography below.

Thomas D. Clareson, ed., *Extrapolation: A Journal of Science Fiction and Fantasy* (The College of Wooster and The Collier Printing Company: Wooster, Ohio, December and May, since 1959). This journal serves both the Modern Language Association Seminar on Science Fiction and the Science Fiction Research Association, publishing scholarly and critical articles, reviews, and bibliographical material. An indispensable tool for study and research.

————, ed., *SF: The Other Side of Realism* (Bowling Green University Popular Press: Bowling Green, Ohio, 1971). The best collection to date of essays on science fiction and fantasy by working scholars.

————, *Science Fiction Criticism: An Annotated Checklist* (Kent State University Press: Kent, Ohio, 1972). The single best source for directing research in the field.

Basil Davenport, ed., *The Science Fiction Novel: Imagination and Social Criticism* (Advent: Chicago, 1959). Provocative essays by the editor and Heinlein, Kornbluth, Bester, and Bloch on science fiction since Wells.

Richard Gerber, *Utopian Fantasy: A Study of English Utopian Fiction Since the End of the Nineteenth Century* (McGraw-Hill: New York, 1973; reissue of the original 1955 Routledge and Kegan Paul edition with updated appendices). A chatty yet scholarly book. The annotated bibliographies of primary materials in the appendices are useful for rare works.

Leslie A. Fiedler, *In Dreams Awake* (Dell: New York, 1975). A "historical-critical" anthology of science fiction from Poe to Ballard, with provocative introduction and commentary by a major critic of American literature and culture.

H. Bruce Franklin, *Future Perfect: American Science Fiction of the Nineteenth Century* (Oxford University Press: New York, 1966). An anthology of science fiction from the era between Shelley and Wells with headnotes and critical introduction.

James Gunn, *Alternate Worlds: The Illustrated History of Science Fiction* (Prentice-Hall: Englewood Cliffs, New Jersey, 1975). An informed and lively study that emphasizes Verne, Wells, and the magazines, written by an accomplished writer of science fiction.

Mark R. Hillegas, *The Future as Nightmare: H. G. Wells and the Anti-Utopians* (Southern Illinois University Press: Carbondale, Illinois, 1967). In addition to Wells, Hillegas considers Forster, Čapek, Zamyatin, Huxley,

Orwell, Lewis, and later dystopian writers in this lucid piece of intellectual history.

David Ketterer, *New Worlds for Old: The Apocalyptic Imagination, Science Fiction, and American Literature* (Doubleday: New York, 1976; reprint of 1974 Indiana University Press edition). A scholarly work that deals with vast amounts of material relating the apocalyptic elements of science fiction to the special qualities of American literary vision.

Damon Knight, *In Search of Wonder* (Advent: Chicago, 1956; enlarged edition, 1967). Essays by a science fiction writer on the work of his colleagues.

Sam J. Lundwall, *Science Fiction: What It's All About* (Ace: New York, 1971; enlarged version of the 1969 Swedish edition, translated by the author). A breezy, readable view of the subject, dealing not only with the novels but with the fanzines, the internationality of the genre, and the relations between popular and elite culture.

R. D. Mullen and Darko Suvin, eds., *Science Fiction Studies* (Indiana State University: Terre Haute, thrice yearly, since 1974). Like *Extrapolation,* this journal publishes criticism, scholarship, and reviews. It is more international in scope, more theoretical in its interests, and more concerned with politics and ideology. It, too, is an indispensable tool for study and research.

Marjorie Hope Nicolson, *Voyages to the Moon* (Macmillan: New York, 1960; reprint of 1948 original). A lucid, scholarly survey of the motif of moon voyaging from ancient times to the early nineteenth century. Valuable for studying the roots of science fiction and for its descriptions of rare works.

Robert M. Philmus, *Into the Unknown: The Evolution of Science Fiction from Francis Godwin to H. G. Wells* (University of California Press: Berkeley, 1970). An important essay in the theory and history of science fiction in relation to the history of ideas.

Robert Plank, *The Emotional Significance of Imaginary Beings* (Chas. C. Thomas: Springfield, Illinois, 1968). A psychoanalytic approach that deals not only with science fiction but with flying saucer cults and Shakespeare.

Eric S. Rabkin, *The Fantastic in Literature* (Princeton University Press: Princeton, New Jersey, 1976). A theoretical study that uses science fiction as one of its major examples.

Mark Rose, ed., *Science Fiction: A Collection of Critical Essays* (Prentice-Hall, Inc., Englewood Cliffs, N.J., 1976). This volume in the Twentieth Century Views series includes essays by Amis, Scholes, Suvin, Lem, Rabkin, Lewis, Sontag, Ketterer, and others.

Robert Scholes, *Structural Fabulation: An Essay on the Future of Fiction* (University of Notre Dame Press: Notre Dame, Indiana, 1975). A wide-ranging essay dealing with the place of science fiction in the development of fiction in general.

Donald H. Tuck, compiler, *The Encyclopedia of Science Fiction and Fantasy Through 1968* (Advent: Chicago, 1974). A bibliographic source of extraordinary completeness listing works under their authors. Unfortunately, only volume 1 (A–L) has so far appeared.

Donald A. Wollheim, *The Universe Makers: Science Fiction Today* (Harper & Row: New York, 1971). A survey and behind-the-scenes look at the field from the advent of the Golden Age by one of the most important editors and publishers of science fiction.

II. SCIENCE FICTION IN OTHER MEDIA

1. COMICS

Arthur Asa Berger, *The Comic-Stripped American* (Penguin: Baltimore, Maryland, 1973). A popular sociological and psychological history of American comics including chapters on Buck Rogers, Flash Gordon, Superman, Batman, and the Marvel Comics Group.

Reinhold Reitberger and Wolfgang Fuchs, *Comics: Anatomy of a Mass Medium* (Little, Brown: Boston, 1972; translation of 1971 Heinz Moos Verlag original). A compendious and well-illustrated history and analysis of the field on both sides of the Atlantic.

2. FILMS

John Baxter, *Science Fiction in the Cinema* (Paperback Library: New York, 1970). A compact historical survey of the major themes of science fiction film with good filmography.

Carlos Clarens, *An Illustrated History of the Horror Film* (Capricorn Books: New York, 1968; reprint of 1967 original). A clear history of the subject with ample illustration and an excellent filmography.

Dennis Gifford, *Movie Monsters* (Dutton: New York, 1968). A breezy survey organized according to type of monster with copious illustration and excellent historical filmographies.

————, *Science Fiction Film* (Dutton: New York, 1968). Another breezy survey with copious illustration but no filmography.

III. SCIENCE BACKGROUNDS

Isaac Asimov, *Today and Tomorrow and . . .* (Doubleday: New York, 1973). For the layman, a thoroughly entertaining collection of essays in the fields of biology, astronomy, chemistry, and physics and some speculation about the nature of science fiction.

J. D. Bernal, *The World, the Flesh and the Devil* (Indiana University Press: Bloomington, Indiana, 1969; reprint of 1929 original with new introduction by the author). This book of breathtaking scientific speculation is probably the single most influential source of science fiction ideas.

Adrian Berry, *The Next Ten Thousand Years* (Mentor: New York, 1974). This fluidly written book provides a great deal of background in modern science in order to justify an uncommonly optimistic view of man's future as aided by technology.

Harold F. Blum, *Time's Arrow and Evolution* (Princeton University Press: Princeton, New Jersey, 1968; an expansion and revision of the 1955 and 1951 editions). This milestone in science writing combines insights from geology, cosmology, thermodynamics, quantum mechanics, biology and even information theory to analyze the constraints on the free play of evolution. Although one of the finest pieces of science writing ever done, it does require a good background education to read easily.

René Dubos, *The Dreams of Reason: Science and Utopias* (Columbia University Press: New York, 1961). This fascinating book by a man who is both an accomplished writer and an important scientist traces in literature and culture the changing attitudes toward science and scientists.

Dennis Gabor, *Innovations: Scientific, Technological and Social* (Oxford University Press: New York, 1970). The author, a Nobel laureate in physics, attempts to predict what must occur, may occur, and needs to occur in the next thirty years.

George Gamow, *Mr. Tompkins in Paperback* (Cambridge University Press: Cambridge, 1969; combined edition of *Mr. Tompkins in Wonderland*, 1940, and *Mr. Tompkins Explores the Atom*, 1945). A witty, nontechnical exposition of the basic concepts of relativity theory and quantum mechanics.

Charles Coulston Gillispie, *The Edge of Objectivity* (Princeton University Press: Princeton, New Jersey, 1960). This is the standard scholarly study of the historically changing assumptions underlying the "empiricism" of science.

Philip Handler, ed., *Biology and the Future of Man* (Oxford University Press: New York, 1970). A massive survey of the whole of modern biology by the members of the National Academy of Sciences. This book not only describes the current state of biological knowledge but relates it to problems of society, psychology, and so forth.

Sir James Jeans, *Physics & Philosophy* (The University of Michigan Press: Ann Arbor, Michigan, 1968; reprint of 1942 Cambridge University Press original). A clear discussion by a man who is both professional physicist and professional philosopher of the dialectic of development of these two fields.

Thomas S. Kuhn, *The Structure of Scientific Revolutions* (University of Chicago Press: Chicago, 1970; enlargement of 1962 original). A milestone in the history of ideas, this book offers an explanation for the way science develops both normally to fill in the data implied by existing theory and in a revolutionary way to create new theories by which to see the world.

S. E. Luria, *Life: The Unfinished Experiment* (Scribners: New York, 1973). Modern breakthroughs in genetics, ethology, and so on have allowed for the beginnings of a unified theory of biology. This short, incisive treatment of all of biology by a Nobel laureate explores this unifying framework and explains it for the lay reader.

Carl Sagan, *The Cosmic Connection* (Dell: New York, 1973). This splendidly decorated book by America's foremost student of the solar system is a connected series of highly informative essays for a popular audience on cosmology, human society, planetary exploration, the nature of life, and prediction of the future. It deals scientifically with many of the science fiction technologies of space exploration.

I. S. Shklovskii and Carl Sagan, *Intelligent Life in the Universe* (Dell: New York, 1966). This scientifically thorough and highly informative work is the standard text in exobiology, the scientific speculation into the nature and existence of life off the Earth. It is a huge book that will teach a lay reader enormous amounts of astronomy and considerable amounts of biology, chemistry, and physics; it is written so compactly, however, that a scientifically sophisticated reader will still be quite satisfied to learn enormous amounts of exobiology.

A. M. Taylor, *Imagination and the Growth of Science* (Schocken: New York, 1970; four lectures given 1964–65 and copyrighted 1967 with a new preface by the author). By examining biographically the activity of discovery in science by such outstanding workers as Aristotle, Kepler, Faraday, Einstein, and Planck the author makes clear what kind of passionate or detached enterprise science might really be, and thus offers both sources for and correctives of some of the stereotypical notions about scientists. Of great reference help is a thirty-page section offering one-paragraph biographies of great physicists and astronomers.

F. Sherwood Taylor, *A Short History of Science and Scientific Thought (with Readings from the Great Scientists from the Babylonians through Einstein)* (W. W. Norton & Co.: New York, 1963; reprint of 1949 original). This nontechnical survey covers the whole history of science including medicine, physics, geology, and so on from the ancients through quantum mechanics and relativity theory. For the nonscientist this is the most efficient beginning point; for those with some scientific training, this is the easiest way to develop a sense of historical perspective.

Peter Wolff, *Breakthroughs in Mathematics* (Plume Books, New American Library: New York, 1970; reprint of 1963 original). By focusing on the work of nine truly revolutionary mathematicians from Euclid to Boole this book both explains many of the fundamental concepts of mathematics from geometry to topology and gives one a sense of the historical development of mathematics as a whole.

IV. AWARD-WINNING SCIENCE FICTION NOVELS

There are three important awards for science fiction writing: International Fantasy Award (1951–55 + 1957) granted by a panel of judges at the British Science Fiction Convention; Hugo Award (1953, 1955–56, 1958–present) granted by fans at the World (formerly U.S.) Science Fiction Convention (Worldcon); Nebula Award (1966–present) granted by mail vote of the approximately three hundred members of the Science Fiction Writers of America. The years in the list below refer not to the year of publication but to the year of award:

1951 *Earth Abides,* George R. Stewart (IFA)
1952 *Fancies and Goodnights,* John Collier (IFA)
1953 *City,* Clifford D. Simak (IFA)
     The Demolished Man, Alfred Bester (Hugo)
1954 *More Than Human,* Theodore Sturgeon (IFA)
1955 *A Mirror for Observers,* Edgar Pangborn (IFA)
     They'd Rather Be Right, Mark Clifton and Frank Riley (Hugo)
1956 *Double Star,* Robert A. Heinlein (Hugo)
1957 *The Lord of the Rings Trilogy,* J. R. R. Tolkien (IFA)
1958 *The Big Time,* Fritz Leiber (Hugo)
1959 *A Case of Conscience,* James Blish (Hugo)
1960 *Starship Troopers,* Robert A. Heinlein (Hugo)
1961 *A Canticle for Leibowitz,* Walter M. Miller, Jr. (Hugo)
1962 *Stranger in a Strange Land,* Robert A. Heinlein (Hugo)
1963 *The Man in the High Castle,* Philip K. Dick (Hugo)
1964 *Way Station,* Clifford D. Simak (Hugo)
1965 *The Wanderer,* Fritz Leiber (Hugo)
1966 *Dune,* Frank Herbert tied with *This Immortal,* Roger Zelazny (Hugo)
     Dune, Frank Herbert (Nebula)
     The Foundation Trilogy, Isaac Asimov (special Hugo for best science
        fiction series)
1967 *The Moon Is a Harsh Mistress,* Robert A. Heinlein (Hugo)
     Babel-17, Samuel R. Delany tied with *Flowers for Algernon,* Daniel
        Keyes (Nebula)
1968 *Lord of Light,* Roger Zelazny (Hugo)
     The Einstein Intersection, Samuel R. Delany (Nebula)
1969 *Stand on Zanzibar,* John Brunner (Hugo)
     Rite of Passage, Alexei Panshin (Nebula)
1970 *The Left Hand of Darkness,* Ursula K. Le Guin (Hugo & Nebula)
1971 *Ringworld,* Larry Niven (Hugo & Nebula)
1972 *To Your Scattered Bodies Go,* Philip José Farmer (Hugo)
     A Time of Changes, Robert Silverberg (Nebula)
1973 *The Gods Themselves,* Isaac Asimov (Hugo & Nebula)
1974 *Rendezvous with Rama,* Arthur C. Clarke (Hugo & Nebula)
1975 *The Dispossessed,* Ursula K. Le Guin (Hugo & Nebula)
1976 *The Forever War,* Joe Haldeman (Hugo & Nebula)

INDEX

248   INDEX